THE
PROPHETIC
LITERATURE

CAROLYN J. SHARP

Abingdon Press
Nashville, Tennessee

D1596833

THE PROPHETIC LITERATURE

This book is printed on acid-free paper.

Library of Congress Cataloging-in-Publication Data has been requested.

978-1-4267-6504-9

Unless otherwise noted, Scripture passages are from the Common English Bible. Copyright © 2011 by
the Common English Bible. All rights reserved. Used by permission. www.CommonEnglishBible.com.

Scripture quotations marked NRSV are taken from The New Revised Standard Version of the Bible,
copyright 1989, Division of Christian Education of the National Council of the Churches of Christ in the
United States of America. Used by permission. All rights reserved.

19 20 21 22 23 24 25 26 27 28—10 9 8 7 6 5 4 3 2 1

MANUFACTURED IN THE UNITED STATES OF AMERICA

Contents

Acknowledgments

My heartfelt thanks are due to Louis Stulman and David Teel for the opportunity to write this volume for the Core Biblical Studies series and for their generosity and wisdom as I prepared the manuscript. For generations, Abingdon Press has provided essential resources in biblical study for theologians, students, and pastors. In an era in which biblical literacy can no longer be assumed even among the ranks of devout believers, the need for a teaching series is urgent. I am delighted to offer this contribution toward that larger pedagogical goal.

I am grateful beyond words for the privilege of teaching the biblical prophets at Yale Divinity School from 2000 to 2017. I cherish the intellectual curiosity and enthusiasm that my students offered in the survey course on the Latter Prophets. In seminars, I learned much from their wisdom and their moments of resistance as we addressed hermeneutics and authority in Isaiah, tradition and ideology in Jeremiah, and theology in Ezekiel; English exegesis of Amos, Hosea, and Jonah; Hebrew exegesis of Isaiah and Micah; and complex topics in feminist interpretation and literary criticism that drew on the biblical prophets. Journeying now into homiletics professionally, I will continue to affirm the witness of the Latter Prophets as an unparalleled resource for contemporary moral vision and theology.

Warm thanks are due to Jeanette Stokes, Rebecca Wall, and all of the wise women of Pelican House at the Trinity Center in Salter Path, North Carolina; they continue to teach me about creativity and risk-taking in writing. This book is dedicated to my brother, Jim Sharp, with admiration for all he has accomplished and gratitude for his loving support.

General Preface

"All beginnings are hard," muses David Lurie in Chaim Potok's novel *In the Beginning*. "The midrash says, 'All beginnings are hard.' You cannot swallow all the world at one time." Whether learning to ride a bike or play an instrument, starting a new job, or embarking on a course of study, beginnings bristle with challenges and opportunities. The Core Biblical Studies series (CBS) is designed as a starting point for those engaged in Old Testament study. Its brief though substantive volumes are user-friendly introductions to core subjects and themes in biblical studies. Each book in the series helps students navigate the complex terrain of historical, social, literary, and theological issues and methods that are central to the Old Testament.

One of the distinctive contributions of CBS is its underlying commitment to bring together our most respected scholars/teachers with students in the early stages of their learning. As we noted in our first book in the series, "Drawing on the best scholarship, written with the need of students in mind, and addressed to learners in a variety of contexts, these books will provide foundational concepts and contextualized information for those who wish to acquaint themselves . . . with a broad scope of issues, perspectives, trends, and subject matter in key areas of interest."

One might think that such an arrangement is commonplace, but this is not always the case. Take, for example, introductory classes at many of our largest universities. Rarely are 101 classes taught by our most experienced instructors. This standard practice is in part a cost-saving measure, but at the same time it misses a unique opportunity. CBS addresses this common oversight by entrusting students' beginnings to mentors who will prepare them for subsequent inquiry.

The books in this series not only serve to introduce beginners to biblical texts but also aim to meet the needs of teachers who are well aware of the complexities of interpreting meaning. The process of meaning making of Old Testament texts is framed and influenced by a range of factors including the workings behind the text (diachronic), within the text (synchronic), and after the text by subsequent reading communities (the so-called *Nachleben*). This dynamic process is refracted through the lens of scholarly methodologies as well as the social location of the reader. No text is an island, and no interpreter stands outside of his or her own particular time and place. An understanding of this amalgam, especially the diversity of interpretive approaches, is rich with possibilities and crucial to informed readings; but at the same time, it can be almost unwieldy in light of time constraints and other limitations. CBS volumes seek to help teachers navigate this complicated terrain in the classroom and so are "unapologetically pedagogical."

The goal of each volume is to help readers encounter the biblical text for themselves and become more informed interpreters, and to set them on a joy-filled trajectory of life-long learning.

Louis Stulman
General Editor

Key Words and Abbreviations

Key Words

BCE . . . . Before the Common Era; the older equivalent was BC, "before Christ"

CE . . . . Common Era; the older equivalent was AD, *anno Domini*, "year of the Lord"

Deuteronomistic . . . . . . related to the Deuteronomistic History (Joshua, Judges, 1 and 2 Samuel, 1 and 2 Kings) or to the scribes who worked on related biblical material

hermeneutical . . . . having to do with textual interpretation

LXX . . . . the Septuagint, an ancient Greek translation of the Hebrew Scriptures

metonym. . . . . figurative: a part that stands for a larger or more complex whole

MT . . . . the Masoretic Text: the group of ancient Hebrew consonantal texts that became the Hebrew Scriptures, with vocalization and accentuation added in the sixth to tenth centuries CE

shalom. . . . . a Hebrew term that can signify peace, flourishing, security, or well-being

theopolitical .... relating to politics in which theological commitments are central or inseparable

traditionist .... a scribe who preserves and elaborates on earlier traditions, oral or written; "tradent" may be used as well, though a focus on transmission of oral traditions is often implied with that term

Yhwh .... the Divine Name revealed to Moses in Exodus 3; known as the Tetragrammaton ("four letters") and translated as "the Lord"

Abbreviations

AB. .... Anchor Bible

AOTC. .... Abingdon Old Testament Commentaries

BibInt .... *Biblical Interpretation*

BibSem .... The Biblical Seminar

CEB .... Common English Bible

HAR .... *Hebrew Annual Review*

ICC. .... International Critical Commentary

IFT .... Introductions in Feminist Theology

Int. .... *Interpretation*

ISBL .... Indiana Studies in Biblical Literature

JBL .... *Journal of Biblical Literature*

JSJSup. .... Journal for the Study of Judaism Supplement Series

JSOTS. .... Journal for the Study of the Old Testament Supplement Series

KJV. .... King James Version

LAI .... Library of Ancient Israel

LHBOTS .... Library of Hebrew Bible/Old Testament Studies

NICOT. . . . . New International Commentary on the
                                       Old Testament

NJPS. . . . . New Jewish Publication Society

NRSV . . . . New Revised Standard Version

OTL . . . . Old Testament Library

SemeiaSt . . . . Semeia Studies

WBC . . . . Westminster Bible Companion

Chapter 1

Introduction: History, Memory, and Prophetic Texts

The word *prophecy* may conjure notions of mysterious communication with the divine, supernatural foresight into events to come, and radical advocacy for justice. What was prophecy in ancient Israel? Was it about predicting the future? Yes—but it was a great deal more than that. Prophets were visionaries who interpreted the past history of the people of God in light of the sacred traditions of Israel. Prophets also looked unflinchingly at the risks and possibilities of the present moment in their communities, whether that was a time of relative security when cultural complacency was pervasive (Amos) or a time roiled by internecine disputes and unsettled leadership (Hosea), a time when the Assyrian empire threatened Judah's stability (early Isaiah) or a time when the Babylonian army had laid siege to Jerusalem and the city had fallen (later Isaiah; Jeremiah, Ezekiel). And yes, prophets did offer visions and words from God about what was coming in the near future and in the far-distant eschatological future, at the end of history. Prophets interpreted the past, looked with keen vision at the present, and foretold the future. In the Hebrew Scriptures, prophetic oracles are framed as a prescient and authoritative communication of the purposes of Israel's God. Especially important in prophetic messages across the centuries were faithfulness to Israel's covenant with

1

God and a deep and active commitment to care for the poor and marginalized, including sojourners, widows, and orphans.

Not only the words of prophets mattered. The actions of the prophets, too, were taken as signs of God working in the community to teach about covenant fidelity, to condemn sin and malfeasance, and to promise hope. Prophets stood between the divine and the human—or, better, between the divine and the whole created order, including human cultures and the natural world. Prophets inhabited a liminal or "threshold" position as intermediaries between the Creator, human communities, and all of creation.

Speaking Truth to Power

The prophets give not only Judaism, but all of Western religion and civilization the legacy of the individual who "speaks truth to power" and thereby places the voice of God in front of acts of injustice and corruption—whether . . . found in the social, political, or religious sphere.

—Stephen Kepnes[1]

Walter Brueggemann has suggested that the prophets were agents of "mediated disruption," responding to crisis and evoking crisis. Prophets saw what was at stake in the sins and failures of leaders and people all around them, and they responded, calling their hearers back to the purposes of God and practices of holiness. But prophets also catalyzed crisis by their words of impending doom and urgent exhortations for their audiences to see clearly, to understand. Brueggemann is certainly right that the prophets "speak in images and metaphors that aim to disrupt, destabilize, and invite to alternate perceptions of reality."[2]

The Hebrew Scriptures represent that the word of the LORD came to dozens of inspired individuals in Israel and Judah over a period of several centuries. Abraham is the ancestor of Israel and, per New Testament traditions, the spiritual ancestor of all who believe (Rom 4). He is portrayed as a Chaldean who migrates to Canaan, the patriarch of what will become a host of countless descendants (Gen 12:1-3). Abraham is a flawed and fearful husband (Gen 12:10-20; 20:1-17) and conflicted father (see Gen 16 and 21) who becomes a powerful chieftain as he obeys the purposes of God. Abraham is also, just once, identified as a prophet who can intercede effectively on behalf of others (Gen 20:7). Moses, a towering figure in the Pentateuch, is portrayed as a bold leader and judge, recipient of God's Law—the Torah—on Mount Sinai, and paradigmatic prophet (see Deut 18:15-22) who intercedes over and over again to save the Israelites from God's wrath. Thus prophecy is anchored in the founding traditions of Israel as covenant people: fleetingly in the patriarchal stories and in a much more sustained way in the narratives of Moses's leadership, Israel's escape from slavery in Egypt (the Exodus), and the wilderness wanderings of Israel on the long journey to Canaan. The biblical books of Samuel and Kings are rich with stories about prophets named and unnamed. Some are famous—who could forget the prophet Nathan's dramatic entrapment of David for his malfeasance in the matter of Bathsheba and Uriah? ("You are that man!"—see 2 Sam 11–12.) Others are more obscure, such as the unnamed "man of God" who prophesies against Jeroboam and the "old prophet" in Bethel who in turn delivers a divine word of judgment against that man of God (1 Kgs 13). False prophecy was a serious problem, in the perspective of the scribes who shaped the biblical traditions. Not every means of intermediation was considered legitimate (see Deut 13:1-5), and not everyone who claimed to be speaking a word of YHWH was authentic (see Deut 18:20-22 and Jer 28, among numerous biblical passages concerned about false prophecy).

Women and men served as prophets in ancient Israel and Judah. There may have been prophets of other genders too; the Hebrew Scriptures do not speak clearly about intersex or genderqueer bodies, hence that aspect of gender history may be lost to us, though we may note with interest the role of the Ethiopian eunuch Ebed-melech in Jeremiah and look at gender roles and conceptions of the body more broadly across the ancient Near East. This volume focuses on the written traditions of the Latter Prophets—Isaiah, Jeremiah, Ezekiel, and the twelve Minor Prophets, all of whom were male, so far as we can guess at how they lived their gender identity. But for the sake of comprehensiveness, you may wish to consider

3

the four named women prophets in the Hebrew Scriptures—Miriam, Deborah, Huldah, and Noadiah—and explore how they have been interpreted in reception history.

- Miriam, the sister of Moses, plays an instrumental role in the survival of baby Moses after his mother puts him into the river in his basket of bulrushes (Exod 2:1-10). She is not mentioned in the Hebrew genealogical text of Exodus 6:20, but the Septuagint (LXX) includes her name there; see also Numbers 26:59 and 1 Chronicles 6:3. After the Israelites have passed through the miraculously divided Red Sea and the LORD has caused the waters to drown the pursuing Egyptian soldiers, Miriam leads the Israelite women in a song of triumph: "Sing to the LORD, for he has triumphed gloriously; horse and rider he has thrown into the sea" (Exod 15:20-21). During Israel's wilderness wanderings, Miriam and Aaron argue with Moses, asserting their own legitimacy as prophets; Miriam alone experiences divine punishment as a result of this conflict (see Num 12). Her death is recorded (Num 20:1), something that underlines her stature in Israel's sacred traditions. Miriam is remembered in Deuteronomy 24:9 and Micah 6:4.

- Deborah, one of the many charismatic warrior-judges whose exploits are recounted in the book of Judges, is identified as a prophet in Judges 4:4. She plays a vital role as military tactician in Israel's defeat of the Canaanite forces of Jabin and his commander, Sisera. Deborah is featured as singer of an epic song of victory that celebrates her role (Judg 5). It has long been noticed that the book of Judges pays close attention to the power and discernment of women (Deborah, Jael, the mother of Samson, Delilah) as well as their vulnerability in the closing chapters of the book (the Levite's concubine, the virgins of Jabesh-gilead, the women dancing at Shiloh). Deborah's role as prophet shows that heeding the LORD does result in victory for Israel, an important signal near the beginning of this book that chronicles Israel's inexorable spiraling into terrible moral chaos.

- Huldah, a prophet during the reign of Josiah of Judah, serves as the catalyst for the religious reforms undertaken by Josiah. When "the book of the law"—usually considered by scholars to have been some form of Deuteronomy—is discovered in the Jerusalem temple, its teachings having been ignored for generations, a stricken Josiah sends officials to consult Huldah. Her oracular response, introduced formally with "Thus says the LORD, the God of Israel" (2 Kgs 22:15), indicts Judah for idolatry and offers an ironic word of comfort to Josiah: his penitence has won him a reprieve from having to see the destruction of Jerusalem. Josiah will die (assassinated during negotiations rather than killed on the battlefield, thus ironically dying "in peace") in 609 BCE, long before the Babylonian onslaught that ends in the fall of Jerusalem in 587. The king's response to Huldah's prophesying is to make a vow of fidelity to the LORD with the people of Judah (2 Kgs 23:3) and to purge Judah of the shrines, personnel, and practices that had supported worship of gods other than YHWH (2 Kgs 23:4-25). Consider that Deuteronomistic editors shaped many texts in the Hebrew Scriptures in light of their goals and ideology. Now: Huldah is the prophet who affirms the rightness of the Deuteronomistic reform and predicts the destruction of the Jerusalem temple. So she is not just some obscure intermediary. Perhaps we should imagine her as closer to a second Moses: a towering prophetic figure who serves to authorize all of the Deuteronomistic writing and amplifying of ancient Israel's sacred texts! Yet in decades of weekly church attendance, not once have I heard Huldah mentioned in a sermon or prayer. Perhaps your experience is different, but I'm guessing that for many communities of faith over many generations, Huldah is not a household name—and she should be.

- Noadiah is mentioned among the prophets who oppose the initiative led by Nehemiah to rebuild the walls of Jerusalem (Neh 6:14). Local antagonism to Nehemiah's efforts constitutes a major theme in the so-called "Nehemiah memoir" in Ezra–Nehemiah, a single unified book in antiquity. The identification of Noadiah by name should be taken as a signal of

5

her significance in the ranks of named adversaries, along with Sanballat the Horonite, Tobiah the Ammonite, Geshem the Arab, and Shemaiah son of Delaiah.

Wilda Gafney has written about the named female prophets in the Hebrew Bible and female prophets who are unnamed, such as the women excoriated as false prophets and duplicitous diviners in Ezekiel 13:17-23. Gafney's 2008 book, *Daughters of Miriam: Women Prophets in Ancient Israel*, is in the "For Further Reading" list at the end of this chapter. Midrashic and Talmudic traditions honor as prophets not only Miriam, Deborah, and Huldah, but also four other women in the Hebrew Bible: Sarah, Hannah, Abigail, and Esther.[3]

Modern scholarship on the biblical prophets is situated within a comparative ancient Near Eastern historical framework. When scholars consider the roles of ancient prophets, scholars have oriented their research toward uncovering historical data about ancient kings, the wars they fought, the monumental buildings they constructed, the politics of the royal court, and the official religious practices that were promulgated in their temples. The study of ancient Israelite prophecy has been enriched in recent years by nuanced literary approaches to the texts, as well as engagement with insights and methodologies of other disciplines in the humanities and social sciences. Cultural anthropology, ritual studies, trauma studies, gender studies, and postcolonial criticism all have enhanced our understanding of the prophetic books of the Hebrew Scriptures. Below you'll find a timeline of some key events in the historical contexts in which the prophetic texts were composed and edited, a span running from the Neo-Assyrian period through the Persian-era shaping of the books in their final forms. Then you will be oriented to insights from particular methodological approaches that have been influential in scholarship on the prophets. This section will prepare you for your own exploration of the prophetic literature. In keeping with the purpose of the Core Biblical Studies series, throughout this volume you'll be invited to consider possibilities for meaning-making via the theological claims asserted in the prophetic literature. Whether a reader of the Latter Prophets belongs to a Christian tradition, a Jewish faith community, another spiritual tradition, or no religious tradition, it's fruitful to consider ways in which these ancient texts speak about community and the power of the Holy.

Study of the biblical prophets requires attention to three interrelated areas of inquiry: historical, hermeneutical, and theological. The terrain of our explorations might be depicted in terms of three overlapping circles:

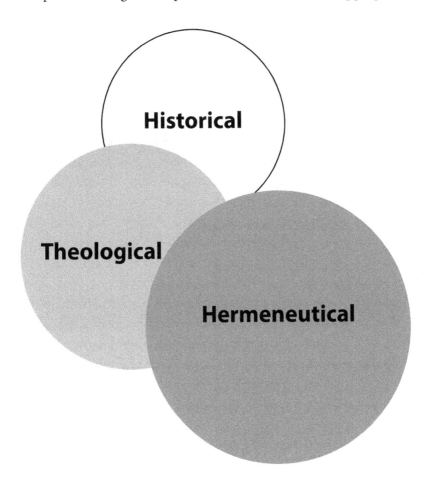

As we engage historical, theological, and hermeneutical (interpretive) questions, we will consider major themes in the Latter Prophets and also wrestle with difficult texts, of which there is no shortage in this material. Because the prophetic literature has been enormously influential in Christian and Jewish traditions and also in Western culture, we should not ignore the risks presented by these texts to communities gathered around Scripture, nor can we dismiss these texts as outdated and irrelevant for the formation and instruction of contemporary readers.

Interpreting the Latter Prophets

Consider the first circle in our model above. Readers of the Bible have questions about the historical contexts out of which and in response to which biblical texts were generated. Keep in mind that the literary framing of a biblical book (the setting, whether explicit or implicit, of the plot of the story) is not the same as when that book was written or edited. This need not pose a drastic challenge to faith—not even for the most literalist reader. Why? Because no biblical book says, "This book was written within a week of the events narrated herein." No biblical book says, "Because these are the words of the LORD to Jeremiah, therefore you must assume that every word in this book was written by Jeremiah himself." The texts do claim to offer authentic and accurate representation of the speech and purposes of God, and they clearly intend—in literary terms—to present reliable voicing and portrayal of the prophets and their circumstances, where the contexts are described. But nowhere do the texts state that no editing or later shaping of the texts happened. In fact, the converse is true. The prophetic corpus is rich with reflections on earlier scriptural traditions, with annotations and interpolations from later scribes, even offering reflection on how complex the processes of producing Scripture had been. On that last point, see Jeremiah 36 and the passages in the book of Isaiah that discuss how God's words should be written down and sealed for future generations.

Historical questions are essential for a clear sense of the layers of meaning in these marvelous composite texts. A sense of history is important for us to interpret language and imagery well, and it's key for comprehending what may have been at stake for the scribes who authored and edited these powerful texts. Historical analysis helps us attend to the needs and hopes of historical communities not our own, something that requires alertness to cultural difference and a posture of openness to the Other. Historical inquiry can serve as a corrective to the unwitting narcissism of readers in diverse times and places who take their own needs and ideas as the supreme reference point for the truth of past history, the significance of the present, and vision for the future. Listening to other voices is important.

Historical questions about the provenance of biblical materials can be complex indeed. If you wish to understand the development of a biblical prophetic book, you'll need to be curious about several different contexts—years, generations, or even centuries apart. In many different times, biblical authors and later editors worked to respond to the truth of God as they understood it. Ancient scribes were skilled in drawing on ancient traditions about God and God's purposes, so their work in the prophetic books is beautifully layered and brimming with allusions. When you read ancient literature, you are getting a sense of history as "The Past" not in some simplistic way, but as a multidimensional and fluid cultural construction. The prophets and the scribal circles that preserved and amplified their prophecies listened, deeply, to many voices clamoring to speak. They wrestled with alternative views of the present and the future as they sought to know their communities and discern the purposes of God in ever-changing circumstances. Another aspect of historical inquiry has to do with understanding your own time and place, your own priorities and commitments as you encounter the biblical witnesses. The best historians are exceptionally clear about the biases, convictions, and conceptual frameworks they bring to the study of their subject.

The second circle in our terrain of three overlapping areas of inquiry has to do with theological issues raised by the material. The Latter Prophets offer a multivocal chorus of theological witnesses to the God of Israel. In the prophetic books we see stirring and disturbing claims about who God is, what God does, and what God expects of the covenant people. None of this is simple. We might think for a moment about the complexity of a single theological notion: the basic idea that God is holy. What did that shared conviction mean for Isaiah and Ezekiel, respectively? In significant ways these two prophetic books couldn't be more different as regards how they witness to the holiness of God and explore the implications of that faith claim. For Isaiah, it is a source of joy and consolation that God is "the

Holy One of Israel." God's holiness is bound up with God's identity as
Creator, the One who "creates weal and makes woe" (Isa 45:7 NRSV), the
One who was from of old, who had spoken and acted from the beginning
of time. Yes, God may have subjected God's people to judgment, purify-
ing a remnant (see Isa 6) that would endure much before returning with
joy to Zion (Isa 35). Divine judgment is painful. But God's holiness is
celebrated as an incomparably powerful place of refuge for God's people,
the luminous divine Presence guaranteeing, according to the tenets of the
royal Zion theology, God's protection of Jerusalem as the seat of God's
holiness.

"O God, Our Help in Ages Past," verses 1 and 2

O God, our help in ages past,
our hope for years to come,
our shelter from the stormy blast
and our eternal home:

under the shadow of thy throne
thy saints have dwelt secure;
sufficient is thine arm alone,
and our defense is sure.

Words: Isaac Watts (1674–1748), alt.; paraphrase of Psalm 90
Tune: St. Anne, melody attributed to William Croft (1678–1727)

For Ezekiel, by contrast, the holiness of YHWH is mysterious and
alarming. The LORD is terrifyingly Other. A vision of the divine Chariot
(Ezek 1) leaves Ezekiel shocked and speechless for seven days. For Ezekiel,
YHWH's jealous protection of the divine holy Name means not consolation
for Israel but precisely the opposite: devastating judgment without mercy,
because the contrast between God's holiness and the people's loathsome
apostasy is so great that YHWH can no longer bear to be in the presence
of the covenant people. YHWH will save, yes. Even Ezekiel cannot avoid
saying that YHWH will save. But the redemption effected by the LORD will
leave the people despising themselves for the terrible unholiness that they

have shown in their breaches of covenant. God's holiness in Ezekiel serves primarily as a signifier of God's inescapable power to destroy and God's fundamental intolerance of human sinfulness. Where the Isaiah traditions sing of the rebuilding of Zion, of the repairing of ancient breaches in the walls and the return of rejoicing exiles to their home, for Ezekiel there can be no contact between God and the abominations that had once taken place in the temple. The LORD must establish a new temple, a new dwelling place for the holiness of God in an eschatological future that is dramatically *not* in continuity with what had gone before. As you read Isaiah and Ezekiel, you'll see two different explorations of the holiness of the LORD and what that means theologically for the LORD's purposes past, present, and future with communities of believers. And that's just one issue out of myriad concerns and possibilities we can explore within the prophetic corpus.

This brings us to the third circle in our diagram: hermeneutics, the art of interpretation. This area of inquiry includes ways in which the biblical material responds to its own traditions exegetically and ways in which our own reading strategies pose particular questions to the biblical material. Every method of reading, and every question we put to a text, comes out of particular ways of viewing the text, the reader, communal norms of interpretation, and history. Centrally involved is the issue of what values and questions readers and reading communities bring to the process of interpretation. As you read, I hope you will examine and develop your own hermeneutical strategies consonant with the strengths and "growing edges" of your own faith tradition if you have one, the meaning-making of other communities of conviction in which you take part (such as artistic, social, or political groups), and your interest in the Bible for cultural and political reasons. What you care about makes you who you are, as a reader of the Bible and as one who can explore the significance of the ancient prophets for contemporary theological, social, and political discourse.

You'll want to understand major points of ancient Near Eastern history during the eras in which the books of the Latter Prophets were written and edited, a span of time from the eighth century to the fifth or fourth century BCE. Every annotated Bible has various timelines and maps, chronological tables of rulers, and so on; I recommend the *New Oxford Annotated Bible*, but other fine annotated Bibles exist. A good history textbook is essential and cannot be reproduced here in summary. There are many competent books on the history of ancient Israel and Judah, written from a variety of perspectives regarding the relationships among archaeological artifacts, ancient texts, and historical memory. In fact, you may wish to have on your desk two books on the history of ancient Israel: one written from a methodological position to which you are sympathetic, and a second volume written from a different perspective that is new to you or with which you disagree. You might read their introductions, then compare their treatments of topics of particular interest. The types of histories available in the scholarly market include historical-critical volumes written by scholars who aim at secular neutrality in their analysis, usually choosing not to identify their own biases and theological commitments. This group includes "maximalist" positions that consider the historiographical material narrated in the Hebrew Bible to be reasonably accurate, with obvious allowances made for ideological influence here and there plus occasional errors where the ancient scribes may not have known something or got something wrong. Also on the market are histories of ancient Israel written from "minimalist" positions. These authors argue that biblical texts are thoroughly ideological productions that can show us little about the historical realities. See the "For Further Reading" list at the end of this chapter: you might take a look at the 2014 volume edited by Bill Arnold and Richard Hess, Rainer Kessler's book on social history, and the textbook by Iain Provan, V. Philips Long, and Tremper Longman.

Every textbook on the history of Israel and Judah will offer extended discussion of the relevant events and issues involved. My own position is that major aspects of the history of Israel and Judah may indeed be glimpsed through the prism of Hebrew Bible texts, but those texts are products of cultural memory, not historical reports, and to read them as if they were empirically verifiable historiography is to put a framework on the texts that they do not themselves require. Ideology is inevitably at play in these texts. This is something that no scholar of the history of ancient Palestine would deny, though there are many gradations of dispute regarding how influential ideological commitments were, how well or poorly the texts reflect history apart from those commitments, and so on. History mattered deeply to the scribes who composed the books of the Latter Prophets, and history is a matter of cultural memory, with many points of contestation and differing perspectives transparently visible in these wonderful ancient texts. Below are some key dates before the Common Era (BCE) important for the Latter Prophets.

1005–965	reign of David, king during the united monarchy
735–715	reign of Hezekiah, king of Judah
721	fall of the northern kingdom of Samaria to Assyria
701	siege of Jerusalem by Assyrian king Sennacherib and his army
640–609	reign of Josiah, king of Judah
612	fall of Nineveh, capital city in the Assyrian empire, to the Babylonians and their allies
608–598	reign of Jehoiakim, king of Judah
605	Battle of Carchemish, at which Babylonian king Nebuchadnezzar II and his forces defeated Egypt and Assyria, securing Babylonian dominance in the Levant
597	deportation of leading citizens of Jerusalem to Babylon by Nebuchadnezzar; deportees included Judean king Jehoiachin and the prophet Ezekiel
597–587	reign of Zedekiah, king of Judah
588–587	siege of Jerusalem by Babylonian king Nebuchadnezzar and his army, resulting in the fall of the city, the subjugation of Judah to the Babylonians, and deportation of many Judean survivors
559–530	the reign of Cyrus II ("Cyrus the Great") of Persia
539	defeat of Babylon by Cyrus
538	edict of Cyrus that Judean exiles may return to Judah
520–515	rebuilding of the Jerusalem temple; its completion inaugurated what scholars call the Second Temple period

Conflict among the major empires—Assyria, Egypt, Babylonia, Persia—was of keen interest to Israelite and Judean rulers and the advisors in their courts. The northern kingdom of Israel and the southern kingdom of Judah were relatively small and vulnerable. Watching the political landscape like hawks, leaders had to position their governments in carefully calibrated alliances, negotiating opportunities for strategic coalition-building and weighing the costs of submission against the risks of political resistance as they sought to preserve their people's lives and secure their communities' economic survival.

History—past, present, and future—is engaged in many creative ways in Israel's prophetic corpus. Many of the books of the Latter Prophets have superscriptions that situate the books historically. These introductory formulas, often with dates, were added by scribes seeking to frame the oracles and other material for their audiences' understanding. As you read the prophetic books, you'll see a rich diversity of ways in which historical contexts are handled. Some oracles are dated to the year, month, and even day when the LORD spoke to that prophet. Other material seems to have been shaped with a goal of not being tethered to a specific date, possibly so the divine word being offered could be heard as relevant to subsequent generations of believers. In those cases, a prophetic oracle might narrate an event without any referent as to the date, or speak of "days of old" when reflecting on the past, or offer a vision for an event "in days to come," without being more precise. Some prophetic material reflects deeply on Israel's past, some oracles reflect God's purposes unfolding in the present moment or near future, and some help their hearers to imagine a distant eschatological future when things will be dramatically different.

Similarly diverse are the ways in which places and personal names are handled. In the book of Hosea, Micah 1, and Jeremiah 48, you'll see many place-names deployed to powerful effect in the poetic oracles; but in vast portions of other prophetic books, few or no place-names come up. In Isaiah, Jeremiah, and Ezekiel, the numbers of personal names of men are drastically different, as the below chart shows. (Past historical figures—Abraham, Sarah, Jacob, Moses, Samuel, David, Rachel, Micah of Moresheth—are not included in this chart; neither are the names of deities and mythological figures such as Lilith. The only woman's name preserved in 166 chapters of material in Isaiah, Jeremiah, and Ezekiel is that of Hamutal, the mother of Zedekiah, in Jeremiah 52.) For some scribal circles, it was crucial to identify who did what; for other scribes or in other oracular situations, clearly that was not a concern. The book of Ezekiel identifies almost no one by name. But in the second half of Jeremiah, political conflict is foregrounded, and it would appear that the preservation of personal names was deemed essential to identify who had supported the prophet and who had been antagonistic or disloyal during the disputes.

Personal Names in the Major Prophets		
Isaiah, son of Amoz	4 kings of Judah king of Israel king of Aram 3 kings of Assyria 1 king of Babylon 1 king of Persia	10 other persons
Jeremiah, son of Hilkiah	6 kings of Judah 2 kings of Babylon 1 king of Ammon 2 kings of Egypt	51 other persons
Ezekiel, son of Buzi	1 king of Judah 1 king of Babylon [Pharaoh does function almost as a personal name in Ezekiel's syntax, but no personal name is given for the king of Egypt]	3 other persons

Prophets and Their Communities

To understand the biblical prophetic books, we'll need to think about the theological and social relationships of ancient Israelite prophets to their communities. The biblical books present us with the prophet as an inspired, charismatic individual responding to God and proclaiming God's messages to Israel and other nations. The book of Isaiah begins with, "The vision of Isaiah son of Amoz, which he saw concerning Judah and Jerusalem" (Isa 1:1 NRSV); you'll see in Jeremiah and Ezekiel, "The word of the LORD came to me" (NRSV), unquestionably positioning the prophet as an individual receiving special revelation. Thus readers and hearers throughout the centuries have been fascinated by the question of who the prophets were. "What Manner of Man Is the Prophet?" is the title of chapter 1 in Abraham Heschel's classic work, *The Prophets*. Heschel writes in eloquent terms of the passionate and tortured psyche of the prophet as inspired individual:

> The world is a proud place, full of beauty; but the prophets are scandalized, and rave as if the whole world were a slum. . . . Why such immoderate excitement? Why such intense indignation? . . . To us a single act of injustice—cheating in business, exploitation of the poor—is slight; to the prophets, a disaster. To us injustice is injurious to the welfare of the people; to the prophets it is a deathblow to existence: to us, an episode; to them, a catastrophe, a threat to the world.[4]

The prophets see what is at stake in immoral behavior, idolatry, and political malfeasance with an acuteness that puts them at odds with their communities. Heschel underlines the hyperbolic nature of the prophetic consciousness:

> Our eyes are witness to the callousness and cruelty of [humankind], but our heart tries to obliterate the memories, to calm the nerves, and to silence our conscience. The prophet is a man who feels fiercely. God has thrust a burden upon his soul, and he is bowed and stunned at [our] fierce greed. Frightful is the agony of [humanity]; no human voice can convey its full terror. Prophecy is the voice that God has lent to the silent agony, a voice to the plundered poor, to the profaned riches of the world. It is a form of living, a crossing point of God and [humanity]. God is raging in the prophet's words.[5]

According to Heschel, the prophet is hypersensitive and courageous in challenging that which may seem to be right but is—per the prophetic sensibility—displeasing to God or out of line with what God intends. As Heschel puts it, "No one is just; no knowing is strong enough, no trust complete enough. The prophet hates the approximate, he shuns the middle of the road. [We] must live on the summit to avoid the abyss. There is nothing to hold to except God."[6]

The prophet as inspired individual is a compelling figure indeed. But the Latter Prophets also show us prophecy as an ancient cultural activity supported by communities for reasons theological and political. The attentive reader of the biblical prophetic books will notice different social groups vying for access to the prophet and will see ideologies clashing, with persons characterized as contesting the prophet's message vigorously when it does not fit with their own social, political, or religious ideas. In *Prophecy and Society in Ancient Israel*, Robert R. Wilson explores sociological dimensions of ancient Israelite prophecy. Wilson argues that societies play a crucial role in supporting and guiding intermediaries such as prophets, shamans, sorcerers, mediums, diviners, priests, and mystics. Through comparative work, Wilson demonstrates that various means are used to control or influence intermediation according to a social group's expectations, including the conferral of political status and economic rewards. Wilson emphasizes that Israelite prophets were engaged in their communities and shaped by their communities' expectations. He objects to "the popular image of the prophet as a divinely inspired individual who reforms society with his radical message and who refuses to be a part of the corrupt social order that he condemns. Clearly, this picture cannot be supported by the anthropological data. . . . If charisma is a 'gift of the gods,' it is also a gift of the society."[7]

As you read the Latter Prophets, you'll see prophets portrayed as charismatic individuals, and you'll see prophecy as a communal phenomenon. Finally, the Hebrew Bible also presents prophecy as a literary heritage—a set of authoritative texts to be heard and pondered, read and re-read, as audiences seek to understand what God had done in the past and to hear God's word afresh in new times and contexts. In these pages, we will consider the ancient prophets as messengers of God's word for particular communities, and prophetic books as cultural productions encoded with particular sociopolitical expectations.

As you read, you'll notice that the prophets function as sentinels pronouncing terrifying words of divine judgment and as visionaries offering words of radiant hope. Judgment oracles are often clothed in graphic images of militarized violence. Oracles of hope often use images of healing, transformation of the natural landscape, or the restoration of political autonomy via a king in the line of David.

Examples of Oracles of Doom and Hope	
I will pour out my wrath against you. With a raging fire I will blow against you, and I will hand you over to those who burn and forge destruction. Fire will consume you, your blood will sink into the earth, and you will no longer be remembered. I, the LORD, have spoken.	DOOM Ezek 21:31-32
Destruction and devastation; the city is laid waste! The heart grows faint and knees buckle; there is anguish in every groin; all the faces grow pale. Look! I am against you, proclaims the LORD of heavenly forces. I will burn your chariots in smoke; the sword will devour your young lions; I will cut off your prey from the earth, the voice of your messengers will never again be heard!	DOOM Nah 2:10, 13
When the oppressor is no more, when destruction has ceased, when the trampler has vanished from the land, a throne will be established based on goodness, and someone will sit faithfully on it in David's dwelling—a judge who seeks justice and timely righteousness.	HOPE Isa 16:4b-5
So you will know that I am the LORD your God, settle down in Zion, my holy mountain. Jerusalem will be holy, and never again will strangers pass through it. In that day the mountains will drip sweet wine, the hills will flow with milk, and all the streambeds of Judah will flow with water; a spring will come forth from the LORD's house and water the Shittim Valley.	HOPE Joel 3:17-18

Prophets also functioned as teachers who helped their communities interpret the traditions that had sustained Israel and Judah in the past. The prophets were reformers and dissenters, as well. The artfully designed and rhetorically powerful books of the Latter Prophets may be understood in the same ways. These texts thunder warnings of judgment and offer visions of hope. They instruct and reform those who gather around them. And they build the capacity of hearers and readers to dissent from those practices that are unethical or unfaithful to sacred tradition.

Tools for Biblical Interpretation

Reading a text is like looking at art and describing what you see in a lively conversation with others. Viewers each have their own background, their own interests, their level of familiarity with artistic conventions, their expertise from other arenas of life, including goals and experiences of possibility and constraint, healing and harm; what they understand and misunderstand; what they can articulate well and can intuit but not express; and so on. Each viewer of art, and each reader of a text, will interpret the work differently than you do, even if there are areas of overlap where you agree. You may have experienced this in a classroom or other setting where dialogue was allowed to flourish, no one dominant perspective was allowed to silence other views, and the leader (whether a professor, pastor, or other facilitator) used their power not to lecture at those in attendance but instead to invite others into voice and model attentive, empathic listening. In such contexts, your companions in the conversation can model acceptance, resistance, and polyphony as essential dimensions of emancipatory learning in community.

Exploration of any text requires clarity about the kinds of questions the interpreter is asking. There are many viable ways to approach biblical texts. There are certain modes of inquiry and frameworks within which some or many in a particular tradition have tended to do their exegetical and analytical work, and other modes of inquiry or frameworks—analytically excellent and spiritually fruitful—that may be newer to those communities of conviction, including the Western academic guild. In every academic, social, artistic, political, and theological tradition, there are staunch defenders of older modes of engagement and passionate advocates of newer approaches. In every art or trade, including the art of interpretation and the trade of making scholarly books, there are historians loyal to what had been, visionaries who thrill to new horizons, and iconoclasts who enjoy dismantling anything that enjoys too long a pedigree or too unblinking a consensus among its adherents.

Historical analysis figures in most methods of biblical interpretation, whether explicitly or implicitly. Even approaches informed by post-modernist understandings rely on underlying assumptions about ways in which ancient historical contexts shaped the texts that were composed and edited in those times. Archaeology, cultural anthropology, political history, and sociological approaches can be of much value in understanding the cultural norms and material experiences that influenced the creative work we read in the prophetic books. Where the reader must be careful, though, is not to follow the naïve assumptions of many historians in biblical studies about how history maps onto text. In introductory textbook after introductory textbook, you'll see the implicit assumption that if we know some of the major public events and figures who were active in a particular time, we can easily see what is going on in a sophisticated and artfully wrought ancient text. Biblical studies as a discipline is notoriously slow to engage newer currents in other disciplines, so I hope you will always bring what you are learning in other settings into engagement with your study of the prophets.

For some readers, understanding the historical setting and authorial/redactional intentions behind a text is essential for understanding meaning. For others, the original intent of a piece of writing can never be fully determined; it is the agency of the reader in constructing associations, perceiving levels of meaning, and so on that creates the meaning of the text. A cheery word of caution regarding the complexity of historical study may be appropriate at the close of this chapter. A number of influential Western scholars, particularly those whose careers were launched in the heyday of uncontested historical empiricism in the twentieth century and who are now approaching retirement, still insist that it is possible to read the Hebrew Bible "on its own terms." I concur that is important to avoid importing personal beliefs and anachronistic cultural assumptions willy-nilly into the ancient texts as if the texts were themselves articulating those beliefs and norms. Cultural and religious narcissism is a risk in every interpretive age. The interpreter should stay vigilant regarding the risks involved in projecting what we already think onto the ancient witnesses. But it is simply impossible for a contemporary reader shaped by postindustrial and late-capitalist values, highly technologized and autonomous living, and a constant stream of globalized news about corporate power and international politics to read "on their own terms" these Iron-Age texts from relatively isolated regions sustained by economies whose forms ranged from subsistence agriculture to centralized trade co-opted by urban elites to militarized extraction under threat of obliteration. The prophets and scribes who together produced Israel's prophetic literature operated under the authority of a series of chiefdoms and sacerdotal lineages that have not been extant for millennia. Translating these texts is, on one level, an exercise in cultural hubris. Even the simplest nouns (*king*, say, or *people of the land*) could not mean to a hearer in the sixth century BCE anything like what they might connote conceptually to a reader in a university context who has any depth of learning in political science, the literatures of other cultures, or sociology. Extensive notes in annotated Bibles go only so far to bridge the gap. When we read the words in translation, we are activating many associations—often unwittingly—that are simply not accurate regarding the Hebrew Bible and might have been unintelligible to a person in antiquity. As for more abstract words and concepts, we cannot know what the text "on its own terms" really signified. How might an ancient Israelite in a subsistence village-based kinship group have understood holiness or social ethics when pondering the effects of drought or the opportunity for trade? We can make educated guesses—Amos tells his people not to exploit the poor, and we can translate that into our contemporary contexts somewhat. But we can never know what it meant on more complex and deeper levels of community, belief, religious praxis, and so on, even bracketing the issue that various ancient persons would have had differing ideas, just as we do today. Contemporary readers may have associations with urban homelessness or struggling laborers under late capitalism that would not map onto the realities in ancient Israel or Judah. So when you encounter a scholar who insists that the Hebrew Bible be read "on its own terms," I encourage you to receive that claim with gentle and courteous skepticism. Such folks do believe what they're saying. It's how they were acculturated in a certain strain of twentieth-century post-Enlightenment rationality, and it seems transparently obvious to them that reading the Bible "on its own terms" is possible. Some of them mean to underline the importance of avoiding cultural narcissism, and that's a valid goal even if it's not fully realizable. But the claim to neutral understanding of an ancient text on its own terms is simply not accurate, as brilliant critical theorists in other disciplines have argued for decades now.

There are many nuanced positions you could take along the spectrum of possibilities regarding the degree to which you seek to interrogate your own reading position and understand cultural difference. Indeed, your position may change depending on what you're reading. You may find historical context and authorial intention important when you are reading a political chronicle but almost impossible to ascertain when pondering a Japanese haiku. The values and assumptions of interpreters, plus the ways in which they construe a larger historical framework and numerous cultural cues, have a great deal to do with the meanings they perceive in texts and other cultural artifacts. Two examples drawn from contemporary Western culture will illustrate the point.

Example 1: King Kong

More than one remake of the film *King Kong* has been released to critical and popular acclaim since the original 1933 film. Reviewers praised a 2005 version for its sensitive portrayal of the loving relationship that develops between an initially threatening giant gorilla and the small blonde woman whom the gorilla captures.

- A feminist interpreter could easily find grounds on which to excoriate the film for its subtext promoting sexually coercive patriarchal power relations. It is a dysfunctional hetero-patriarchal fantasy (the feminist might say) that a captured and physically threatened woman, completely in the power of a primitive male far stronger than she, may be afraid initially but will come to love her captor and choose to be with him.

- An animal rights advocate might praise the film for its perceived ironic undermining of the notion that humans rightly exercise dominion over animals' bodies (see Gen 1:26). The giant gorilla, while admittedly violent against property and antagonists, shows himself capable of connecting in a gentle and meaningful way with a human, while most of the humans in the film are portrayed as exploitative, cruel, or voyeuristic.

• A racial justice activist might deplore the film's subtle reinforcement of subterranean racist views regarding relationships between black males and white females, views that were prevalent in racist white society in the United States when the original movie was filmed in 1933. African American comedian Greer Barnes offers just that opinion of the movie, quoted in the *New York Times* on January 3, 2006, by Anthony Ramirez: " 'You know what the moral of the movie is, right?' asked Mr. Barnes, who is black. 'Ain't no monkey, no matter how big he is, is going to come from Africa and take our white women' " (p. B2). A study of racial politics in *King Kong* might well arrive at a conclusion not too different from the one he expressed.

Which of these perspectives on *King Kong* is correct? There is merit to each of them, depending on how you frame the hermeneutical questions and how you construe the context in which you are considering the film. This is not the same as "relativism." It is an acknowledgment that truth is constructed according to a host of factors having to do with the interpreter's perspective regarding the object being studied, the relevant cultural setting(s) in which interpretation is taking place, and the interpreter's understanding of the act of interpretation itself.

Example 2: The Volkswagen Beetle

A story by Natalie Angier in the *New York Times* of January 3, 2006, described how "cuteness" constitutes an evolutionarily effective development. Huge eyes, disproportionately large heads, fuzzy round bodies, uncoordinated limbs, and other such traits signal to parents (whether human or other) that little ones need caretaking. Cultural uses of "cuteness" can be seen in countless products marketed to children and adults. Angier invited us to consider the clash of cultural codes and interpretations in the design of the Volkswagen Beetle automobile in its original context decades ago in Germany, and its remaking in the last few years. "As though the original Volkswagen Beetle [weren't] considered cute enough, the updated edition was made rounder and shinier still. 'The new Beetle looks like a smiley face,' said Miles Orvell, professor of American studies at temple University in Philadelphia. 'By this point its origins in Hitler's regime, and its intended resemblance to a German helmet, [have been] totally forgotten'" (p. F8). Interpretations are diverse, and appropriately so. Historical dimensions always come into play in our interpretation of cultural texts and other artifacts, whether those dimensions are overtly influential, misunderstood, or largely forgotten.

Through my work for a master's degree and my first year of doctoral studies at Yale, Brevard Childs was teaching at Yale Divinity School. A kind man and dedicated teacher, Professor Childs had two ways of obliterating another scholar's position concerning a biblical text. One was to characterize it as "flat," by which he meant that the argument or position did not yield an adequately full and rich sense of the theology of the passage under investigation. The other thing Childs would say is that a particular reading or method provided a view that was "out of focus." He meant it was bringing issues into the foreground that the biblical text itself did not privilege or emphasize, and thus this flawed reading was substituting the reader's own priorities, ignoring the text's invitation to focus on something else. Now, Childs was roundly criticized in the guild for suggesting that the "text" was doing something that, to external observers, just happened to match up nicely with his own hermeneutical biases. Childs was not one for going deep into the ideological constructedness and contextualization of all readings, including his own. But I found fruitful his way of speaking about readings as "flat" or "out of focus." As a feminist literary critic, I take that pedagogical gold from my admired professor with appreciation and work with it in new ways, relying on a metaphor not of a single authorized view but, rather, a prism or multiple vantage points from which to gaze on something that our gaze(s) help to construct. I aver that readings that fail to attend to the complex gendered dimensions of these ancient texts are "flat." Readings that fail to engage the dynamic contestations and arguments percolating within biblical texts, instead constructing a homogenized master narrative in a single voice as if that were the biblical text, are "out of focus." Readings that summarize the surface content of biblical poetry without plumbing the depths of metaphorization and the power of ellipsis are very much "out of focus." Readings that substitute a bland overview of archaeology and ancient military history for the catalytic ways in which biblical prose works narratologically to construct character and community are deplorably "flat." Conversely, scholarship that draws on the rich insights and lived wisdom of readers from many social and theological locations—from feminist, womanist, queer, and postcolonial "sites" academic and nonacademic, and from interdisciplinary university locations in African American Studies and Comparative Literature and Gender Studies and Political Science—aid immensely in creating readings that are multilayered and deep rather than flat, readings that can be brought into breathtakingly sharp focus through the use of different hermeneutical lenses and epistemologies from other disciplines.

As you read further in biblical studies, you'll encounter varieties of literary criticism. In the arena of narratology, skilled literary critics pay attention to metaphors and symbols. They consider narratorial voice, reported discourse, and dialogue among characters. Literary critics reflect on dimensions of setting, plot, and characterization. They analyze cues as to the expectations of the implied audience and the many ways in which those expectations may be affirmed, subverted, or redirected through literary art. Literary critics work to understand both straightforward uses and ironic manipulation of genre in texts; they notice qualities of openness or closure in story endings; and much more. The field of narratological analysis is huge even within biblical studies alone, and your wisdom in reading biblical stories will be incalculably deepened if you study literary theory in the humanities more broadly. Within narratological study of the Hebrew Scriptures, scholars who have contributed a great deal include Robert Alter, Yairah Amit, Mieke Bal, Timothy K. Beal, Danna Nolan Fewell, Harold Fisch, David Gunn, Tod Linafelt, and Meir Sternberg; many others could be named as well.

In analysis of biblical Hebrew poetry, skilled literary critics pay close attention to the elliptical, "gapped" nature of poetic expression: so much is left unsaid, and so much context is left unexpressed, that poetry creates space for catalytic connections and deep possibilities for significance, and allows for the play of ambiguity in the process of interpretation. Literary critics also consider parallelism and other formal structural features of biblical poetry: repetition and juxtaposition are vitally important to ancient poetic art. The pairing of clauses, lines, and larger blocks for rhetorical effect and artistic beauty achieves many marvelous effects in prophetic oracles. Among those effects are artful restraint, "heightening" or progressive intensification, and the establishment of equivalences and differences on many levels—phonological, morphological, grammatical, syntactical, semantic—in word-pairs, clauses, lines, whole verses, and larger blocks of text. What James Longenbach says about a poem by Andrew Marvell is beautifully true of biblical poetry: "the language feels inexplicably complex by virtue of its restraint, by virtue of implications the language raises but does not acknowledge having raised."[8] Scholars who have made influential advances in the study of biblical poetry in recent decades include James Kugel, Adele Berlin, and F. W. Dobbs-Allsopp.

Below you will find guidance on two sets of approaches to the Latter Prophets. We will consider methods focused on the compositional history of biblical books in their ancient contexts and methods focused on the analysis of ideologies constructed within and beyond the biblical text. For extensive treatments of methods in biblical studies and how to apply them, begin with the works listed in "For Further Reading," in the knowledge that many fine books on methods of biblical study exist.

Methods Focused on Compositional History

Source criticism, tradition history, and redaction criticism are modes of inquiry that can be vitally important for understanding how the prophetic books came to be in the form in which we read them today. It is highly likely that many prophetic books were composed in stages, drawing on various sources that may have existed independently at an earlier point in time. Later scribal editing—"redaction"—shaped the texts of many of the prophetic books as the books were cherished and preserved in prophetic or other circles.

Source criticism operates on the assumption that, in ways unique to each particular biblical book, scribes may have utilized existing written sources as they created these witnesses within the prophetic tradition. Evidence from the three major prophets suggests that oracles against other nations were expected in literary collections of prophecies. Each set of oracles (in Isa 13–23, Jer 46–51, and Ezek 25–32) seems to have relatively little in common with the themes of the rest of the prophetic book in which it is embedded. Many scholars have worked to show macrostructural links and literary connections between oracles against other nations and other oracles in the relevant books, but other scholars have suggested that these collections of oracles against foreign nations may have circulated independently, something that cannot actually be proved. Scholars have also wondered about the songs of the Suffering Servant in the book of Isaiah (42:1-4, 49:1-6, 50:4-9, and 52:13–53:12), although there, the rhetorical and theological linkages are plentiful with other oracles in Isaiah. Another case sometimes regarded as evidence of an independent source is Jeremiah 27–29. The name of the Babylonian king in those three chapters is spelled *Nebuchadnezzar*, whereas in all the other chapters of Jeremiah, it's spelled *Nebuchadrezzar*. Whether chapters 27–29 were edited later by a scribe who knew the name as *Nebuchadnezzar* from the Deuteronomistic History, or whether the coherent story the scribe tells, with its governing motif of "yoke," was originally a stand-alone set of narratives is impossible to know. Older scholarship on Jeremiah made confident assertions about separate sources in that book. In a 1914 book that was enormously influential, Sigmund Mowinckel (1884–1965) gave labels as follows for the book of Jeremiah: "A" for most of the poetry, "B" for biographical prose, "C" for hortatory or sermonic prose, and "D" as a catch-all label for disparate later materials. Even for those who do not follow Mowinckel's schema, the poetic oracles of doom in the first half of the book are usually considered to have been composed early, hortatory and biographical chapters coming later from another scribal hand or hands, with poetic oracles of promise and the oracles against the nations considered to be even later additions.

Archiving of Ancient Materials

On analogy to what is known about recording practices in other ancient Near Eastern cultures, it is likely that that records of oracles, omens, visions, dreams, and communications received by ecstatics would have been filed away in temple libraries [and] in royal archives if they involved the king directly. . . . It is logical to assume, then, that the creators of individual prophetic books accessed the preserved archives, chose oracles, omens, visions, dreams and communications received by various specialities of priestly personnel that suited their larger purposes, and then expanded them to make them especially relevant to their own historical circumstances and ideology.

—Diana Edelman[9]

The gift of source criticism to biblical studies is the important idea that ancient authors or scribal schools might well have worked on different blocks of material at different times, perhaps utilizing pre-existing sources that were a known part of their heritage. Much of the theory regarding ancient sources is speculative, but in some cases we can see from comparing ancient Hebrew and Greek manuscripts that indeed, in one stream of the tradition, material had been missing that seems to have been added later.

Tradition history addresses literary motifs and cultural tropes in biblical texts. Echoing or reworking received tradition gives a literary text a depth and grounded relevance that can make its narratives or its poetic expression all the more powerful. When considering the history of traditions and their use, scholars examine intertextual quotations and allusions within the biblical corpus and also the wider ancient Near Eastern context for cognate literatures. The Exodus tradition, for example, was clearly known and used by Amos, who holds his people accountable for their moral failings by the God who brought Israel out of Egypt; a series of ironic reversals in Amos is meant to annihilate his hearers' complacency about the history of deliverance on which they rely. Exodus motifs were used in a very different way by those who created the oracles in the second half of Isaiah that sing of a joyous procession through the wilderness.

There, Judeans' return from the Babylonian diaspora is imaged as a new journey through the wilderness, with springs of water bubbling up and the vegetation bursting into bloom as God's beloved people pass by on their way home. Mythological traditions from across the ancient Near East are artfully reworked in the prophetic books. The Bible is a richly layered collection of texts that refer to other texts and traditions, and it can be truly fascinating to study the ways in which the prophets and scribal circles worked with what was available to them.

Redaction criticism studies the textual evidence that scribal circles edited and supplemented existing literary texts during the process that yielded the biblical books we now have. The redaction critic looks for moments of textual awkwardness that might suggest interpolation, an editor having added something—a new thought, an explanation, a correction—that doesn't fit entirely well in its context. Some redactional changes may have been for local textual reasons, but those who study the editing of biblical books also look for series of additions that, taken together, seem to show a distinctive ideological purpose. In some instances, prose explanations seem to have been added to clarify mysterious poetic oracles—this seems to be the case in some places in Jeremiah. In some instances, oracles directed against the northern kingdom of Israel seem to have been updated with brief mentions of their applicability to Judah as well (see for example Hos 6:11). Textual disruptions flag editorial work, such as in the middle of Jeremiah 29, where a lengthy addition in the middle of 29:15 appears in the Hebrew text tradition but is not represented in the Septuagint. Redaction is fascinating because it gives clues to the earliest reception history, as it were, of biblical texts, when the texts were still in development. With every complex biblical text that shows signs of scribal reworking, we have a polyphony of witnesses to the ways in which earlier sacred tradition was heard and God's purposes were understood for particular historical contexts.

Methods Focused on Ideology Critique

A number of interpretive methods are excellent for exposing the ideologies that have shaped particular perspectives, arguments, and images within texts and the political, social, religious, and other commitments that have influenced how texts have been received. Below are offered necessarily brief pointers to feminist and womanist interpretation, postcolonial criticism, trauma studies, and disability studies. Each of these constitutes a complex set of approaches in biblical studies that developed through its own unique history of scholarship in the humanities more generally. Feminist interpretation and postcolonial criticism have generated vast bibliographies over many decades for readers at the college level and beyond. Womanist interpretation, queer criticism, trauma studies, and disability studies are considerably newer within biblical scholarship, but each of those modes of inquiry has at least two decades of scholarship behind it in the humanities and social sciences. If one or more of these methods beckons in a compelling way to you: pursue it! Space constraints in the present volume require that I gesture only briefly toward these important and fascinating pathways here.

Not every biblical studies classroom or faith community welcomes intellectual inquiry framed in feminist-, womanist-, postcolonial-, queer-, or disability-studies terms. Professors have their own values and biases, the areas in which they have developed expertise and the questions that they dismiss or may be ill-equipped to engage. All readers have things they see clearly and things they do not understand, intellectual strengths and prejudices, and norms that have been inculcated in them during their schooling. This goes for every author whose work you read, every peer with whom you engage in dialogue, and every teacher. Not every teacher will address this; many are uncomfortable reflecting on how their course design and other pedagogical choices, their scholarly training, and their institutional context are driven by implicit wisdoms and unwritten cultural biases, issues of authority and disenfranchisement that are variously claimed, disavowed, or unrecognized, and embedded hierarchies of epistemologies (some ways of knowing are considered more valuable than others).[10] Indeed, scholarship itself, with its moments of clear insight and its inevitable and pervasive biases, constitutes an appropriate object of analysis within ideological criticism. When learners glimpse a broader view of the development

30

of the Western scholarly guild, you are better able to assess the claims of the scholars you're reading and the implicit claims and priorities of your professors' syllabi. If you are interested in the history of biblical scholarship, with its idiosyncratic characters, its "Eureka!" moments and failures of vision, its instances of unexamined consensus and its bitter disputes, here are three books you might appreciate:

- Burke O. Long, *Planting and Reaping Albright: Politics, Ideology, and Interpreting the Bible*. University Park: The Pennsylvania State University Press, 1997.

- Rudolf Smend, *From Astruc to Zimmerli: Old Testament Scholarship in Three Centuries*. Tübingen: Mohr Siebeck, 2007.

- Stephen D. Moore and Yvonne Sherwood, *The Invention of the Biblical Scholar: A Critical Manifesto*. Minneapolis: Fortress, 2011.

Fair warning: after reading any of the above works, you may no longer be able to nod in agreement when you hear someone claim that biblical scholarship is objective, if indeed you ever believed that claim. Ideology is at work everywhere: in the biblical texts, in the methods we use to engage and illuminate those texts, and in the ways in which interpretive claims are expressed and evaluated in the academic guild and in communities of faith.

Ideology and Hermeneutics

We understand more clearly than many of our predecessors how what is perceived in the so-called "real world" is inevitably connected with the knowledge, the prejudices and the ideologies that the perceiving person brings with [them]. We understand also how the myth of "the neutral, uninvolved observer" has functioned and continues to function as an ideological tool in the hands of those whose political and economic interests it has served.

—Iain Provan[11]

The interrogation of ideology always requires that we ferret out and examine veiled assumptions about meaning, power, and which voices are privileged. Ideology is unavoidable; the important thing is to strive to recognize ideological commitments and analyze their effects.

Feminist biblical interpretation, which has existed in many forms and expressions for centuries, has made remarkable gains as regards the increasing refinement of its methodologies in the past fifty years. Early work was focused on claiming and honoring women's experience. This often meant lifting up the voices and stories of women biblical characters. As the subfield grew in strength and sophistication, feminist interpreters continued their resistance of gendered dynamics of oppression as those were identified in ancient sociohistorical contexts, interpretive traditions over the centuries, and norms in the modern guild of biblical studies. An informative resource here is Susanne Scholz's 2007 book, *Introducing the Women's Hebrew Bible*, which traces a brief history of key developments in feminist biblical scholarship from the late nineteenth century in the United States to contemporary interpretation, en route offering a fascinating glimpse into the careers of four influential feminist biblical scholars: Phyllis Trible, in the United States; Athalya Brenner, formerly of the Netherlands and now in Israel; Elsa Tamez, in Costa Rica; and Marie-Theres Wacker, in Germany. With the growing influence of feminist analysis and gender theory work done outside of biblical studies, recent years have witnessed the emergence of sophisticated critical attention to the role of gender—feminine, masculine, and other—in the formation of biblical subjects and implied audiences, reader agency in the construction of meaning, and reading practices as culturally situated performances.

The conversation has moved from the foundational work of second-wave feminist biblical scholars to gender analyses that take into account late-modern and postmodern understandings of gender, sex, power, the body, and textual authority. Within this purview, queer readings are still developing within biblical scholarship; see "For Further Reading" for two key resources. As is the case with literary criticism, so too in feminist interpretation, your skills will be honed and your knowledge deepened in crucial ways if you engage this area of inquiry in the humanities more broadly. There are many volumes of essays in feminist biblical criticism going back to the 1980s—far too many to identify here, which is a wonderful sign of the richness and vitality of this mode of interpretation. There are so many important contributors that one risks giving offense by naming some at the expense of others. Nevertheless, I offer that for the novice wishing to gain expertise in this area, feminist interpreters of the Hebrew Scriptures whose work has been especially generative include Athalya Brenner, L. Juliana Claassens, Esther Fuchs, Christl Maier, Phyllis Trible, and Gale Yee. I should also mention two New Testament feminist scholars whose work has been influential for their Hebrew Bible colleagues: Kwok Pui-lan and Elisabeth Schüssler Fiorenza. Within the subfield of masculinity studies, Rhiannon Graybill's 2016 book, *Are We Not Men? Unstable Masculinity in the Hebrew Prophets*, is an essential resource.

Womanist interpretation emerged as a powerful set of approaches informed by feminism but deeply dissatisfied with the failures of second-wave White feminists to recognize the White supremacy and unintended racial prejudices that deformed Western feminism's vision of emancipatory cultural work and social advocacy. Grounded in the lived experience of African American women and other women of color, womanist biblical interpretation may be traced back to African American women preachers such as Jarena Lee (1783–1864), Julia A. J. Foote (1823–1900), and Anna Julia Cooper (1858–1964). Womanist interpretation seeks to interrogate and resist performances of power that subjugate Black women and others. In a variety of ways, womanist interpreters offer readings of biblical texts and analyses of histories of interpretation that can dismantle oppression, creating and sustaining inclusive communities committed to justice for all persons. Building on the important early work of Katie Cannon, Renita Weems, and Delores Williams, womanist interpreters whose work you might consult today include Kelly Brown Douglas, Wilda Gafney, Nyasha Junior, Eboni Marshall Turman, and Emilie Townes.

Postcolonial criticism has developed in the humanities from foundational works such as *Black Skin, White Masks* (1952) and *The Wretched of the Earth* (1961) by Frantz Fanon, *Orientalism* (1978) by Edward Said, *The Location of Culture* (1994) by Homi Bhabha, and *A Critique of Postcolonial*

Reason: A History of the Vanishing Present (1999) by Gayatri Chakravorty Spivak. It had long been recognized in biblical studies that the threats and lures of empire were negotiated in a variety of ways in the literature of the Hebrew Scriptures. This is quite evidently the case in the prophetic corpus: Isaiah and Jeremiah, in particular, work hard to promote particular theopolitical approaches regarding alliances with or against the empires that surrounded their small and threatened nation. The devastations wrought in Israel and Judah by the imperial predations of Assyria and Babylon can be seen throughout the Hebrew Bible. But in sophisticated analysis of the multiplicity of effects and distortions of colonial subjugation in the sacred texts of Israel and Judah, the guild of biblical scholars has lagged far behind their colleagues in Comparative Literature, English, and History departments. This situation is improving as biblical scholars develop the skills to move away from simplistic historicism. The horizon is open for more nuanced interpretation of the oblique effects of ideologies in the shadow of empire, not only as may be seen in the actual plot of biblical stories, but also in the narratology and poetics of these ancient texts and the ways in which they strive to form the subjectivity of their implied audiences. For keen analysis that addresses colonialism and postcoloniality in interpretation of biblical texts, the novice might start with the work of Musa W. Dube, Judith E. McKinlay, Fernando F. Segovia, and R. S. Sugirtharajah.

Trauma studies seeks to analyze ways in which texts reveal and mask that they were produced in, or marked by, situations of trauma on social, cultural, or political levels. National and local catastrophes can sear the memories of individuals and social groups for generations. In any culture, meaning-making through traditional verbal arts such as storytelling, song, and liturgy can be profoundly affected by protracted anxiety, anguish, and loss in the ranks of those who create and lead during a time of crisis, and by their children and their children's children as memories of horror or devastation are passed down, through active recounting or through the oblique communication of stunned silence. Trauma studies helps us analyze some of the ways in which remembered trauma has left marks on the texts of the Hebrew prophets, who remembered—literally and figuratively—the grievous harm done by Assyrian military assaults and deportations in the eighth century BCE and the unspeakable suffering caused by the Babylonian army in the years before the first deportation of Judeans in 597, as troops broke through the walls of Jerusalem, defiled and destroyed the cultural structures that upheld communal life in that place, and slaughtered or deported the citizens cowering in the ruins. Attending to the residue of those times of terror and noting the social formations and deformations that were deemed vital for survival, we can "read" what the threat of obliteration did to the cultural heritage of Israel and Judah. We see traces of fear, rage, conflict, and loss in these texts' depictions of ancient cultural norms of political leadership, their promotion of particular political responses to experiences of vulnerability and cultural anxiety, and their vivid portrayals of Judean life pitched in the intersections of woundedness, resilience, and creativity.

Forged in Remembered Trauma

The prophetic literature is survival literature for postwar communities living through monstrous events. Coarse language of violence together with penetrating images of cultural ruin run through the literary terrain. Shocking scenes of brutality give the corpus its erratic and discontinuous quality. Put concretely, written prophecy bears witness to unmanageable social and symbolic dissonance as a result of colonizing forces located on the Tigris and Euphrates. . . . Its multiple voices are often raw, unpredictable, and violent because savage forces perceived as both human and divine have devastated symbolic and social worlds. From the testimony of survivors, both ancient and contemporary, we know that such wreckage not only causes physical and emotional havoc, but it also evokes probing questions about meaning: the meaning of atrocity; the meaning of moral chaos; the meaning of divine silence.

—Louis Stulman and Hyun Chul Paul Kim[12]

Disability studies assesses what we can know of communal values and cultural norms through assessing the ways in which bodies and capacities are represented as healthy, strong, or normative in desirable ways, or sick, weak, or nonnormative in ways considered undesirable. Theorizing disability involves understanding that implicit or overt valuations of bodies and capacities are constructed socially. Values may be articulated in a host of ways, in literature and in interpretations. We can analyze idealization of the "normate" (the form or ability considered standard), ways in which

35

texts or interpretations ignore or suppress difference, the marginalization of bodies or capacities considered undesirable, and cultural mechanisms of outright abjection—that is, the exclusion or even violent expulsion of the nonnormative from a social system.

Within disability scholarship on the Hebrew Bible, historians assess medical and social practices in antiquity regarding the regulation and treatment of bodies, and the religious and political norms developed on the basis of various ancient conceptions of wellness, illness, and injury, contagion, purity and impurity, and related issues. Literary analyses of disability look at metaphors, plot, and characterization for cultural cues about ancient Israelite notions of bodiedness (in all its dimensions, including mental), exploring the implications of difference or impairment within the plots of biblical stories and on a meta-narrative level as expressed or implied in concepts of viable membership in the covenant community, constraints on social relationships, and theological ideas regarding what pleases or displeases God. Scholars of disability examine cultural assumptions and values encoded in Torah legislation, for example, in the prohibitions against sacrificing to YHWH animals considered "blemished" or otherwise inadequate and the legislation regulating female bodiedness in language that may imply that the healthy heterosexual male body is the normate over against which aspects of female, nonnormative male, and other bodied experience are construed as problematic or needing remediation. A scholar of disability studies who offers an excellent comprehensive overview is Rebecca Raphael. Her 2008 book, *Biblical Corpora: Representations of Disability in Hebrew Biblical Literature*, is an example of scholarship that engages well with traditions of physical difference, ability and impairment, holiness, purity and impurity, and so on, considering ways in which normality and alterity are represented in biblical narratives and rhetoric. Another leading disability studies scholar who has done important work on the Latter Prophets is Jeremy Schipper. Schipper's 2011 book, *Disability and Isaiah's Suffering Servant* (see the bibliography of the Isaiah chapter in this book) is essential reading for those considering the prophetic body and the social body of Israel.

Moving Forward into the Prophetic Books

As you prepare to read and reread the prophets, remember that all texts are culturally freighted acts of communication. The relationship between historical contexts and textual representations is wondrously complex. Any simple pronouncement or claim about an overarching theme in a prophetic text is bound to be inadequate to the richly complicated nature of these books. And remember that literary aspects of meaning in texts are rich indeed. Meaning is created by numerous interactions among a huge variety of factors within and outside of texts, all of these as construed by the interpreter. The intertextual and intercultural web of connections, associations, and resonances that can be discerned—even just within the ancient context, and all the more as you move into the history of interpretation—is vast. I hope you find that vast horizon unsettling in productive ways, and intellectually exciting.

When you are hiking, cycling, or driving, you may encounter signs that enhanced caution or advanced skills are required ahead. The hiker might see a gentle reminder to STAY ON TRAIL or a more sobering CAUTION! DIFFICULT TERRAIN AHEAD. Drivers in remote areas may come across more elaborate warnings, like this:

or like this:

```
╔══════════════════════════════════════╗
║                                        ║
║      EXTREMELY ROUGH                   ║
║      ROAD AHEAD — VEHICLE              ║
║      TRAFFIC DISCOURAGED               ║
║      ─────────────                     ║
║                                        ║
║      4 x 4 WITH EXPERIENCED            ║
║      DRIVERS AND NARROW                ║
║      WHEEL BASE ONLY                   ║
║                                        ║
╚══════════════════════════════════════╝
```

Just as a pleasant road can turn into a winding course that requires laser focus and artisanal driving skills, or a broad, flat hiking path can yield to more demanding terrain, so too, interpretive terrain can become challenging to navigate as one moves away from the well-marked trails of scholarly consensus. Now, for those who enjoy untangling scholarly debates and probing for the logic underlying competing claims, advanced expeditions into contested issues are invigorating. Fascinating discoveries lie around every bend, and the vistas are magnificent! But those new to biblical study may not be fully equipped to undertake the journey into the complexities of biblical scholarship. The section titled "For Further Reading" at the end of each chapter will help guide you as your journey continues. If you want to attend closely to the biblical text at first, rather than launching immediately into scholarly abstractions, start with the influential book of Walter Brueggemann, *The Prophetic Imagination*, which came out in 2018 in a fortieth anniversary edition.

As we move forward together, be aware of the vast scope of material we'll be covering. Isaiah, Jeremiah, and Ezekiel differ from one another in literary style and offer strikingly different theologies. Hosea, Amos, Jonah, and Nahum couldn't be more different from one another, on numerous counts. Nevertheless, I've heard many students say that the prophets all blur together in their minds, at least at first, and I honor that. Learning is a complex process. When we learn, we are assimilating a great deal of new information; we are working to reconfigure or nuance our previous understanding of a topic; and we may be struggling with ideas that challenge us and with the magnitude of what we still do not know. Doubt and questioning are not obstacles to learning but, instead, integral parts of learning and maturing in wisdom. We might think of Jeremiah's initial objection to his call to prophetic ministry: "Ah, Lord GOD! Truly I do not know how to speak, for I am only a boy" (Jer 1:6 NRSV). His humility and awareness of his limitations made him all the more appropriate as God's servant. The below hymn, created in 2005 by Yale Divinity School students Dianne Bilyak[13] (text) and Alan C. Murchie (music), reminds us that disorientation is an important part of the learning process and can be spiritually significant for us as learners.

Help My Unbelief

When the darkening sorrows have led us to night,
When the absence of presence has covered the light,
When the ground underneath us is not always firm,
And we sink and it takes us a long time to learn

That the way that we trust and the way that we grow,
Is to give up our need to be sure and to know,
Like the lines that we crossed and lines that we traced,
That at times became lifted by hands made of grace.

And we see that confusion can turn us about,
And we face our belief in the shadows of doubt,
And we fall on our knees and look straight at the fear
and make peace with the mystery that carried us here.

For Further Reading

Arnold, Bill T., and Richard S. Hess, eds. *Ancient Israel's History: An Introduction to Issues and Sources.* Grand Rapids: Baker Academic, 2014.

Avalos, Hector, Sarah J. Melcher, and Jeremy Schipper, eds. *This Abled Body: Rethinking Disabilities in Biblical Studies.* SemeiaSt 55. Atlanta: Society of Biblical Literature, 2007.

Becker, Eve-Marie, Jan Dochhorn, and Else K. Holt, eds. *Trauma and Traumatization in Individual and Collective Dimensions: Insights from Biblical Studies and Beyond.* Studia Aarhusiana Neotestamentica. Göttingen: Vandenhoeck & Ruprecht, 2014.

Blenkinsopp, Joseph. *A History of Prophecy in Israel.* Rev. Ed. Louisville: Westminster John Knox, 1996.

Boer, Roland. *The Sacred Economy of Ancient Israel.* LAI. Louisville: Westminster John Knox, 2015.

Brown, William P. *A Handbook to Old Testament Exegesis.* Louisville: Westminster John Knox, 2017.

Brueggemann, Walter. *The Prophetic Imagination.* 40th anniversary ed. Minneapolis: Fortress, 2018.

Gafney, Wilda C. *Daughters of Miriam: Women Prophets in Ancient Israel.* Minneapolis: Fortress, 2008.

Graybill, Rhiannon. *Are We Not Men? Unstable Masculinity in the Hebrew Prophets.* Oxford: Oxford University Press, 2016.

Heschel, Abraham J. *The Prophets.* New York: Harper & Row, 1962.

Hornsby, Teresa J., and Ken Stone, eds. *Bible Trouble: Queer Reading at the Boundaries of Biblical Scholarship.* SemeiaSt 67. Atlanta: Society of Biblical Literature, 2011.

Junior, Nyasha. *An Introduction to Womanist Biblical Interpretation.* Louisville: Westminster John Knox, 2015.

Kessler, Rainer. *The Social History of Ancient Israel: An Introduction.* Translated by Linda M. Maloney. Minneapolis: Fortress, 2008.

Macwilliam, Stuart. *Queer Theory and the Prophetic Marriage Metaphor in the Hebrew Bible.* Oakville, CT: Equinox, 2011.

McKenzie, Steven L., and John Kaltner, eds. *New Meanings for Ancient Texts: Recent Approaches to Biblical Criticisms and Their Applications*. Louisville: Westminster John Knox, 2013.

O'Brien, Julia M. *Challenging Prophetic Metaphor: Theology and Ideology in the Prophets*. Louisville: Westminster John Knox, 2008.

Provan, Iain, V. Philips Long, and Tremper Longman III. *A Biblical History of Israel*. 2nd ed. Louisville: Westminster John Knox, 2015.

Raphael, Rebecca. *Biblical Corpora: Representations of Disability in Hebrew Biblical Literature*. LHBOTS 445. New York: T & T Clark, 2008.

Scholz, Susanne. *Introducing the Women's Hebrew Bible*. IFT 13. New York: T & T Clark, 2007.

Sharp, Carolyn J., ed. *The Oxford Handbook of the Prophets*. Oxford: Oxford University Press, 2016.

Sugirtharajah, R. S. *Exploring Postcolonial Biblical Criticism: History, Method, Practice*. Oxford: Wiley-Blackwell, 2012.

Thompson, Thomas L. *The Mythic Past: Biblical Archaeology and the Myth of Israel*. New York: Basic Books, 2000.

Chapter 2

Isaiah:
Prophet of Restoration

The dramatic book of Isaiah is a compelling work of ancient literature. The Isaiah traditions span several centuries during which Israel struggled to find its way in challenging political circumstances. Isaiah of Jerusalem prophesied in the eighth century BCE, but his witness was deemed powerfully authoritative in subsequent generations, for the oracles of Isaiah of Jerusalem, along with prose traditions linked to the Isaiah materials, were preserved, shaped, and further elaborated as Israel's historical circumstances changed. From the Assyrian period through the rise of Babylonian dominance and on into the Persian period, Isaiah's words of challenge and consolation were important to the scribes who preserved Israel's spiritual heritage in written prophetic books.

Over the centuries, attentive readers have noticed major differences of theological and political emphasis in different blocks of material within Isaiah. Since the pioneering work on Isaiah done in 1892 by Bernhard Duhm (1847–1928), scholars have referred to different sections with specific names, tying the authorship of each section to a particular historical setting from the eighth century through the sixth century BCE or a bit later. Many scholars still use the following divisions: Isaiah 1–39 is called First Isaiah, Isaiah 40–55 is called Second Isaiah (or Deutero-Isaiah), and Isaiah 56–66 is called Third Isaiah (or Trito-Isaiah). Most scholars agree that Isaiah 1 and Isaiah 66 serve as a kind of framing structure for the entire book; further, numerous theological connections and thematic links can be discerned across the three major sections. Certainly those charged with preserving the Isaiah traditions in ancient Judah took great care to weave disparate subcollections of material together into a majestic whole. Many other structural proposals have been developed since the work of Duhm—it's the kind of work that structurally minded scholars find important and energizing. Below are three alternatives, simply as a gesture toward a larger landscape of pathways through which the diverse materials of Isaiah may be understood:

- John N. Oswalt believes that Isaiah 56–66 was "written in the full knowledge of the entire preceding corpus and function[s] to unify that corpus. . . . In chaps. 1–39 a right relationship with God is only possible in the light of admission of the sin which has broken the relationship, a whole-hearted renunciation of that sin, and an equally wholehearted commitment to living a life of obedience. . . . Chaps. 40–55 present a radically different picture. They seem to suggest that obedience to the laws of God plays no part in either securing or maintaining a relationship with Him. The only sin is the sin of giving up hope, and the only failure is failure to remember the infinite power and creativity of the Creator. . . . [In chaps. 56–66,] righteous living is still required, but now it is to be the gift of God's grace. . . . [56–66] represents a circling back in an effort to tie the two sections together."[1]

- David L. Petersen proposes that Isaiah 1–32 and 36–66 be seen as two sections treating Zion in different ways: the first part deals with the "travails of Zion," and the second part with the personified city's restoration. Isaiah 33–35 functions as a complicated kind of hinge that muses theologically on the traditions that occur in the earlier part and the traditions that occur in the latter part. Petersen characterizes the book as a "grand diptych," his metaphor alluding to art made with hinged panels of ivory or painted wood.[2]

- Ulrich Berges argues that Isaiah 36–39 constitute the theological center of the book, which should be envisioned not as a diptych but "as a literary cathedral in which the reader is invited to witness Zion's past history and future destiny." The other chapters, in the view of Berges, are arranged in this structure:

- Act I, Isaiah 1–12: Zion and Jerusalem between judgment and salvation;
- Act II, Isaiah 13–27: Zion's enemies and friends— Yнwн's kingship;
- Act III, Isaiah 28–35: The divine king and the congregation of Zion;
- Act IV, Isaiah 36–39: The threat to and deliverance of Zion and Jerusalem;
- Act V, Isaiah 40–48: The [servant] Jacob/Israel in Babylon and his liberation by Cyrus;
- Act VI, Isaiah 49–54: The restoration of Zion and the work of the [servant];
- Act VII, Isaiah 55–66: The division in Israel and the fate of the [servants].[3]

A number of scholars find the arguments weak regarding different sections of Isaiah if those are seen as discrete, either wholly independent or only lightly connected. Benjamin D. Sommer has objected, "I dispute . . . the practice (especially prevalent in criticism of Isa 1–33 and 56–66) of finding a patchwork of textual fragments in passages that make better sense as they stand. The disjunctions and contradictions that allegedly establish the composite nature of prophetic texts often result from hyper-sensitive reading rather than genuine critical acumen."[4] It is assuredly not difficult to find powerful theological connections across the book of Isaiah. For just one example, Brevard Childs offers: "The prophetic author [of Third Isaiah], who is not just a learned scribe, follows Second Isaiah in keeping his identity anonymous when performing his role as a faithful tradent of the prophetic tradition of Isaiah. He lays claim to the same divine spirit that was given to his predecessor in 42:1, and he identifies fully with his same mission."[5] Now, "identifies fully" may be a bit overstated, given that we can see pronounced differences of theme and emphasis in Isaiah 56–66. But there is continuity here, and Childs is saying that continuity is the point in this complex Isaianic tradition. That's not the same as claiming that the same historical prophet wrote all of the book of Isaiah. But it is to say that, theologically speaking, the continuity of witness in the Isaiah traditions over several centuries is more important for the text than identifying the specific individuals who were involved in proclaiming that witness.

Another kind of focus may be found in the divine purposes enacted in history. According to all of the Isaiah texts, the LORD is at work in history. In events of great magnitude in Israel's life and in more minor events whose details have been forgotten, the LORD has been at work, redeeming and teaching the covenant people generation after generation, even if the lessons to be learned—the theological formation, if you will—may differ as Israel's and Judah's contextual challenges change. One implication of reading this magnificent, complex prophetic book as a whole is that the historical actions of God with God's people are worth remembering in their particularity. According to Isaiah, God's historical agency and purposes can be discerned or ignored in the choices of Israel in every age, with profound consequences through history from "of old," from ancient days, into every present moment—whether that be the present moment of eighth-century Isaiah of Jerusalem, or the present moment of Second Isaiah reflecting on those older traditions and elaborating on their significance, or a future moment.

Many attentive readers would agree with Ulrich Berges that "the book of Isaiah is too disparate to be regarded as unified, and too unified to be regarded as purely disparate."[6] Whatever you find most plausible about how the book of Isaiah came to be, I'd encourage you to consider that the final form of the book of Isaiah has been shaped as a gorgeously complex unity, and it invites us to read its disparate parts and voices in relationship to one another. Isaiah expressly fosters a hermeneutic of attentiveness to connections within the book across time, which is one of the features that makes this ancient prophetic text fascinating to read and reread.

Isaiah 1:1 suggests that Isaiah of Jerusalem prophesied for about forty years. The prophet relayed the word of the LORD and enacted his dramatic sign-acts in the reign of Judean king Uzziah (who reigned 783–742 BCE) and on through the reigns of Jotham (742–735), Ahaz (735–715), and

Hezekiah (715–687). Isaiah 6 speaks of the prophet receiving his commissioning to the prophetic vocation in 742. Two military crises disrupted political and social life in Jerusalem in the years that followed. The Syro-Ephraimite war created grave anxiety in Judah from 735 to 732. Assyrian pressure on Judah and neighboring groups in the region catalyzed the creation of a resistance coalition of Aram (Syria—that's the "Syro-" part in the name of this war) and the northern kingdom of Israel ("Ephraim"). The coalition sought to coerce Ahaz of Judah into joining them; Ahaz was terrified and needed the reassurances of the prophet Isaiah in order to "stand firm in faith" (Isa 7 NRSV; see 2 Kgs 16 for an account of Ahaz's confirmation of Judah's vassal loyalty to Assyria and payment of tribute to the Assyrian king). Continuing instability in the region meant that rebellion against Assyria continued to percolate, after some years leading to a second crisis: an assault on Jerusalem in 701 by Sennacherib and his army. Isaiah 36–37 and the parallel narrative in 2 Kings 18–19 say that Sennacherib's siege of Jerusalem was thwarted by divine intervention. In the interests of fairness, I note here a case of dueling narratives, for Sennacherib's own account describes the military campaign as having been successful, the Assyrian king boasting in an inscription on a royal monument that he had shut up Hezekiah within Jerusalem "like a bird in a cage."

Some material in Isaiah 1–39 does not reflect events of the eighth century. The Isaiah 23 oracle against Tyre, the wealthy Phoenician city-state, speaks of Tyre and its harbor having been destroyed, Tyre then to be "forgotten for seventy years, the lifetime of one king" (23:15), but we don't know of events that fit that description until the conquest of Tyre by Alexander the Great in 332. Nebuchadnezzar, the king of Babylon, besieged Tyre for thirteen years in the time of the prophet Ezekiel, from 585 to 573, but Tyre was not destroyed. This is acknowledged in Ezekiel 29:17-20, in which an oracle dated to 571 says, "Nebuchadrezzar of Babylon made his army labor hard against Tyre; every head was made bald and every shoulder was rubbed bare; yet neither he nor his army got anything from Tyre to pay for the labor that he had expended against it" (29:18 NRSV), so the LORD promises to give Egypt to Nebuchadnezzar as a consolation prize. In any case, the decimation of Tyre was not an event of eighth-century history. You may read the Isaiah 23 oracle, then, as predicting the future, as reflecting an earlier situation in hyperbolic language, or—with many scholars—as having been composed later than its literary setting in the book of Isaiah might suggest.

Other historical events that shaped the book of Isaiah include the waning of Assyria's power in the latter part of the seventh century and the rise of Babylon to dominance in the region, a power shift fully effected by 605 with Babylon's defeat of Egypt at the Battle of Carchemish. Later chapters of Isaiah (chaps. 35 and 40 onward) clearly know the fall of Jerusalem to Babylon in 587, the rise of the Persian empire and its defeat of Babylon, and the decree of King Cyrus of Persia in 538 that the Judean exiles in Babylon may return home.

Theological Themes

Several themes serve as theological anchors and unifying trajectories across the sixty-six chapters of Isaiah. Below are discussions of three such themes. Focusing on these may help you to organize your understanding of this complex book as you wade into the stirring poetic oracles and dramatic prose stories of the Isaiah traditions.

God as the Holy One of Israel

God is called "Israel's holy one" or "the holy one of Israel" dozens of times in the book of Isaiah. Below are some important instances. Notice that this special theological title comes up across the entire book, not just in one section.

> Doom! Sinful nation, people weighed down with crimes, evildoing offspring, corrupt children! They have abandoned the LORD, despised the **holy one of Israel**; they turned their backs on God. (1:4)

> Doom to those who drag guilt along with cords of fraud, and haul sin as if with cart ropes, who say, "God should hurry and work faster so we can see; let the plan of **Israel's holy one** come quickly, so we can understand it." (5:18-19)

Therefore, as a tongue of fire devours stubble, and as hay shrivels in a flame, so their roots will rot, and their blossoms turn to dust, for they have rejected the teaching of the Lord of heavenly forces, and have despised the word of **Israel's holy one**. (5:24)

On that day, what's left of Israel and the survivors of the house of Jacob will no longer depend on the one who beat them. Instead, they will faithfully depend on the Lord, the **holy one of Israel**. (10:20)

Shout and sing for joy, city of Zion, because **the holy one of Israel** is great among you. (12:6)

These are rebellious people, lying children, children unwilling to hear the Lord's teaching, who say to the seers, "Don't foresee," and to the visionaries, "Don't report truthful visions; tell us flattering things; envision deceptions; get out of the way; step off the path; let's have no more 'holy one of Israel.'" (30:9-11)

Therefore, the Lord God, **the holy one of Israel**, says: In return and rest you will be saved; quietness and trust will be your strength—but you refused. (30:15)

Don't fear, worm of Jacob, people of Israel! I will help you, says the Lord. **The holy one of Israel** is your redeemer. (41:14)

I am the Lord your God, **the holy one of Israel**, your savior. I have given Egypt as your ransom, Cush and Seba in your place. (43:3)

The Lord, **the holy one of Israel** and its maker, says: Are you questioning me about my own children? Are you telling me what to do with the work of my hands? (45:11)

The children of your tormenters will come bending low to you; all who despised you will bow down at your feet. They will call you The Lord's City, Zion, of **the holy one of Israel**. (60:14)

The incomparably powerful holiness of God suffuses the book of Isaiah with light and strength. The ancient authors of these traditions use this theme to render risible the arrogance of all who might dare to oppose God's purposes, whether those be international enemies or the unjust within Judean society. No human pride will be able to stand against the divine plan:

> The LORD of heavenly forces has planned a day:
>> against all that is prideful and haughty;
>>
>> against all that is lofty,
>>
>> and it will be laid low;
>>
>> against all the cedars of Lebanon, high and lofty;
>>
>> against all the oaks of Bashan;
>>
>> against all the high mountains;
>>
>> against all the lofty hills;
>>
>> against every tall tower;
>>
>> against every fortified wall;
>>
>> against all the ships of Tarshish;
>>
>> against all the wonderful boats.
>
> People's pride will be brought down
>> and human arrogance humiliated.
>
> The LORD alone will be exalted on that day;
>> the idols will completely pass away. (2:12-18)

Spiritual complacency, political scheming, arrogance: all will fall before the incomparable power of Israel's God.

Prophetic Critique of Idolatry

The prophetic rejection of idolatry—the worshipping of false gods—is articulated in two different ways in Isaiah, with a special intensity in Isaiah 40–55. First, the prophet ridicules idols in scathing terms as inanimate

50

statues, making those who utilize idols in ritual worship look foolish. Consider the ludicrous scene sketched in Isaiah 44:

> Who would fashion a god or cast an image that can do no good? Look, all its devotees shall be put to shame; the artisans too are merely human. . . . The ironsmith fashions it and works it over the coals, shaping it with hammers, and forging it with his strong arm; he becomes hungry and his strength fails, he drinks no water and is faint. . . . He plants a cedar and the rain nourishes it. Then it can be used as fuel. Part of it he takes and warms himself; he kindles a fire and bakes bread. Then he makes a god and worships it, makes it a carved image and bows down before it. Half of it he burns in the fire; over this half he roasts meat, eats it and is satisfied. . . . The rest of it he makes into a god, his idol, bows down to it and worships it; he prays to it and says, "Save me, for you are my god!" No one considers, nor is there knowledge or discernment to say, "Half of it I burned in the fire; I also baked bread on its coals, I roasted meat and have eaten. Now shall I make the rest of it an abomination? Shall I fall down before a block of wood?" (44:10-12, 14-17, 19 NRSV)

Now, those of us who worship in liturgical traditions in which sanctified or honored objects play a role might bridle at this mockery. When the Torah is processed through a gathered congregation in a synagogue, the believers stand and face it, and some reach out to touch its velvet mantle with their fingertips or kiss it as a gesture of reverence. In my own liturgical tradition, the Episcopal Church, many bow prayerfully as the processional cross goes by in worship; a few worshippers genuflect to the tabernacle on the high altar each time they enter or leave their pew. In none of these cases do believers think that God is being worshipped as actually present in the object itself as something that could then "come and save them." Clearly Second Isaiah's broadside is highly tendentious. It would have been memorable, as well as insulting or amusing, to his ancient audience. The prophetic indictment against idolatry continues in Isaiah 46:

> To whom will you liken me and make me equal, and compare me, as though we were alike? Those who lavish gold from the purse, and weigh out silver in the scales—they hire a goldsmith, who makes it into a god; then they fall down and worship! They lift it to their shoulders, they carry it, they set it in its place, and it stands there; it cannot move from

its place. If one cries out to it, it does not answer or save anyone from trouble. (46:5-7 NRSV)

Again, few ancient believers were likely to have thought that as they prayed before a liturgical object, the icon or statue would jump down from its pedestal to save them. But Isaiah's blistering sarcasm was crafted for rhetorical effect. One effect assuredly would have been to render absurd the worship of deities other than Israel's God, strengthening the bonds of faithfulness in the covenant community that heard the prophet's words.

A second way in which Second Isaiah makes idolatry untenable for the implied audience involves repeated assertions that only Israel's God has predicted what would happen "from of old." Only the LORD knows what happened in primordial times and in Israel's past history, the "former things." Only the LORD knows the "new things" that will happen in the future. Idols are insensate blocks of wood; they do not understand what has been and cannot foretell what will come to pass, and those who worship them are like them. Second Isaiah is relentless in his polemic about how useless idolatry is in this regard.

On idolaters bringing their "proofs" that other gods can be powerful:

> Let the idols approach and tell us what will happen.
> The prior things—what are they?
>> Announce them, and we'll think about them and know their
>> significance.
>> Or proclaim to us what is to come!
> Report things that will happen in the future,
>> then we'll know that you are gods.
> Do good! Or do bad!
>> Then we will all be afraid and fearful.
> Look! You are nobody, and your deeds are nothing.
>> Whoever chooses you is disgusting. (41:22-24)

> The things announced in the past—look—they've already happened,
>> but I'm declaring new things.
>> Before they even appear, I tell you about them. (42:9)

Don't remember the prior things;

> don't ponder ancient history.

Look! I'm doing a new thing;

> now it sprouts up; don't you recognize it?

I'm making a way in the desert,

> paths in the wilderness.

The beasts of the field, the jackals and ostriches, will honor me,

> because I have put water in the desert and streams in the wilderness.
>> (43:18-20)

Remember the prior things—from long ago;

> I am God, and there's no other.

I am God! There's none like me,

> who tells the end at the beginning,

> from ancient times things not yet done,

> saying, "My plan will stand;

> all that I decide I will do,"

I call a bird of prey from the east,

> a man from a distant land for my plan.

As surely as I have spoken, I'll make it happen. (46:9-11)

Past things I announced long ago;

> from my mouth I proclaimed them.

> I acted suddenly, and they came about.

Because I know that you are stubborn,

> your neck is made of iron,

> and your forehead is bronze.

I informed you long ago;

> before they came about I proclaimed them to you

> so you wouldn't say, "My idol did them;

> my wood statue and metal god commanded them." (48:3-5)

Look! I'm creating a new heaven and a new earth:

   past events won't be remembered;

   they won't come to mind.

Be glad and rejoice forever in what I'm creating,

   because I'm creating Jerusalem as a joy

   and her people as a source of gladness. (65:17-18)

All of history—everything that has occurred and will occur to Israel over the centuries—has been purposed by the Creator, who alone has control over history's unimaginable expanse. Second Isaiah reassures a traumatized people who may have believed that the fall of Jerusalem and the slaughter or deportation of so many of their loved ones was the result of Israel's God having been defeated by the god Marduk of Babylon or other deities. The prophet's point is not just that Yнwн had never been bested by the gods of Israel's enemies, nor only that Yнwн is strong enough to redeem the traumatized Judean survivors from Babylonian captivity. More than that, all that Israel has endured is dwarfed within the cosmic sweep of the purposes of God. All that has existed and all that will ever come into being are woven together in the mind of the One who now, through Second Isaiah, speaks good news of deliverance to Israel.

Daughter Zion, Wounded and Restored

Across the ancient Near East, cities were personified as female in many cultures' scribal literatures. Personification may have achieved a number of rhetorical goals, including making oracles more dramatic or poignant and stirring up in ancient hearers a sense of solidarity or loyalty toward the center of religious and political power. Jerusalem, often named *Zion* in poetry, is characterized in Isaiah by means of several evocative metaphors: pejoratively in the metaphor of defiant sex worker (English translations still use the terms *whore* or *prostitute*); in terms of vulnerability as a daughter or wife in need of protection; as a barren, bereaved, or forsaken mother who comes to know the joy of many children; and as a bejeweled and honored queen resplendent in her radiance. Below are some of the passages in Isaiah in which Jerusalem is personified in poetic terms as Daughter Zion.

> Daughter Zion is left like a small shelter in a vineyard,
>> like a hut in a cucumber field,
>> like a city besieged. (1:8)

> This faithful town has become a prostitute!
> She was full of justice;
>> righteousness lived in her—
>> but now murderers. (1:21)

> What will one say to that nation's messengers?
>> The LORD has founded Zion;
>> the oppressed among God's people will find refuge there.
>>> (14:32)

> Since you prayed to me about Assyria's King Sennacherib, this is the message that the LORD has spoken against him:
> The young woman, Daughter Zion, despises you and mocks you;
>> Daughter Jerusalem shakes her head behind your back. (37:21-22)

> But Zion says, "The LORD has abandoned me;
>> my Lord has forgotten me." (49:14)

> Awake, awake, put on your strength, Zion!
> Put on your splendid clothing, Jerusalem, you holy city;
>> for the uncircumcised and unclean will no longer come into you.

Shake the dust off yourself;

> rise up; sit enthroned, Jerusalem.

Loose the bonds from your neck, captive Daughter Zion! (52:1-2)

This is what the LORD announced to the earth's distant regions: Say to
Daughter Zion, "Look! Your deliverer arrives, bringing reward and
payment!" (62:11)

Whoever heard of such a thing?

> Whoever saw such things as these?

Can a land come to birth in one day?

> Can a nation be born all at once?

Yet as soon as birth pangs came,

> Zion bore her children.

Will I open the womb and not bring to birth? says the LORD.

> Will I, who create life, close the womb? says your God.

Celebrate with Jerusalem; be happy with her,

> all you who love her!

Rejoice with her in joy,

> all you who mourn over her,
>
> so that you may nurse and be satisfied from her comforting
> breasts,
>
> that you may drink and be refreshed from her full breasts.
> (66:8-11)

For many in ancient Judah, Jerusalem is to be honored as God's chosen dwelling place forever. This tenet, which scholars call the "royal Zion
theology," underlines God's enduring faithfulness to Jerusalem and to the
throne of David as expressed with translucent clarity in 2 Samuel 7.

The Royal Zion Theology: 2 Samuel 7

The narrative here presents this as the word of the LORD to the prophet Nathan:

So then, say this to my servant David: This is what the LORD of heavenly forces says: I took you from the pasture, from following the flock, to be leader over my people Israel. I've been with you wherever you've gone, and I've eliminated all your enemies before you. Now I will make your name great—like the name of the greatest people on earth. I'm going to provide a place for my people Israel, and plant them so that they may live there and no longer be disturbed. Cruel people will no longer trouble them, as they had been earlier, when I appointed leaders over my people Israel. And I will give you rest from all your enemies. And the LORD declares to you that the LORD will make a dynasty for you. When the time comes for you to die and you lie down with your ancestors, I will raise up your descendant—one of your very own children—to succeed you, and I will establish his kingdom. He will build a temple for my name, and I will establish his royal throne forever. I will be a father to him, and he will be a son to me. Whenever he does wrong, I will discipline him with a human rod, with blows from human beings. But I will never take my faithful love away from him like I took it away from Saul, whom I set aside in favor of you. Your dynasty and your kingdom will be secured forever before me. Your throne will be established forever. (2 Sam 7:8-16)

Jerusalem as religious and political center is a focal point for prophetic poetry that dramatizes the divine purpose for God's beloved people who have endured exile and yearn for a new future. Noting the image of Zion as bereaved mother in Lamentations, Christl Maier writes:

The idea of Zion's motherhood is intrinsically connected to the exilic situation as well as to all efforts to overcome this experience of pain and death. The motherly role of the city is crucial to the survival of those who escaped or were exiled and helped to shape the memory of the postexilic community. . . . Texts in Second Isaiah recall the image of mother Zion in their effort to promote a message of restoration and renewal of the divine–human relationship. In the context of Second Isaiah, the reinstallation of the city as queen and consort of YHWH corresponds to the vision that Zion's children are brought back and that Zion resumes her motherly role.[7]

Thus the female personification of Zion is crucial to the Isaiah traditions, and it counts as a multivalent organizing motif across the book.

Other expressions of the royal Zion theology do not trade on the personification of Zion as such but underline the honor due Jerusalem as God's eternal dwelling place. To fill out the portrayal of this stream of theological tradition, I direct your attention to the following three texts. As you read Isaiah, you'll notice other relevant passages as well.

At the beginning of Isaiah 16, amid oracles of doom against Moab, we see an exhortation—ironic? it seems earnest—that the inhabitants of Jerusalem should let Moabite fugitives and outcasts make their way to Zion "like scattered nestlings" (NRSV) to settle safely there. Then comes a majestic oracle of promise in the diction of the royal Zion theology:

> Let the outcasts of Moab live among you.
>
> Be a hiding place for them from the destroyer.
>
> When the oppressor is no more,
>
>> when destruction has ceased,
>>
>> when the trampler has vanished from the land,
>
> a throne will be established based on goodness,
>
>> and someone will sit faithfully on it in David's dwelling—
>>
>> a judge who seeks justice and timely righteousness. (16:4-5)

God has chosen the Davidic line for eternity and will uphold that royal line. Remarkably in Isaiah 16, the resulting peace might even offer security to fugitives from enemy nations. A second example of the Zion theology can be seen in Isaiah 31:

> The Lord has said to me:
>
> When the lion growls,
>
> the young lion, over its prey,
>
>> though a band of shepherds is summoned against it,
>>
>> isn't scared off by their noise or frightened by their roar.
>
> So the Lord of heavenly forces will go down

to fight on Mount Zion and on her hill.

Like birds flying aloft,

> so the Lord of heavenly forces will shield Jerusalem:
>
> shielding and saving, sparing and rescuing. (31:4-5)

The biblical title "Lord of heavenly forces" is a military title. It signals that God is the head of the heavenly armies and is mighty in battle.

For our third example, consider the images in Isaiah 33. Verse 14 depicts sinners in Zion trembling at God's might. God holds the covenant people to a standard of righteous behavior: those who will withstand divine judgment are "those who walk righteously and speak uprightly, who despise the gain of oppression, who wave away a bribe instead of accepting it, who stop their ears from hearing of bloodshed" (33:15 NRSV). Ethical comportment is here directly connected to the promise of the royal Zion theology, namely, safety and flourishing: "their refuge will be the fortresses of rocks; their food will be supplied, their water assured" (33:16 NRSV). Those are the things you'd need in a siege: the point is that the Lord will protect the righteous in Jerusalem. Then comes a description of the Zion theology almost hypnotic in its lyricism:

> Gaze upon Zion, our festival town.
>
> > Your eyes will see Jerusalem, a carefree dwelling,
> >
> > a tent that is not packed up,
> >
> > whose stakes are never pulled up,
> >
> > whose ropes won't snap.
>
> The Lord's majesty will be there for us:
>
> > as a place of rivers, broad streams
> >
> > where no boat will go,
> >
> > no majestic ship will cross.
>
> The Lord is our judge;
>
> > the Lord is our leader;
> >
> > the Lord is our king—
> >
> > he will deliver us. (33:20-23)

Anomalous Note: Isaiah 19:24-25

Each biblical prophetic book is artfully complex and theologically rich. I will lift up three central themes for each book, but we shouldn't go too far in the direction of homogenizing what are marvelously complicated collections. To talk about "the" message of any prophetic book would be reductionist and would impoverish the ancient witness. To drive that point home, for each major prophet (Isaiah, Jeremiah, and Ezekiel), we will consider an anomalous theological note: a passage unusual in its diction and ideas, decidedly uncharacteristic and yet important. These anomalous notes, along with others you may discover as you read, can be used fruitfully to interrogate any narrow or unduly simplistic view of the relevant prophet.

In Isaiah, an anomalous note is struck at the end of chapter 19, in an oracle that speaks of an eschatological day of universal blessing on which Israel and its implacable enemies will be united in their receiving of God's grace:

> On that day, Israel will be the third along with Egypt and Assyria, a blessing at the center of the world. The LORD of heavenly forces will pronounce this blessing: "Bless Egypt my people, and Assyria my handiwork, and Israel my inheritance." (19:25)

Just before this are verses that say Egypt will come to know the LORD and will return to the LORD, and God will "hear their pleas and heal them" (19:22). Some commentators have heard the phrase "a blessing at the center of the world" as a theological reflection on the covenant with Abram in Genesis 12:3, which was to be a source of blessing for all the families of the earth. This refiguring of intractable enemies Egypt and Assyria in terms of their flourishing may be understood as an invitation to those enemies (rhetorically) to participate fully in the covenant that God has established with Israel. This is uncharacteristic of the book of Isaiah and, though we might nod at Isaiah 2 and Micah 4, rare in the prophetic corpus generally. Even in stirring Second Isaiah passages about nations streaming to Zion and bringing Judean exiles back, the images are of the subjection of the nations to God's authority and to Israel: foreign kings and queens will bow to Israel and "lick the dust" of Israel's feet (49:23). So these verses at the end of Isaiah 19 are decidedly unusual. Reach for these striking words of promise when you wish to use a biblical text to contest the militarized xenophobia and bloodcurdling cries for vengeance that we see elsewhere in the Bible and, tragically, in many conflict zones across the world in the present day.

Isaiah 1–39

Isaiah 1 functions as a *précis* or illustrative summary of the entire book of Isaiah, the first part of a framing structure that interpreters see as mirrored by either chapter 66 alone or chapters 65–66 taken together. Theological notes are sounded in the opening chapter that will play out more fully throughout Isaiah. Mark the following motifs as you read Isaiah 1, then look for them as you read the rest of the book:

- Israel's sinfulness and failure to understand who the LORD is

- the prophetic call for repentance and justice

- juridical language (1:18, "settle this"; 3:13 "the LORD rises to accuse")

- the use of female-gendered and sexualized metaphorical language for Israel's sin

- beautiful restoration language and interest in beginnings (1:26)

- continued judgment after restoration: a pattern also in Isaiah 60–66

Be prepared for transitions to seem awkward or precipitous. For example, in Isaiah 4, at one moment there is a scene of desperation with Zion under siege, and next, we read a glorious oracle of restoration. You will encounter such moments of literary tension or awkwardness frequently as you read the biblical prophets. In some cases, disjuncture results from different traditions having been brought together literarily into a collection.

Other times, there may be a subtle narrative "plot" or underlying theological logic to such juxtapositions that is not immediately apparent.

Prophetic Vision versus Impaired Spiritual Perception

Beginning with Isaiah 1 ("But Israel doesn't know; my people don't behave intelligently," 1:3), in the prophet's commissioning in Isaiah 6, and on throughout the book of Isaiah, we encounter the idea of impaired spiritual perception. Often using metaphors of "blindness" and "deafness," a number of texts excoriate Israel for limited vision, lack of literacy (actual and metaphorical) in their theological traditions, and failure to "hear" the word of God. The metaphors of blindness and deafness are constructed from the perspective of sighted and hearing scribes who understood blindness and deafness as wholly negative deficits, which we may name as a position of prejudice or unwitting distortion from the perspective of contemporary disability studies. Metaphors of blindness and deafness come up in Isaiah's commissioning in Isaiah 6: the prophet is to be sent to a people who will not understand and who will be destroyed as a result. Some have compared this troubling passage to the problematic aspect of God's hardening Pharaoh's heart in the Exodus, a text that has played havoc with Christian theological views of free will for many centuries. In Isaiah 6:10, the problem is even more acute: it is not just one enemy king but an entire people that will be addressed by a prophet who knows in advance that he will not be able to make them understand: "Make the mind of this people dull, and stop their ears, and shut their eyes, so that they may not look with their eyes, and listen with their ears, and comprehend with their minds, and turn and be healed" (NRSV). The motif is elaborated further in Second Isaiah, especially in Isaiah 42 through 44, where Israel's spiritual blindness is worked out as a consequence of the people's idolatry. Isaiah 6 is pivotal not only for understanding the prophet's commissioning but also for understanding the people's relationship to the revelation of God performed by means of the prophetic word through much of Isaiah.

Dramatic contrasts play throughout Isaiah 6. Standing on the threshold between the divine and human realms, Isaiah sees a vision of God, a theophany majestic and beyond comprehension. The six-winged seraphim, supernal fiery creatures, fly about continually praising the LORD of hosts; the temple is filled with smoke, and the threshold itself shakes from the tremendous sound of those calling out praise to God. It is an extraordinary scene, one that has been represented richly in art and liturgical music across the ages.

"Let All Mortal Flesh Keep Silence," verses 3 and 4

Rank on rank the host of heaven
spreads its vanguard on the way,
as the Light of Light descendeth
from the realms of endless day,
that the powers of hell may vanish
as the darkness clears away.

At his feet the six-winged seraph;
cherubim with sleepless eye
veil their faces to the Presence,
as with ceaseless voice they cry,
"Alleluia, alleluia!
Alleluia, Lord Most High!"

Words: Liturgy of St. James, para. by Gerard Moultrie (1829–1885)
Tune: Picardy, seventeenth-century French carol

Isaiah's first response is a cry of doom: he understands that he is not pure, not capable of being present to the glory of the LORD without harm. His lips then are purified with a burning coal taken from the altar, and Isaiah offers to do holy work: "Here am I; send me!" (6:8 NRSV). Isaiah, the servant of the LORD, stands as paradigmatic prophet and as an icon of the covenant people, who will be "read" in Second Isaiah as servant of this Holy One.

The dramatic temple scene is contrasted then, starkly, with the fate of the earth after the LORD's punishment of sin. "How long?" the prophet asks. "Until cities lie waste without inhabitant, and houses without people, and the land is utterly desolate; until the LORD sends everyone far away, and vast is the emptiness in the midst of the land" (6:11 NRSV). A grim vision, perhaps suggesting not just the local devastation of Judah but a reversal of the creation story in the garden of Eden. Isaiah the prophet, poised with agonizing clarity of vision on the threshold between the divine and the human, can perceive the magnificence and radiance of the heavenly beings thronged around the LORD with thunderous hymns of praise—and he can see the appalling devastation and desolation, the silence and abandonment of human culture because the people do not understand who God is. It is the role of the prophet, as it will become the role of the suffering servant, to experience blindness and deafness, and from that position to proclaim the Holy One of Israel, teaching the people so that they know to worship the LORD alone as their Redeemer.

The Assyrian Threat

Prophets not only foretold the future but also offered assessments of the current circumstances (social and political as well as religious) of their people. There are similarities but also striking differences between Isaiah and some of the Jeremiah traditions regarding the appropriate political position to take vis-à-vis an invading enemy. One similarity is that both prophets view victorious enemies as the instruments of the LORD's purposes. In Isaiah 10:5-6 we hear this: "Doom to Assyria, rod of my anger, in whose hand is the staff of my fury! Against a godless nation I send him; against an infuriating people I direct him to seize spoil, to steal plunder, and to trample them like mud in the streets."

Harsh words, and profoundly troubling on a theological level for contemporary readers. So also Jeremiah will say, centuries later, that the invading Babylonian army storming the gates of Jerusalem has been dispatched there by the LORD to perform the LORD's purpose: to destroy God's own people for their stubborn sinfulness over many generations. But where Jeremiah will counsel submission to Babylon, Isaiah's politics is different. Isaiah insists that Judah and its leaders must trust in God, neither fearing the enemy nor negotiating with human allies. The LORD is the one who should be feared, and that means not yielding in a pragmatic position of accommodation but—Isaiah's advice to Ahaz in Isaiah 7—instead standing firm in faith, else "you shall not stand at all" (7:9 NRSV).

When we read Isaiah 7, we see a self-consciously theological interpretation of history, specifically the events of the Syro-Ephraimite War, the crisis that arose when Judah declined to join Syria and the northern kingdom of Israel in its alliance against Assyria. In Isaiah 7:10-11, the Lord tells King Ahaz of Judah, who is terrified of the Syro-Ephraimite coalition, to ask God for a sign: "Ask a sign of the Lord your God: let it be deep as Sheol or as high as heaven" (7:11 NRSV). God is eager to show the divine purpose at work in the political events unfolding before Ahaz's eyes. But Ahaz will not ask: he opts for a pragmatic position. He says, "I will not test the Lord," which suggests that he doesn't necessarily want the answer: Ahaz would be compelled to think theologically about the situation he is in, to consider God's purposes rather than his own military options. Isaiah, impatient, says that God will give a sign anyway: a young woman will give birth to a child whose name is Immanu-el, "With us is God." Many read this oracle in Isaiah 7 as good news, and Christian liturgies use it during Advent in the well-known hymn "O Come, O Come, Emmanuel." But in fact, the "Immanuel" sign is steeped in irony. The child's maturation period (see 7:15; about three years until weaning) will also be the period during which God will accomplish God's purposes. Now, disastrously, those purposes are not going to be about consolation for Ahaz and restoration for Judah. Or they will in one sense, but as is so often the case with irony, what is said that is true is not the most significant part of the communication. Isaiah had "comforted" Ahaz, saying that Rezin of Aram and Pekah of Israel would not succeed. True; but then it becomes clear that Assyria's defeat of the Syro-Ephraimite coalition is not the good news that Ahaz might have thought it would be.

Following are three remarkable images of the Assyrian incursion, each showing how uncontrollable is the Lord's power at work via deployment of an enemy. The ancient audience would have been terrified in three different ways in rapid succession with these metaphors.

65

- **Stinging insects:** "On that day, the LORD will whistle for the flies from the remotest streams of Egypt and for the bees that are in the land of Assyria. They will come and settle in the steep ravines, in the cracks of the cliffs, in all the thornbushes, and in all the watering holes" (7:18-19).

- **A sharp razor:** "On that day the Lord will shave with a razor hired beyond the Euphrates—the king of Assyria" (7:20): this heightens the drama and highlights the irony of Ahaz getting what he wanted but also more than he bargained for. The razor will not only shave the head and the hair of the feet but also take off the entire beard: a forcible and deeply shaming removal of the warrior's beard. That is, the power of Assyria will not be confined to Judah's enemies. The land will be devastated, stripped bare.

- **Flood waters:** This image heightens the sense of disastrous, out-of-control threat: "Because this people . . . melt in fear before Rezin and the son of Remaliah" (8:6 NRSV)—that is, because the people are afraid of the Syro-Ephraimite coalition instead of understanding that God is the one with power here— "therefore, look, the Lord is raising up against them the powerful floodwaters of the Euphrates, the king of Assyria and all his glory. It will rise up over all its channels, overflowing all its banks, and sweep into Judah, flooding, overflowing, and reaching up to the neck. But God is with us; the span of his wings will cover the width of the land" (8:7-8).

There is devastating irony here. God is indeed with the people—to defeat the threatening Syro-Ephraimite coalition, yes, but also to overtake the land of Judah as well. God's floodwaters of destruction, namely, Assyria, will flood the entire land. "O Immanuel" (8:8 NRSV), this sarcastic name now flung at the people, twists the knife. Does this people not understand that the LORD is with them for all of the divine purposes that are wrought in history, for not just weal but also woe? Isaiah 8:12 makes the point clear: "Don't call conspiracy all that this people calls conspiracy. Don't fear what they fear, and don't be terrified. It is the LORD of heavenly forces whom you should hold sacred, whom you should fear, and whom you should hold in awe" (8:12-13).

Israel needs to learn to stand in awe and obedience before the power of the Holy One, who alone shapes history. Any perspective on history in the book of Isaiah has to understand that as the nonnegotiable starting point.

With Isaiah 8, we come to the first of two sign-acts Isaiah of Jerusalem is commanded to perform to embody the purposes of the LORD in visual and material ways to the people of Judah. Sign-acts occur also in Jeremiah and Ezekiel. Prophetic sign-acts may have served as dramatic performance art, street theater that created embodiments of the word of the LORD as tableaux in front of an audience comprised largely of folks who could not read or who may not have paid attention to complex oracular poetry.

Sign-Acts in Isaiah	
Isaiah is to write "Belonging to Maher-shalal-hash-baz" on a tablet and have the inscription witnessed. This becomes the name of the son Isaiah subsequently fathers. The name, translated as "The spoil speeds, the prey hastens," serves as a sign that the Syro-Ephraimite coalition will be defeated and the wealth of its countries plundered by Assyria.	8:1-4
Isaiah is said to have walked naked and barefoot for three years as a sign of the futility of an alliance with Egypt and Ethiopia against the Assyrian empire: the defeated inhabitants of those countries will be led naked and barefoot into exile by Assyria.	20:1-6

In the pages of the Bible, we have only the narration of sign-acts; we cannot see them enacted in person. The literary representation of these moments of ancient performance art gains new audiences capable of sustained attentiveness as the acts themselves become part of written tradition on which the scribes, and later readers, can reflect. Connections with other oracles—such as Isaiah's oracles against Ethiopia in chapter 18 and against Egypt in chapter 19—may then be traced, and the prophetic word all the more confirmed, as later audiences turn to the study of the scroll of Isaiah.

Notice the messianic prophecy in 9:2-7. Those of you who have sung Handel's *Messiah* may know this passage by heart. Messianic hopes are articulated throughout the prophetic corpus, but nowhere with such staggering beauty as in the book of Isaiah. The royal and messianic imagery of 9:2-7 with its stirring "for unto us a child is born" passage (KJV), and of 11:1-9, the glorious "Peaceable Kingdom" passage, would have bolstered the spirits and resolve of the ancient audience, whether in the time of the Assyrian threat or in later periods of crisis.

Isaiah 13–23 comprises harsh cries for vengeance against the nations, with also some oracles about Judah's impending destruction. Brutal oracles of judgment against foreign nations seem to have been an expected literary feature in ancient prophetic works: they can be found in Isaiah, Jeremiah, Ezekiel, Amos, and several smaller biblical prophetic books. The presence of such oracles in sacred literature presents serious theological challenges for readers who do not believe that God delights in the wholesale slaughter of human beings.

Enduring Prophetic Witness

At key moments, the book of Isaiah offers the written prophetic word as something to be preserved through trials and tribulations and then retrieved, or finally understood, in a future time. The word of God is not just for the present. It is also for future generations of believers to hear and understand, even if it had been unintelligible in the time in which it was originally offered. This meta-consciousness about the enduring prophetic word is a fascinating dimension of the book of Isaiah, something fairly unusual in the Hebrew Bible.

> Bind up the testimony; seal up the teaching among my disciples. I will wait for the LORD, who has hidden his face from the house of Jacob, and I will hope in God. (8:16-17)

> This entire vision has become for you like the words of a sealed scroll. When they give it to one who can read, saying, "Read this," that one will say, "I can't, because it's sealed." And when the scroll is given to one who can't read, saying, "Read this," that one will say, "I can't read." (29:11-12)

Now go, write it before them on a tablet,

    inscribe it on a scroll,

    so in the future it will endure as a witness.

These are rebellious people, lying children,

    children unwilling to hear the LORD's teaching,

    who say to the seers, "Don't foresee,"

    and to the visionaries, "Don't report truthful visions;

    tell us flattering things;

    envision deceptions;

    get out of the way;

    step off the path;

    let's have no more 'holy one of Israel.'" (30:8-11)

Consult the LORD's scroll and read:

    Not one of these will be missing;

    none will lack its mate.

    God's own mouth has commanded;

    God's own spirit has gathered them. (34:16)

Isaiah prophesies that the land of Edom will be devastated; "from generation to generation it will lie waste" (34:10), and it will be possessed by a veritable menagerie of wild creatures: hawks, ravens, ostriches, hedgehogs, jackals, wildcats, owls, hyenas, and buzzards.

The written record of prophecy is important, especially since the prophetic word is understood, in some passages in Isaiah, to be hidden or to be intelligible only to a select few. It is esoteric knowledge that needs to be preserved for future generations to consult as an authoritative resource. Of the Isaiah 8 passage, Brevard Childs writes,

> In this confession of Isaiah one can . . . discern the beginnings of a sense of "canon consciousness." By this is meant that the prophetic witness that was not received when first proclaimed has been collected and preserved in faith for another generation. These collected testimonies retain their truth and authority in spite of the passing of time and continue to serve as God's word for a future age.[8]

Of the Isaiah 29 quotation, Childs says, "The message of God to Israel has become a closed document that is either sealed or given to someone who cannot read. . . . Divine revelation has now been carefully related to the vehicle of a written scroll. The effect of hardening is that Israel can no longer understand its scriptures."[9]

The theme of written prophecy comes up near the end of Isaiah, in the Lord's judgment on idolaters within Israel and which says, "Look, this stands written before me. I won't be silent, but I will repay; I will repay in full measure (65:6). "This stands written before me" may refer to indictments of Israel in earlier chapters of Isaiah or to earlier authoritative traditions in the sacred texts of ancient Israel more generally. Either way, Isaiah underlines the authority of written prophetic revelation.

Eschatological Imagery

Isaiah 24–27 has sometimes been called the "Apocalypse of Isaiah." Apocalyptic rhetoric and thought flourished toward the end of the period of formation of the Hebrew Bible and on into the intertestamental period, the span of several hundred years between the finalization of Hebrew Bible traditions and the composition of the earliest New Testament traditions. Defining features of *apocalyptic* (that word can function as an adjective or a noun) include:

- esoteric knowledge imparted to a seer by a heavenly figure;

- the use of allegorical symbolism for political figures and events contemporaneous with the writing of the apocalyptic text (which is not necessarily the same as the historical setting within the plot of the story);

- a vision of God's cataclysmic inbreaking into human history to vindicate the righteous.

We glimpse early Jewish apocalyptic tradition in Ezekiel 38–39, which comes from the postexilic period or later. Apocalyptic material is more fully developed in Zechariah 1–8 and Daniel 7–12, corpora that constitute the latest material in the Hebrew Scriptures. Here in Isaiah 24–27, imagery that seems to gesture toward apocalyptic thinking, though certainly stopping short of full-blown apocalypticism, are:

- the cosmic scope of events God's punishing of personified astral bodies ("They will be gathered together like prisoners in a pit, shut into a prison, and punished after many days," 24:22) and defeat of monsters ("On that day, the LORD will take a great sword, harsh and mighty, and will punish Leviathan the fleeing serpent, Leviathan the writhing serpent, and will kill the dragon that is in the sea," 27:1).

- divine transformation of history this includes gestures toward set periods of time ("punished after many days") (24:22); "On that day, a great trumpet will be played. Those who were lost in the land of Assyria and those who were scattered in the land of Egypt will come. They will bow to the LORD at his holy mountain in Jerusalem" (27:13).

Note the theological themes that arise in a discernible literary progression in Isaiah 24–27. In Isaiah 24, the effects of human sin are not just social but ecological and cosmological: "The earth lies polluted under its inhabitants, for they have disobeyed instruction, swept aside law, and broken the ancient covenant" (24:5). The earth will be utterly laid waste by the LORD, who will punish the heavenly forces and the kings of earth. Isaiah 25 offers a surprising shift to praise: "LORD, you are my God. I will exalt you; I will praise your name, for you have done wonderful things, planned long ago, faithful and sure" (25:1). God has been a refuge for the poor and has silenced the ruthless. The devastation of the whole earth may be read, then, as the LORD enacting justice on behalf of the powerless, something we glimpse in the oracle about a coming eschatological feast in Isaiah 25, often read at Christian funerals:

> On this mountain, the LORD of heavenly forces will prepare for all
>> peoples a rich feast. . . .
> He will swallow up on this mountain the veil that is veiling all peoples,
>> the shroud enshrouding all nations.
> He will swallow up death forever. . . .
> They will say on that day,
> "Look! This is our God, for whom we have waited—
>> and he has saved us!" (25:6-9)

In Isaiah 26, then, we see a shift to a focus on Judah:

> On that day, this song will be sung in the land of Judah:
>> Ours is a strong city!
>> God makes salvation its walls and ramparts.
> Open the gates and let a righteous nation enter,
>> a nation that keeps faith.
> Those with sound thoughts you will keep in peace,
>> in peace because they trust in you.
> Trust in the LORD forever,
>> for the LORD is a rock for all ages. (26:1-4)

In Isaiah 27, the power of God as Creator is highlighted: the defeat of the sea monster Leviathan shows God's power in the trope of the mythical battles at creation that we know from ancient Near Eastern literature more generally; then there is a renewed focus on Israel, where God promises to care for the vineyard that is Israel, so long as Israel renounces idolatry. Finally comes the last note in Isaiah 24–27, "On that day, the LORD will beat grain from the channel of the Euphrates up to the Valley of Egypt. You will be collected, Israelites, one by one" (27:12): all of the exiles of God's people will be brought home. These four chapters were structured along an artful literary trajectory that does the following:

- establishes the LORD's power to destroy the whole earth;

- celebrates the LORD's power over death itself;

- acclaims divine justice, the LORD as agent on behalf of the poor and needy;

- prophesies the restoration of Judah, including the ingathering of the exiles.

The making of military alliances is abhorrent to the God of Isaiah:

> Doom to you, rebellious children, says the LORD,
>> who make a plan, which is not mine;
>> who weave a plot, but not by my spirit, piling up sin on sin;
>> setting out to go down to Egypt without consulting me,
>> taking refuge in Pharaoh's refuge and hiding in Egypt's shadow.
> Pharaoh's refuge will become your shame,
>> hiding in Egypt's shadow your disgrace.
> Though their officials are in Zoan,
>> and their messengers reach Hanes,
>> all will become shamed because of a people who can't assist them.
> They are no help; they are no profit;
>> rather, shame and disgrace. (Isa 30:1-5)

Verses 15 and 16 of the same chapter underscore the point: "Therefore, the Lord GOD, the holy one of Israel, says: In return and rest you will be saved; quietness and trust will be your strength—but you refused. You said, 'No! We'll flee on horses'—therefore, you will indeed flee—'and we'll ride off; on swift steeds we will ride'—therefore, your pursuers will be swift" (30:15-16).

The sarcasm here is just brutal: You want to flee on horses? Fine, but the point is, you'll be fleeing for your lives. You trust that your horses will be swift? Guess what? The horses your pursuers ride will be swift too.

For Isaiah, relying on international military alliances was a faithless move that shows Israel did not trust in God. The point is dramatized beautifully in Isaiah 36–39, a prose section that appears almost verbatim in 2 Kings 18–20 as well. First, in Isaiah 36 and 37 is the story of the siege of Jerusalem pressed by King Sennacherib of Assyria in 701. Read the extraordinary mocking speech of the Rabshakeh, an Assyrian officer, that is designed to destabilize Judah and leave them prepared to surrender. Within the plot, this speech is sheer military genius. Considered as an artful work within the book of Isaiah, it is a gem of ancient scribal expertise. The Rabshakeh says to Hezekiah: "It appears that you are trusting in a staff—Egypt—that's nothing but a broken reed! It will stab the hand of anyone who leans on it! That's all that Pharaoh, Egypt's king, is to anyone who trusts in him. Now suppose you say to me, 'We trust in the LORD our God.' Isn't he the one whose shrines and altars Hezekiah removed?" (36:6-7). This is a reference to Hezekiah's religious reforms. Hezekiah was said to have torn down local altars in order to centralize worship, according to good Deuteronomistic principles, in Jerusalem. The Rabshakeh is cleverly twisting this to imply that God is angry that God's altars were removed: "So now, make a wager with my master, Assyria's king. I'll give you two thousand horses if you can supply the riders!" (36:8). Here the Rabshakeh derides Judah's military strength: we'll even give you the warhorses, if you really want to fight! It may also be countering ancient Israelite holy-war ideology, which maintained that since the LORD fights for Israel, one can winnow out the ranks of the warriors because it is God's strength in any case, not your own, that allows you to prevail in battle. "Moreover," he continues, "is it without the LORD that I have come up against this land to destroy it? The LORD said to me, Go up against this land and destroy it" (36:10 NRSV). The Rabshakeh is using Israel's own theology against the people of God. More Assyrian rhetorical pyrotechnics ensue; all seems hopeless . . . and then Jerusalem is saved by divine intervention: "The LORD's messenger went out and struck down one hundred eighty-five thousand soldiers in the Assyrian camp. When people got up the next morning, there were dead bodies everywhere" (37:36).

In 7:3, Isaiah had met Ahaz at "the end of the channel of the Upper Pool, by the road to the field where laundry is washed." In 36:2, when the Rabshakeh and the Assyrian army come to taunt Hezekiah, they, too, meet "at the water channel of the Upper Pool, which is on the road to the field where clothes are washed." Another explicit linkage of Ahaz and Hezekiah may be seen in 38:1-8. Hezekiah is sick and is on the brink of death. Hezekiah cries out to the LORD, who hears his prayer and heals him. The sign of this miraculous healing? "Once the shadow cast by the sun descends on the steps of Ahaz, I will make it back up ten steps" (38:8). Time is going to be reversed!

These linkages constitute textual signals that we are to read the story of Ahaz and the story of Hezekiah together, as contrasting models. The first king failed to trust God and Assyria swept into Judah like a flood, delivering from the Syro-Ephraimite coalition but being a force for harm in Judah rather than deliverance. The second king, Hezekiah a few generations later, did trust in God, and Jerusalem was miraculously spared.

Isaiah 40–55

Isaiah prophesies that the LORD—the incomparably powerful holy one of Israel—is at work in history, supremely in control of all and capable of creating either weal or woe. Isaiah 7 had underlined the importance of trusting in God rather than in political alliances with other nations. God is the one to fear: the Holy One of Israel is the only one who can deliver. Isaiah 7 through 39 is framed by two prose stories of kings: one was fearful (Ahaz) and was dominated by the enemy, while the other did trust (Hezekiah) and was delivered. This literary shaping presents the early part of the book of Isaiah as a debate about how to trust in God for deliverance. That's a key point to understand before the reader enters into Isaiah 40, the world of Second Isaiah, with its glorious message of comfort and hope for a people who can trust that their God is saving them from exile in Babylon and bringing them home in triumph. Isaiah 40 is considered by many scholars to be the formal "starting point" for the oracles of Second Isaiah, a postexilic prophet (or prophetic group) that cherished the traditions of First Isaiah, working to expand their meaning as the Babylonian exile came to an end and Judeans in diaspora were allowed to return home. This chapter and the ones that follow brim with stirring oracles of restoration, tidings of good news to the Judeans who had endured threats and deportations, the destruction of Jerusalem (587), and, depending on whether one had been deported or not, either a poor life in the ruined Judah or a difficult life in exile in Babylon or Egypt. In Second Isaiah, we also see a marked emphasis on God as the Creator whose wisdom and power put to shame all other contenders (for example, 40:12-26). Much here is resonant with claims about God that are made in the book of Job and in biblical wisdom literature generally. In wisdom passages, what comes to the fore are the claims for God's limitless creative power over the forces of nature and God's universal dominion.

A New Exodus

Second Isaiah speaks of God leading God's exiled people back through the wilderness to the Promised Land, to Judah. But this is no terrified escape with Babylonian pursuers, analogous to Israel's hasty escape by night during the Exodus, with the Egyptians in pursuit. No, this is a joyous procession accompanied by singing and miraculous healings. We see in Isaiah 35:1-10 a beautiful description of this triumphal march: the wilderness becomes a place of pools of water and abundant springs as the glory of the LORD passes through at the head of the caravan of God's beloved people. We do hear an echo of holy-war tradition in 35:3-4: "Strengthen the weak hands, and support the unsteady knees. Say to those who are panicking: 'Be strong! Don't fear! Here's your God, coming with vengeance; with divine retribution God will come to save you.'" Conflict may lie ahead, but the LORD of heavenly forces will be with them. The desert will bloom all around them, and the way has already been prepared for Israel: "A highway will be there. It will be called The Holy Way. . . . no lion will be there, and no predator will go up on it. None of these will be there; only the redeemed will walk on it. The LORD's ransomed ones will return and enter Zion with singing, with everlasting joy upon their heads. Happiness and joy will overwhelm them; grief and groaning will flee away" (35:8-10).

The desperation of the older Exodus is decisively transformed in this moment of deliverance, as 52:11-12 makes clear: "Depart! Depart! Go out from there! Unclean! Don't touch! Get out of that place; purify yourselves, carriers of the LORD's equipment! You won't go out in a rush, nor will you run away, because the one going before you is the LORD; your rear guard is the God of Israel." This Exodus is transformed also in scope, for God's people shall return from all four corners of the globe: the LORD promises, "Don't fear, I am with you. From the east I'll bring your children; from the west I'll gather you. I'll say to the north, 'Give them back!' and to the south, 'Don't detain them.' Bring my sons from far away, and my daughters from the end of the earth" (43:5-6). The redemptive power of the holy one of Israel knows no limits. From every earthly place of captivity and enslavement, the LORD is mighty to save.

Wilderness as Metaphor in Second Isaiah

Second Isaiah uses the metaphor and motif of "wilderness" to describe the multifaceted experiences of exile. The wilderness is a place of vulnerability and wandering. It is an arid terrain in which survival is always in question. Indeed, the wilderness is a place of danger, testing, and scarcity. . . . While living in the barren and uninhabitable wilderness, perhaps figuratively and topographically, the exiles can lament and grieve. In the rugged hills and parched plains (Isa 40:4; 41:17), disconsolate refugees can reclaim their lives and reinvest their energy in meaning- and mission-making. In the desert, the exiles can behold the stars, hear the tempest, and learn the constancy of their God. The valleys and rough terrain are stark reminders of how ephemeral human power structures actually are; and in the desert the exiles can rediscover their true identity as God's children. . . . Although many see nothing but death and despair in the desert, the prophet discerns the steadfast love and fidelity of YHWH.

—Louis Stulman and Hyun Chul Paul Kim[10]

Cyrus II, king of Persia, is lauded in Second Isaiah as the LORD's "shepherd" (44:28). Cyrus has been divinely anointed to liberate the captives. See the hymn to Cyrus in Isaiah 45: "The LORD says to his anointed, to Cyrus, whom I have grasped by the strong hand, to conquer nations before him, disarming kings, and opening doors before him, so no gates will be shut: I myself will go before you, and I will level mountains. I will shatter bronze doors; I will cut through iron bars" (45:1-2). Here we have a foreign king acclaimed for his role in releasing God's captive people and leading the exiles of Judah back to their home, fulfilling the purposes of the God of Israel even though Cyrus himself may be unaware of that (45:4-5). Here we see a strong reaffirmation of the notion that foreign rulers are the unwitting instruments of the Lord. In Isaiah 10, Assyria is mocked for its arrogance: the enemy does not realize that the reason it has been able to pulverize the northern kingdom of Israel is because Yhwh has appointed it to do so, and Yhwh will also appoint its destruction when the "ax [vaunts] itself over the one who wields it" (10:15 NRSV). Here in lyrical oracles of promise, we see Cyrus celebrated as an instrument of the Lord's purposes though he may not realize the source of his military success.

The Servant Songs

The four Servant Songs, which are found in Isaiah 42:1-4, 49:1-6, 50:4-9, and 52:13–53:12, have attracted interpretive attention for many centuries. These powerful poems articulate an unusual combination of themes of messianic power, evangelistic mission, and suffering on behalf of others. The Servant may be a royal figure, since throughout the ancient Near East, it was a primary responsibility of the king to establish justice, as the first Servant Song tells us. The Servant has a messianic vocation to save others through teaching Torah, teaching not only Israel but all the nations of the world, for the "coastlands" wait for his teaching, it says in the first Servant Song. The Servant has an evangelistic mission, as seen in the commissioning of the Servant, not only to bring Israel back to the Lord but to be a "light to the nations," per the third Servant Song. And he suffers on behalf of others in order somehow to effect their vindication, as is maintained in the fourth Servant Song.

Interpreters have been fascinated not least because the identity of the Servant remains mysterious. The question of the Servant's identity becomes particularly complex when readers take into account the numerous mentions of God's "servant" in Isaiah that do not occur in the Servant

Songs proper. Clearly, in some of those instances the entire people of Israel is meant. Many other proposals have been made over the centuries, and no consensus has been reached. Below are some of the options.

(a) The Servant is the prophet Isaiah or another prophet—perhaps Jeremiah. Interpreters have long pondered the resonance between Isaiah 49:1, "The LORD called me before my birth, called my name when I was in my mother's womb," and Jeremiah 1:5, where the LORD says to the prophet, "Before I created you in the womb I knew you; before you were born I set you apart; I made you a prophet to the nations."

(b) The Servant is the people Israel, portrayed in poetic terms as a single figure.

(c) The Servant was originally Israel and is never not Israel. Nevertheless, when Israel failed in its mission as a light to the nations, later Isaiah traditionists effected a "transfer" of the mission of the Servant to an individual figure who has been commissioned to teach Israel.[11]

(d) The Servant is a royal or messianic figure whose identity will never be known.

(e) The first Servant Song speaks of Cyrus of Persia. When Cyrus's rule fails to meet the expectations of the Isaiah community, those responsible for editing the Isaiah traditions added new Servant material that recast the Servant as a prophetic figure presented in deliberate contrast to Cyrus.[12]

(f) Isaiah envisions a long historical progression of various Servants. Israel was the first entity so commissioned, back in the time of the bondage in Egypt; Moses was the second; and Cyrus is the latest. The four Songs present a biography of Moses in four stages.[13]

(g) The Servant is an eschatological figure who may be best understood, from a history-of-interpretation viewpoint, as a prophecy of Jesus of Nazareth. Many Christian traditions have taken this position and find it a rich and meaningful way to understand the Servant Songs.

Other options could be added to the list. Especially noteworthy are positions that postulate some kind of development in the understanding of the Servant. Such a suggestion of gradual growth in understanding and changes in the Isaiah traditions over time may be the best model for understanding the genesis and elaboration of this figure in the book. We turn next to Isaiah 56–66, where what has been predicated of the individual "Servant" yields to a new emphasis on plural "servants" within a postexilic community riven by conflict.

Isaiah 56–66

The first note struck in Isaiah 56 is a lyrical note of inclusion welcoming into the worshipping community anyone who is loyal to the LORD and honors the Torah, especially the mandate to observe the sabbath. Foreigners and eunuchs will be welcomed, not excluded as per Deuteronomy 23:1-8 and other texts such as Ezra–Nehemiah. The extravagant promise in Isaiah 56:5, "I will give them a monument and a name better than sons and daughters. I will give to them an enduring name that won't be removed," assures the faithful (including those who cannot have children) that they will endure and be remembered forever. The Hebrew there for "a monument and a name" is *yad vashem*, which is the name given to the Holocaust memorial site outside of Jerusalem. Yad Vashem, established in 1953, draws on the biblical promise of God's faithfulness and memory in community to counter the horrific destruction of Jewish and other families in the Holocaust. Isaiah 57–59 then offers a turbulent mix of vitriolic invective against sinners within Israel and beautiful promises of healing and restoration.

Isaiah 60–62 resonates with the stirring oracles of salvation that we had read in Isaiah 40–55, and the first-person speaker seems to be continuing the first-person voice of the Suffering Servant. These three chapters offer distinctly new imagery and stylistic features, including a particular focus on the vindication and glorification of Zion. Note that 61:1-2 was later read aloud by Jesus of Nazareth in the Nazareth synagogue as being about himself and his ministry (see Luke 4:16-21). Isaiah 63:1-6 surprises us: it is an oracle about God's vengeance on Edom. Edom had been a powerful local antagonist up through the fall of Jerusalem. By the time Third Isaiah was composed—in the postexilic period or later—"Edom" may be beginning to function as an iconic figure for enemies more generally, as happens with "Rome" in the Christian era. The terrifying image of God coming bloody from the winepress has been refracted in reception history in rich and startling ways, including in poetry and art that depicts the crucified Christ's blood being forced out of him as if in a winepress.

The Agony

Philosophers have measur'd mountains,
Fathom'd the depths of seas, of states, and kings,
Walk'd with a staff to heav'n, and traced fountains:
⠀⠀⠀But there are two vast, spacious things,
The which to measure it doth more behove:
Yet few there are that sound them; Sin and Love.

⠀⠀⠀Who would know Sin, let him repair
Unto mount Olivet; there shall he see
A man so wrung with pains, that all his hair,
⠀⠀⠀His skin, his garments bloody be.
Sin is that press and vice, which forceth pain
To hunt his cruel food through ev'ry vein.

⠀⠀⠀Who knows not Love, let him assay
And taste that juice, which on the cross a pike
Did set again abroach, then let him say
⠀⠀⠀If ever he did taste the like.
Love is that liquor sweet and most divine,
Which my God feels as blood; but I, as wine.

—George Herbert (1593–1633)[14]

Judgment material gives way to a communal lament in 63:7–64:12, a recital of the LORD's saving deeds on behalf of Israel in the past and a plea for the LORD to save once again. In Isaiah 65–66 you will see a polemical contrast drawn between the fate of the servants of the LORD and the fate of the disobedient.

Reflecting on the entire book of Isaiah, you may notice points of contact between the last eleven chapters and Second Isaiah. For example, in Third Isaiah's emphasis on the righteousness of God's "servants," we glimpse reflection on the figure of the Servant and an implicit broadening of the mission of that individual, particularly as regards establishing justice within the community as a whole. We also see textual gestures toward earlier Isaiah material:

- There is a contrast between former things and new things (65:16-17).

- The prophet sings of the return of those scattered abroad in diaspora, along with the political subjection of enemy monarchs (see for example 60:14: "The children of your tormenters will come bending low to you; all who despised you will bow down at your feet"). You'll remember that the theme of the exiles processing back from diaspora is a major motif in Second Isaiah.

- At the end of Isaiah 65 is explicit echoing of First Isaiah's promises about God's holy mountain from Isaiah 11: a reiteration of this promise, now centuries old in the historical framework of the book, that God will inaugurate an eschatological reign of peace centered on God's holy mountain.

In Isaiah 63–64, we see a movement away from the first-person voice to a communal voice that addresses God in supplication directly, with diction that sounds like a communal psalm of lament such as Psalms 44, 74, and 79:

Where are your zeal and your might?. . .

Your holy people took possession for a little while,

> but now our adversaries have trampled down your sanctuary.

We have long been like those whom you do not rule,

> like those not called by your name.

O that you would tear open the heavens and come down. . . .

Our holy and beautiful house,

> where our ancestors praised you,

has been burned by fire,

> and all our pleasant places have become ruins.

After all this, will you restrain yourself, O Lord?

> Will you keep silent and punish us so severely?

> (Isa 63:15, 18-19; 64:1, 11-12 NRSV)

Here we hear the bold pleading of the righteous, who hold God accountable for the disproportionate suffering they have endured. In view here are surely the horrific siege and destruction of Jerusalem in 588–587, the Babylonian exile, and perhaps other traumas and disasters reflected on in the book of Isaiah as a whole. The shift to this communal voice is a powerful literary and theological move that invites the implied audience fully into the witness of the book. It invites us not only to acknowledge the truth of the Isaiah traditions but also to begin to speak with them, to identify with the "we" of this community and begin to merge our own voices with theirs.

Eschatological promises in Isaiah 65 hark back to the "former things/new thing" distinction in oracles earlier in the book and echo the stirring imagery of the Peaceable Kingdom from Isaiah 11 (see 65:25). The glorious passion of the material promising vindication of Zion is matched by the ferocity of the concluding verse of the book, which promises a fiery judgment awaiting all those who rebel against the Lord.

For Further Reading

Berges, Ulrich. "Isaiah: Structures, Themes, and Contested Issues." In *The Oxford Handbook of the Prophets,* edited by Carolyn J. Sharp, 153–70. Oxford: Oxford University Press, 2016.

Childs, Brevard S. *Isaiah.* OTL. Louisville: Westminster John Knox, 2001.

Maier, Christl M. *Daughter Zion, Mother Zion: Gender, Space, and the Sacred in Ancient Israel.* Minneapolis: Fortress, 2008.

Schipper, Jeremy. *Disability and Isaiah's Suffering Servant.* Biblical Refigurations. Oxford: Oxford University Press, 2011.

Stulman, Louis, and Hyun Chul Paul Kim. "Isaiah as Messenger of Faith amid Doubt" and "Vision of Homecoming amid Diaspora." In *You Are My People: An Introduction to Prophetic Literature,* 27–94. Nashville: Abingdon, 2010.

Chapter 3

Jeremiah:
Prophet of Struggle

The prophet Jeremiah is one of the most dramatic figures in all of Scripture. In the book that bears his name, we find his passionate outpourings of oracles of judgment against Judah and oracles against foreign nations; some beautiful chapters of consolation material are also attributed to him. We also have riveting prose narratives about the conflictual ways in which the prophet interacted with kings Jehoiakim and Zedekiah and other court officials, notably the powerful Shaphanides—several generations in the family of Shaphan the scribe—during the turbulent years immediately preceding the fall of Jerusalem in 587 BCE. From this prophet's example, the term *jeremiad* was coined to describe a prolonged diatribe or bitter complaint. We see the pathos of Jeremiah—his suffering because of his adversaries and on behalf of his people—most transparently in his laments, sometimes also called the "confessions" of Jeremiah, a form with which his name has become closely associated in the history of interpretation. The vivid poetic oracles and prose tableaux in Jeremiah are rich with the theological voicing of anguish. Indeed, Abraham Heschel has suggested that we see in many passages in Jeremiah not only the suffering of the prophet but also the pathos of God, whose "sorrow rises again and again to unconcealed heights of expression."[1] Else Holt pursues the implications of this position in her work on the prophetic "persona," analyzing how biblical books present the living figures of the prophets in ways consonant with their books' overarching goals. Holt writes,

> Jeremiah is the prophet with the most complete "biography" in his book, from information about his birthdate and birthplace via his showdowns with the ruling classes in Jerusalem before and during the Babylonian siege until his disappearance in Egypt. . . . The word of God and the prophet merge into one persona, and the prophet's *vita* serves as an authorization of the divine word-become-flesh . . . the prophetic persona representing and incarnating the divine persona.[2]

The oracles and prose narratives of the book of Jeremiah unquestionably were shaped by traditionists other than the prophet himself. The figure of the scribe Baruch, and a number of other cues in Jeremiah 36 and elsewhere in the book, signal the book's self-conscious awareness about the role of scribal activity in transmission of the Jeremiah material. Alongside first-person speech by Jeremiah, there are many stories about Jeremiah in the third person, so there is no warrant for insisting that the entire book was composed by the prophet himself: the book itself does not make that claim at all. Jeremiah was born into a priestly lineage rooted in Anathoth, a village northeast of Jerusalem. He may have begun his prophetic ministry around 627 BCE (see Jer 1:2), or considerably later; there are "gapped" years not represented in the book, and the material we do have focuses on his prophesying from around 605 through the fall of Jerusalem and shortly thereafter from diaspora in Egypt, whence he was taken (see Jer 42–43) against his will. The book of Jeremiah is an excellent literary site within the Latter Prophets to see just how closely interwoven were theology and politics in the world of the prophets. In Jeremiah, prophecy was not a simple pointing to the purposes of God but the promulgation of detailed and complex views regarding what was happening in the prophet's own time. Every prophet wrestled with how leaders and people should interpret their ancient traditions to help them respond to contemporaneous events. In Jeremiah, that political wrestling is especially visible, not just between the lines but quite dramatically in the plot.

The book of Jeremiah has had a complex history of composition. It reveals intense interest in the person of the prophet himself, a notable concern with which officials were adversaries and which were allies, and in how his actions and oracles should be construed. The book is a fascinating mix. There are grim oracles of judgment against Israel and other nations; biographical stories about the prophet that seem to center on conflict with officials; hortatory prose material constituting impassioned "sermons" delivered by the prophet in public places around Jerusalem; radiant oracles of consolation and promise; and prose narratives about conflicts in the political life of Judeans in Jerusalem, Babylon, and Egypt. Many scholars have seen evidence of Deuteronomistic redaction in Jeremiah, and there certainly are sustained connections among Deuteronomy, the book of Kings, and Jeremiah. Christl Maier has shown that Jeremiah is portrayed as a teacher of Torah, in keeping with ways in which that teaching office is understood in Deuteronomy. Because there are a number of important distinctions to be drawn between the language and themes of the prose in Jeremiah and the language and themes of Deuteronomy and the Deuteronomistic History, many of us now prefer the term *Deutero-Jeremianic* when we're discussing material in Jeremiah that has come from later traditionists.

Jeremiah as Teacher of Torah

The image of prophets as moral teachers and interpreters of the Torah is rooted in the biblical books and especially in the book of Jeremiah. . . . Jeremiah appears as a prophet who teaches the people how to amend their ways. . . . The prophet voices God's care for the socially disadvantaged and grounds their rights in the God-given torah.

—Christl Maier[3]

The materials in Jeremiah often seem to be in tension with each other, offering strikingly different emphases from poetry to prose and contestatory ways of framing issues within the Deutero-Jeremianic prose. Many readers find the book of Jeremiah to be a confusing welter of traditions that seem to tumble over one another. Louis Stulman has argued for an overarching structure from the first half of the book, with its emphasis on breaking down social structures and judgment, to the second half of the book, with an emphasis on rebuilding symbol systems.[4] Many readers assent to some form of that macrostructure, pointing to the commissioning language in Jeremiah 1 as a signal of literary and theological goals in the book writ larger:

> This very day I appoint you over nations and empires,
>> to dig up and pull down,
>> to destroy and demolish,
>> to build and plant. (1:10)

Even given this organizing motif of breaking down and rebuilding, there is an undeniably turbulent quality to the streams and fragments of tradition and ideology that we encounter in Jeremiah. Oracles at the beginning of the book are both dramatic and vague. The prose material, by contrast, seems vitriolic and hyperspecific. The "Book of Consolation" (Jer 30–31) comes as a surprise in the middle of the book, with its lyrical poems of restoration and unity framed on both sides by prose narratives of threat, enmity, and conflict. While a few scholars have argued that this promise material constitutes the "center" of the Jeremiah traditions, many others believe those chapters to have been added late and sit somewhat awkwardly in their current literary context. Oracles of judgment against foreign nations occur near the end in the Hebrew text tradition (chaps. 46–51) but in the middle (spliced into chap. 25) in the Septuagint. The book of Jeremiah is volatile and complicated, in its final literary form, in its divisive ideology, and also in its history—or histories—of transmission. Variations may reflect not just minor scribal differences but two different major streams of political and theological thought in the scribal groups that preserved and amplified the Jeremiah traditions in the exilic and postexilic periods.

Theological Themes

The book of Jeremiah surges with tides of invective and theological judgment, shot through by crosscurrents of political conflict alongside which flows a small but persistent stream of hope. Because the book is so turbulent, it may be productive to focus your attention on several broad themes in this unpredictable material. First, the Jeremiah traditions are deeply concerned with the idolatry and stubborn infidelity that, according to the prophet's characteristically hyperbolic rhetoric, have been embraced by the covenant people for many generations. Second, Jeremiah is concerned with God's word for Judah and Jerusalem at a time when the Babylonians are threatening the city, so the role of prophecy as a vital resource in Judah's political history is front and center. And third, you will see a continual back-and-forth dynamic—we could say "dialectic," except that the voices are speaking past each other rather than to each other—within which the doom of Judah is set in tension with the possibility that repentance might, in fact, save the people and Jerusalem.

Persistent Idolatry

In Jeremiah 2:8 we see the prophet's indictment of the political and religious rulers: "The priests did not say, 'Where is the LORD?' Those who handle the Law did not know me; the rulers transgressed against me; the prophets prophesied by Baal, and went after things that do not profit" (NRSV). A few verses later, the prophet weaves a poignant image of the futility of idolatry: "My people have committed two crimes: They have forsaken me, the spring of living water. And they have dug wells, broken wells that can't hold water" (2:13). In an arid, dusty environment where life-giving water had to be fetched from springs or wells and carried, sometimes laboriously over rugged terrain, back to thirsty family and livestock, this image of idolatry evokes inexplicable choices. Why would someone turn their back on a ceaseless fountain of streaming, splashing cool water in order to dig and build a stone-lined well that is so cracked that water leaks out of it underground? The LORD had been Judah's redeemer, a God mighty to save, as Isaiah also says:

Surely God is my salvation;

I will trust, and will not be afraid,

for the Lord GOD is my strength and my might;

he has become my salvation.

With joy you will draw water from the wells of salvation.

And you will say in that day,

Give thanks to the LORD,

call on his name;

make known his deeds among the nations,

proclaim that his name is exalted. (Isa 12:2-4 NRSV)

On this theme, we can see a characteristic difference between the diction of Isaiah and the diction of Jeremiah. Isaiah makes visible, in beautiful and beckoning language, the joy of choosing rightly. Jeremiah makes visible, with angry and shaming language, the terrible consequences of choosing poorly. Jeremiah 2 goes on to rail at the people about what they expect to gain by making alliances—idolatry in this book signifying worship of false deities but also trusting in political alliances with other nations. Where Isaiah invites the people to imagine a future luminous with the *shalom* of God, Jeremiah berates them for doing something "terribly bitter," for "acting like a prostitute," for acting like a female animal in heat (2:20).

Prophecy in Political History

The Jeremiah traditions are transfixed by the problem of how to understand the role of the prophets in political history. This is a major concern in the book of Kings as well; it was of urgent interest to scribal circles trying to make sense of the tragedies and challenges of the sixth century BCE and later. The political life of Israel and Judah should have been centered, per the priests and the prophets, on the Redeemer who had brought Israel out of slavery in Egypt, transforming that experience of political subjugation. When Israel seemed to forget who had delivered them—or seemed to fail to trust in the LORD as new threats arose, from the wilderness time onward—the same LORD who had delivered them underlined the authority of Moses as prophet and then sent other prophets as well, all to point Israel back to the truth of their heritage. The people are portrayed in Jeremiah as having been steadfast in their refusal to acknowledge the power of their own traditions and the witness of the prophets:

The LORD proclaims:

Stop at the crossroads and look around;

ask for the ancient paths.

Where is the good way?

Then walk in it and find a resting place for yourselves.

But you said, "We won't go!"

Still, I have appointed watchmen to warn you.

But you said, "We won't listen!" (6:16-17)

In the Deutero-Jeremianic prose, you'll see an important trope deployed in six different chapters in roughly the same words: the idea that over and over again throughout history, Israel has stubbornly failed to heed the LORD's "servants the prophets." In Jeremiah 7, the LORD thunders, "From the moment your ancestors left the land of Egypt to this day, I have sent you all my servants the prophets—day after day. But they didn't listen to me or pay attention; they were stubborn and did more harm than their ancestors" (7:25-26; compare 25:4-6; 26:4-6; 29:16-19; 35:15; 44:4-6). This tradition is an important structuring motif in the book. In Jeremiah 7, it highlights the recalcitrance of a community that will not listen to Jeremiah. In Jeremiah 25, it serves as justification for the LORD deploying Babylonian troops against the LORD's own people. In Jeremiah 26, it functions in a conditional sentence—"If you don't listen to me . . ." —in a larger narrative drama about who stands with the prophet and who opposes him. In Jeremiah 29, it is deployed with surgical precision to excoriate Zedekiah and those who remained in Jerusalem after the 597 deportation. In Jeremiah 35, the motif is used to underscore that heeding the prophets means honoring sacred tradition rather than compromising one's integrity out of fear. In Jeremiah 44 the motif, wielded almost as a weapon, is used to show continuity between idolatry before the fall of Jerusalem and the ongoing practices of diaspora Judeans in Egypt.

It is intriguing to observe that in the biblical book of Kings, prophets address their oracles to kingly houses and the prophetic word is invariably effective: it is an unstoppable performative word that always brings about that which the LORD has intended. The difference between that efficacious prophetic word and the ignored prophetic word in the Jeremiah traditions could not be starker. In Jeremiah, we see over and over again that the prophets have not been successful—they have not been heeded generation after generation, and God's word has gone ignored. The only place in the Deuteronomistic History where we see a picture of prophecy like that in the prose of Jeremiah is in 2 Kings 17.

The Jeremiah traditions also illumine the role of prophecy in Judah's political history through reflecting on the threat posed by false prophecy and ways to verify when a prophetic word may be true. The basic problems are articulated in Deuteronomy 13 and 18:

> Now if a prophet or a dream interpreter appears among you and performs a sign or wonder for you, and the sign or wonder that was spoken actually occurs; if he says: "Come on! We should follow other gods"—ones you haven't experienced—"and we should worship them," you must not listen to that prophet's or dream interpreter's words, because the LORD your God is testing you to see if you love the LORD your God with all your mind and all your being. You must follow the LORD your God alone! Revere him! Follow his commandments! Obey his voice! Worship him! Cling to him—no other! That prophet or dream interpreter must be executed because he encouraged you to turn away from the LORD your God who brought you out of Egypt, who redeemed you from the house of slavery; they tried to lead you away from the path the LORD your God commanded you to take. Remove such evil from your community! (Deut 13:1-5)

> The LORD your God will raise up a prophet like me from your community, from your fellow Israelites. He's the one you must listen to. . . . I myself will hold accountable anyone who doesn't listen to my words, which that prophet will speak in my name. However, any prophet who

arrogantly speaks a word in my name that I haven't commanded him to speak, or who speaks in the name of other gods—that prophet must die. Now, you might be wondering, How will we know which word God hasn't spoken? Here's the answer: The prophet who speaks in the LORD's name and the thing doesn't happen or come about—that's the word the LORD hasn't spoken. That prophet spoke arrogantly. Don't be afraid of him. (Deut 18:15, 19-22)

Jeremiah and his compatriot Ezekiel are deeply concerned about false prophecies, whether those be oracles offered in the name of a deity other than YHWH or misleading assurances of *shalom* given by opportunistic intermediaries to their rulers or the people, saying that all would be well. According to Jeremiah and Ezekiel, social injustice and idolatry were rampant, the Torah-grounded covenant community was on the brink of collapse, and Judah's leaders refused to align their policy decisions with the purposes of God. All was far from well. In fact, dire catastrophe threatened and would come to pass:

> In the prophets of Samaria I saw something shocking:
>> They prophesied by Baal and led astray my people Israel.
> In the prophets of Jerusalem I saw something horrible:
>> They commit adultery and tell lies.
>> They encourage evildoers so that no one turns from their
>>> wickedness. . . .
> The LORD proclaims:
> Don't listen to the prophets who are speaking to you;
>> they are deceiving you.
> Their visions come from their own hearts,
>> not from the LORD's mouth.
> They keep saying to those who scorn God's message,
>> "All will go well for you,"
> and to those who follow their own willful hearts,
>> "Nothing bad will happen to you." (Jer 23:13-14, 16-17)

The challenge of adjudicating whether prophecy was true or false is something with which the book of Jeremiah wrestles early and late in its literary structure. We glimpse some of this conflict early on, in an astonishing accusation that the prophet levels against the LORD in Jeremiah 4: "Lord GOD, no! You have utterly deceived this people and Jerusalem by promising them peace even though the sword is at their throats" (4:10). Here, false prophecy is prophesying *shalom* ("it will be well with you"), whereas true prophecy calls the people's attention to their impending doom. A narrative of prophetic conflict in Jeremiah 28 emphasizes that the inexorable approach of doom is precisely what is prophesied by authentic prophets. When Hananiah prophesies falsely that the exile of the first deportees will be over in two years and the temple vessels will be returned, Jeremiah counters with this:

> Get married and have children; then help your sons find wives and your daughters find husbands in order that they too may have children. Increase in number there so that you don't dwindle away. Promote the welfare of the city where I have sent you into exile. Pray to the LORD for it, because your future depends on its welfare. The LORD of heavenly forces, the God of Israel, proclaims: Don't let the prophets and diviners in your midst mislead you. Don't pay attention to your dreams. They are prophesying lies to you in my name. I didn't send them, declares the LORD. (29:6-9)

Regarding how to understand Jeremiah himself and his message, within the Deutero-Jeremianic prose we can glimpse two opposing factions struggling to shape the prophet's legacy in line with their own distinct theopolitical views. The dominant voice is the voice of the diaspora group in Babylon: the political, religious, and scribal elites taken into captivity beginning in 597 and joined by a second wave of deportees after the fall of Jerusalem in 587. This scribal group is working as hard as it possibly can to underwrite its own authority as the "true Israel," using several rhetorical strategies. Chief among them is the "submit to Babylon and live" policy—which is what they have done as a traumatized group of political prisoners seeking to survive under conditions of subjugation in a foreign land. Another rhetorical strategy the Babylonian diaspora elites have worked into the Deutero-Jeremianic prose is to denigrate the Judeans who were left behind in Judah or who fled to Egypt. This dominant voice can be heard clearly in Jeremiah 24, 27, 29, and 44. Those chapters promote the goodness of those who have had to submit to Babylonian hegemony (see 24:1-7) and the despicable nature of those who remained in Judah (24:8-10; 29:16-19) or who went to Egypt (44:11-14). The ferocity of the arguments suggests that there were very high stakes politically in all of this, possibly relevant to the reconstitution of Judah in the postexilic period. A late addition to the book of Jeremiah (29:16-20, not present in the LXX text) shows that these disputes among different Judean factions were raging in the postexilic period.

The dominant voice in the Deutero-Jeremiah prose is shouting "submit to Babylon and live," this *Realpolitik* platform aggressively underwriting the exiles' political authority as God's chosen remnant from devastated Judah. But there is also a more submerged and marginal counter-voice in the Deutero-Jeremianic prose. These folks saw the coming destruction as inevitable and had no interest in pragmatic accommodationist politics. Countless countries and regions throughout history have faced the terrible choice about whether to submit to an imperial onslaught and seek to ingratiate themselves with their conquerors or, instead, fight the idealist fight even if it means their own destruction. There are many creative possibilities for how to respond to militarized colonization, as Homi Bhabha and other postcolonial scholars have shown. Those who work openly with the enemy are often called traitors by those who have thrown in their lot with resistance or seek simply to endure with integrity. We see this dramatized in Jeremiah 37:

> Now when the Babylonian army had withdrawn from Jerusalem due to Pharaoh's advance, Jeremiah set out for the land of Benjamin to secure his share of the family property. He got as far as the Benjamin Gate in Jerusalem when the guard there named Irijah, Shelemiah's son and Hananiah's grandson, arrested the prophet Jeremiah, saying, "You are deserting to the Babylonians."
>
> "That's a lie," Jeremiah replied. "I'm not deserting to the Babylonians." But Irijah wouldn't listen to him. He arrested Jeremiah and

brought him to the officials, who were furious with him. They beat him and threw him into the house of the scribe Jonathan, which had been turned into a prison. So Jeremiah was put in a cistern, which was like a dungeon, where he remained a long time. (37:11-16)

Jeremiah is accused of treasonous behavior, and the same charge might be leveled at much of the Deutero-Jeremianic prose. Three times in Jeremiah, the king who is commanding the invading Babylonian troops, Nebuchadnezzar, is called the LORD's "servant" (25:9, 27:6, and 43:10), something that would have shocked ancient hearers. Now, take a look at the ideology affirmed in Jeremiah 29:

Build houses and settle down; cultivate gardens and eat what they produce. Get married and have children; then help your sons find wives and your daughters find husbands in order that they too may have children. Increase in number there so that you don't dwindle away. Promote the welfare of the city where I have sent you into exile. Pray to the LORD for it, because your future depends on its welfare. (29:5-7).

On a level that goes deeper than the plot of the narrative, the book of Jeremiah is struggling mightily to justify those who did go to Babylon and assimilate into the culture of the cruel conqueror. "Praying for the *shalom*" of Babylon—working in an assimilationist way toward the flourishing of the enemy that had broken through the wall of Jerusalem, killed and maimed so many Judeans, and plundered the temple—would have been an utterly repugnant notion to those left in the ruins of Jerusalem and to those who had fled elsewhere.

The resistance position may have been politically suppressed during the transmission process that preserved and elaborated on the Jeremiah traditions, but it is still visible. We can hear echoes of this position in subtle uses of metaphors and diction that are unlike the stock of the dominant voice; but proof of this second faction's ideology is harder to muster, because they are more marginal in the final form of the book. Whatever you decide about the tensions that percolate through the book of Jeremiah, there can be no question that Jeremiah is the complicated product of a traumatized and bitterly divided scribal community.

Tension between Doom and Repentance

The prose passages in Jeremiah are riven by a fierce theological tension that the book is trying to work out. It is an urgent matter, involving survival or death within the plot of the book and authorization of a particular ideology in the postexilic context in which it was finally shaped. The scribes that worked over the legacy of Jeremiah did not all agree on how to understand what had happened to Judah and Jerusalem. Bitter partisan politics are narrated even as part of the plot, so this is not an overly subtle conclusion. A theological issue at the core of the partisan disputes has to do with whether the trauma that befell Judah and Jerusalem had been inevitable or could have been avoided through the people's repentance. This question constituted a vital debate having to do with political authority and culpability in the wake of trauma. Struggling with the question was crucial—so it must have seemed—for understanding how the postexilic future of the community might be embraced and lived with new purpose.

First, here are some passages that suggest that doom is inevitable, including passages in which Jeremiah is forbidden to exercise the classic prophetic role of intercession on behalf of the people.

> Just go to my sanctuary in Shiloh, where I let my name dwell at first, and see what I did to it because of the evil of my people Israel. And now, because you have done all these things, declares the LORD, because you haven't listened when I spoke to you again and again or responded when I called you, I will do to this temple that bears my name and on which you rely, the place that I gave to you and your ancestors, just as I did to Shiloh. I will cast you out of my sight, just as I cast out the rest of your family, all the people of Ephraim. As for you, don't pray for these people, don't cry out or plead for them, and don't intercede with me, for I won't listen to you. (7:12-16)

> You have as many gods as you have towns, Judah, and you have as many shameful altars for worshipping Baal as you have streets in Jerusalem. As for you, don't pray for these people, don't cry out or plead for them, for I won't listen when they cry out to me on account of their distress.

What are my loved ones doing in my temple

while working out their many evil schemes?

Can sacred offerings cancel your sin

so that you revel in your evil deeds? (11:13-15)

In a sign-act, Jeremiah is to wear a new loincloth, then hide it in a rocky place at the Euphrates (the river coursing past Babylon, and hence quite some distance from Jerusalem) or else near a local town whose name sounds the same as "the Euphrates" in Hebrew; the wordplay may be intentional. After a long time, he is to retrieve it and see that it is ruined. The lesson:

> Then the LORD's word came to me: The LORD proclaims: In the same way I will ruin the brazen pride of Judah and Jerusalem! Instead of listening to me, this wicked people follow their own willful hearts and pursue other gods, worshipping and serving them. They will become like this linen garment—good for nothing! Just as a linen undergarment clings to the body, so I created the people of Israel and Judah to cling to me, declares the LORD, to be my people for my honor, praise, and grandeur. But they wouldn't obey. (13:8-11)

Robert Carroll has suggested that this sign-act may be a "dramatic reenactment of exile in Babylon" itself ruining the people.[5] If he is right, the perspective in Jeremiah 13 would be robustly antagonistic to the position of the accommodationist partisans who say that the Babylonian exiles are "good figs" (24:4-7; 29:16-19) and who urge the exiles to pray for the *shalom* of Babylon (29:7):

> The LORD said to me: Don't pray for the safety of these people. When they fast, I won't pay attention to their pleas, and when they offer entirely burned offerings and grain offerings, I won't accept them. Instead, I will devour them with war, famine, and disease. (14:11-12)

> The LORD said to me: Even if Moses and Samuel stood before me, I wouldn't change my mind about these people. Send them away from me. Let them go! And if they say, "Go where?" tell them, This is what the LORD proclaims:

Those marked for death—to death,

those marked for war—to war,

those marked for famine—to famine,

   and those marked for exile—to exile.

I will appoint over them four agents of death, declares the Lord: soldiers to kill, dogs to drag off, and vultures and wild animals to devour and destroy. (15:1-3)

Because you have not obeyed my words, I am going to send for all the tribes of the north, says the Lord, even for King Nebuchadrezzar of Babylon, my servant, and I will bring them against this land and its inhabitants, and against all these nations around; I will utterly destroy them, and make them an object of horror and of hissing, and an everlasting disgrace. (25:8-9 NRSV)

Now compare the below passages suggesting that repentance can still avert the coming disaster. These are interwoven with passages threatening inevitable doom, so this is not a simple matter of historical sequence, repentance having initially been possible but later being foreclosed as the enemy drew near. No: the heavily edited book of Jeremiah gives the impression of being an active "site" of contestation about these theological and political issues. That's one reason it's hard to read. Consider:

This is what the Lord of heavenly forces, the God of Israel, says: Improve your conduct and your actions, and I will dwell with you in this place. (7:3)

If you truly reform your ways and your actions; if you treat each other justly; if you stop taking advantage of the immigrant, orphan, or widow; if you don't shed the blood of the innocent in this place, or go after other gods to your own ruin, only then will I dwell with you in this place, in the land that I gave long ago to your ancestors for all time. (7:5-7)

The Lord proclaims: Do what is just and right; rescue the oppressed from the power of the oppressor. Don't exploit or mistreat the refugee, the orphan, and the widow. Don't spill the blood of the innocent in this place. If you obey this command, then through the gates of this palace will come kings who occupy the throne of David, riding on chariots and horses along with their entourage and subjects. (22:3-4)

Jeremiah said to all the officials and to all the people, "The LORD sent me to prophesy to this temple and this city everything you have heard. So now transform your ways and actions. Obey the LORD your God, and the LORD may relent and not carry out the harm that he's pronounced against you." (26:12-13)

When a group experiences slaughter and forced displacement on a catastrophic scale, the trauma wreaked by the enemy can be mirrored, almost reenacted, by harmful dynamics within the community as the survivors seek to understand what has happened. Many in traumatized families and communities reach for blaming mechanisms as they struggle with anguish and rage. That's one reason why the Babylonian exiles so viciously disenfranchise their traumatized compatriots back home in Judah and those who fled to Egypt. It can be painful to read Jeremiah 24, 29, and 44, once you realize that it is a known psychological effect of disaster that communities, groups, and families can turn on one another, becoming fiercely divided in a kind of blaming or "splitting" that is a maladaptive response to trauma. The fear generated by the Babylonian incursions, the deaths of so many Judeans during the siege and fall of Jerusalem, the multiple deportations of Judean citizens, and the dehumanizing dimensions of life in captivity in Babylon must have done terrible damage to the cultural fabric of the community. Wrenching grief and burning rage must have been experienced by the scribes who preserved and argued over the heritage of Jeremiah. Some had firsthand experience of the disaster. If the book of Jeremiah reached its final form in the postexilic period, many scribes would have witnessed the agonizing grief of their parents or grandparents. Some would have seen relatives or friends dealing with maiming injuries; the youngest might have been enculturated through hearing only silence whenever someone skirted too close to a subject that caused anguish to the older generation.

Effects of Trauma

Traumatic violence comes as a shocking blow, a terrifying disruption of normal mental processes, distorting reality, even as it becomes the only reality. Disasters brought about by traumatic violence disturb what people think, feel, and believe. They distort perceptions and shut down ordinary life. . . . These memories can be neither forgotten nor escaped, even though they exist as shattered moments of experience. . . . The unutterable nature of the wounds is a second form of violence and related to fragmented memories. Often it is impossible for victims to tell what happened to them, to name their experiences, or to depict in words the terrors that have overwhelmed them.

—Kathleen O'Connor[6]

Anomalous Note: Jeremiah 31:22

As we move forward into Jeremiah material that includes ferocious indictments of traumatized Judah and vitriolic disputes among the community's leadership, we may be sustained by an anomalous note in the book that reminds us that newness and transformation are possible and cannot be obliterated even by the harshness of surrounding material. Our anomalous note in this book is in Jeremiah 31, where we find one of the most mysterious verses (31:22) in all of Scripture. NRSV translates it as, "For the LORD has created a new thing on the earth: a woman encompasses a man." That second clause is the one that seems impossible to understand, though the words and syntax are clear enough. Here are other translations and explanations:

- "Faithful daughter Israel, though wayward and promiscuous in times past . . . at last embraces or 'encompasses' her God." (Louis Stulman)[7]

- "Virgin Israel will once again embrace her God!" (CEB)

- "A woman courts a man." (NJPS)

- "A female courts a man." (Leslie Allen)[8]

- "A woman protects a man." (Robert Carroll)[9]

- "A female shall encompass a hero." (William Holladay)[10]

- "A woman is turned into a man." (William McKane)[11]

- "The female protects the man." (Jack Lundbom)[12]

Kathleen O'Connor rightly observes that the clause may be generative of multiple layers of meaning, depending on how the reader relates it to other motifs and metaphors in Jeremiah 31.[13] The best translation, in my view, is, "Female surrounds warrior-male." The first noun is certainly to be translated "female"; the Hebrew there is not the word more commonly used for *woman*, but the sexed term *female* that is juxtaposed with *male* in Genesis 1:27 and thus, many agree, having to do with the (sexual) fruitfulness to which the first ancestors were called in the garden of Eden. The second noun has the semantic valence of strength (thus: man of valor, strong man, hero, male soldier), and that nuance is crucially important here. I read the line in the semantic environment of a repeated refrain in Jeremiah that has the same root verb, *s-b-b*, "to surround, to encompass." The repeated refrain *māgôr missābîb* occurs five times in Jeremiah. It is translated as "Terror all around!" and occurs in contexts that describe fear of enemy invaders (Jer 6:25; 46:5; 49:29) and also violent political disputes within the community that threaten the protagonist (Jer 20:3, 10; see also Ps 31:13). The same verb is used of enemy sieges, when hostile troops surround a city, just as the Babylonian army surrounded and besieged Jerusalem.

Reading Jeremiah 31, we move through images of some from "all the families of Israel" (31:1) having survived the sword (31:2), the survivors being led by a loving God back home from diaspora with singing (31:3-13). Bereaved mother Rachel is to be comforted (31:15-17), the fallen northern kingdom (Ephraim) will be restored, and this is to be a "new thing on the earth": "female surrounds warrior-male." Now, sexual reproduction could not plausibly be called "a new thing on the earth" in itself, nor could simple restoration from exile, nor could the metaphor of Zion nurturing her returned children. Many texts celebrate those things. Jeremiah 31:22 is far more radical. For it to be true that this is a "new thing on the earth," something never before seen in human culture, we have to be more daring in our interpretation. In the fuller context of Jeremiah 31, and taking 31:22 as a powerful reversal of all the ways that Judah, Jerusalem, and the prophet himself have been surrounded, beaten, incarcerated, enslaved, and otherwise "mastered" by violence: we must understand 31:22 as prophesying that female fruitfulness, as shown—from the dawn of creation itself—in childbirth and nurturing, will finally overcome the ceaseless violence that has dominated the world via male-warrior culture. Jeremiah 31:22 is an extraordinarily bold proclamation of *shalom*. It should be read along the lines of Isaiah 2:4 and Micah 4:3, "Nation will not take up sword against nation; they will no longer learn how to make war" (Isa 2:4). What a mighty word of consolation to a nation utterly broken by war, by captivity, and by vicious internecine disputes generated by fear! This mysterious oracle of hope constitutes the most profound reversal that a prophet could possibly envision in the relations of power that constitute human communities. As you move back into the harsh polemics and vivid conflicts narrated in the rest of the book of Jeremiah, I hope you will remember 31:22 as an indestructible prophecy of hope. It may be received as a word of cosmic newness for every female, male, genderqueer, and other-gendered body; for every family and social group; and for every community within reach of God's holy word.

Jeremiah 1–25

In Jeremiah 1, notice the commissioning of the prophet. The work that lies before Jeremiah is described with six verbs that invite the reader to undertake a journey through the terrain of the entire book. Jeremiah's commissioning gestures toward a preponderance of judgment material (four verbs: "to dig up and pull down, to destroy and demolish," 1:10) and some luminous restoration material as well (two verbs: "to build and plant," 1:10). Here we glimpse the inevitability of the prophetic vocation: the LORD has known Jeremiah since before he was formed in the womb and has consecrated him as a servant of the divine purpose before he was born.

Jeremiah will come to experience the presence of the LORD as exhausting and coercive. You might note also an unusual phrase in the commissioning of Jeremiah: "I made you a prophet to the nations" (1:5). The biblical prophets ordinarily prophesied to their own people—to kings, or, as in the Latter Prophets, to the people of Israel and Judah more generally. There are collections of oracles against foreign nations, but many scholars think that those would never have been heard by enemies in real terms and were intended to serve as "good news" for Judean audiences instead. The vast majority of prophetic material we have in both the Former and Latter Prophets is directed at domestic audiences, not at the nations of the world. Here, the range of the word of God is clearly envisioned—theologically and politically—as reaching across the known world, including Egypt and Babylon, two countries that play vitally significant roles later in the book of Jeremiah. This "prophet to the nations" phrase signals the importance of international politics in the vocation of the prophet Jeremiah, an interest amply borne out in the prose of the rest of the book.

In 1:6, Jeremiah objects, " 'Ah, Lord GOD,' I said, 'I don't know how to speak because I'm only a child.' " And the LORD responds, "Don't say, 'I'm only a child.' Where I send you, you must go; what I tell you, you must say. Don't be afraid of them, because I'm with you to rescue you" (1:7-8). We see similar objections to experiences of divine call in the stories of Moses, Gideon, and Isaiah. These objections are fascinating. The objection always emphasizes the inadequacy of the "clay vessel," the prophet or judge (in the case of Gideon), and the LORD's response underlines the performative power of the divine word and the illimitable drive of the divine purpose. God's word is mighty and effective, no matter how flawed or inadequate the commissioned individual may be. Each objection has to do with the particular task and what is at stake theologically in the vocation of each person called. Moses worries, "My Lord, I've never been able to speak well, not yesterday, not the day before, and certainly not now. . . . Please, my Lord, just send someone else" (Exod 4:10, 13). In response to the first objection, the LORD gives Moses three signs to perform. The signs are vitally important, not only to Israel, but also to Pharaoh, as demonstrations of the LORD's power. In response to the second of Moses's objections, the LORD thunders, "Who gives people the ability to speak? Who's responsible for making them unable to speak or hard of hearing, sighted or blind? Isn't it I, the LORD? Now go! I'll help you speak, and I'll teach you what you should say" (Exod 4:11-12). This is arguably a foreshadowing of the Law that Moses will receive on Sinai: the divine teaching that Moses will pass on to all Israel. And the third objection ("just send someone else") is met with the LORD appointing Aaron as spokesperson, foreshadowing the way in which the Law has been given to prophets like Moses and to priests like Aaron. Gideon's objections in Judges 6:15 focus on how he understands himself as powerless, an unimpressive individual in a weak clan. This objection flags a key premise of holy war: the LORD does not need powerful fighters in order to accomplish the divine purpose, since it is the LORD who fights the battle. Isaiah's objection in Isaiah 6:5 has to do with him and his people being impure: he is purified with a burning coal taken, as it were, from God's own holiness, which is an important theme in Isaiah. So too in Jeremiah, we see an objection met by reassurance in terms that orient the reader to major issues in the book writ larger. Jeremiah does not know how to speak, but the response comes that he shall indeed speak what the LORD commands. Jeremiah is afraid he will not be able to withstand the adversarial dynamics within the community, but the LORD reassures him: he will be triumphant, not over other nations, but domestically: "Today I have made you an armed city, an iron pillar, and a bronze wall against the entire land—the kings of Judah, its princes, its priests, and all its people. They will attack you, but they won't defeat you, because I am with you and will rescue you, declares the LORD" (1:18-19). Thus, the objection of Jeremiah seems to have been shaped as having to do with fear of internecine opposition to his message.

In 2:18-19, Jeremiah insists that political alliances will not avail—a posture so different from the "submit to Babylon and live" platform of the later accommodationist prose: "So why take the path to Egypt to drink water from the Nile? Why travel the path to Assyria to drink water from the Euphrates? . . . Don't you understand how terribly bitter it is to abandon the LORD your God and not fear me? declares the LORD of heavenly forces." In the same chapter, notice a classic statement of the notion of retributive justice: "I have disciplined your children in vain; they have rejected my correction. You have devoured your prophets like a hungry lion" (2:30). Death and disaster are works of God intended to bring the people back to God, an ideology that is pervasive in the Latter Prophets. It is given a particularly memorable expression in Amos 4, where the LORD complains that repeated acts of disastrous punishment had not achieved their intended effect: the LORD struck the covenant people with famine, drought, blight, mildew, pestilence, and defeat in battle, "yet you didn't return to me, says the LORD" (Amos 4:6).

Jeremiah 2 and 3 raise a problem that is visible throughout the prophetic corpus and particularly acute in Ezekiel: patriarchal gendered language that portrays faithless Judah as a woman whose sexuality cannot be controlled by men and whose sins have polluted the whole land, leaving it ripe for punishment and defilement by enemies. Idolatry and moral sin were considered to defile the community and its territory. Some passages in Jeremiah portray the land, or even the whole earth (the word is the same in Hebrew), defiled by corpses lying unburied, this as a way of signaling the depth of corruption of the people and their leaders:

> At that time, declares the LORD, the bones of the kings of Judah and its officers, the bones of the priests and the prophets, and the bones of the people of Jerusalem will be taken from their graves and exposed to the sun, the moon, and the whole heavenly forces, which they have loved and served and which they have followed, consulted, and worshipped. Their bones won't be gathered for reburial but will become like refuse lying on the ground. (8:1-2)

> The LORD roars on high;
>> from his holy place he thunders.
> He roars fiercely against his flock,
>> like the shouting of those who tread on grapes, against everyone
>> on earth.
> The uproar is heard far and wide,

because the LORD is bringing a lawsuit against the nations.

He's entering into judgment with all people,

sentencing the guilty to death, declares the LORD.

The LORD of heavenly forces proclaims:

Look! Disaster travels from nation to nation.

A terrible storm comes from the far ends of the earth.

At that time, those struck down by the LORD will fill the earth. And no one will mourn for them or prepare their bodies for burial. They will become like refuse lying on the ground. (25:30-33)

Reading the oracles of Jeremiah presents quite a hermeneutical challenge. With their changes in addressee, sharp shifts in focus, and so on, now are we to understand the literary connections among them? Why do some verses seem to comment on other verses, while others seem disconnected from the surrounding material in their literary contexts? William McKane has argued that the book of Jeremiah gradually achieved its final, extremely complicated form through a gradual process of accretion of smaller units here and there. He calls this the "rolling corpus" model. A passage might pick up later commentary, or material that affirms or contests or modifies its position, as various scribal circles continued to preserve, amplify, and elaborate on the Jeremiah traditions. McKane's model was intended to address the indisputable circumstance that no one overarching theory can account for all that goes on in Jeremiah. Even my own theory of fierce contestations, which I've argued are visible along several different trajectories and expressed through several kinds of literary tensions, cannot fully account for everything in the book. McKane's position may be critiqued for proposing a slightly too random view of how the book has been shaped, and for not seeking to anchor particular scribal interventions more firmly in a concrete social context. Yet in a significant number of places in Jeremiah, it certainly seems that processes of local accretion are what have yielded the final form. This and other models of compositional growth of Jeremiah may be fruitful for the reader who is baffled by this complex prophetic book.

Deconstrucing Israel

The indictments brought against Israel in Jeremiah 1–25 articulate the LORD's expectations of covenant faithfulness and describe, often in vivid detail, the ways in which Judah has frustrated or disappointed those expectations. The people are excoriated for idolatry, for reliance on military alliances instead of on YHWH, and for moral corruption and social injustice:

> Be wary of your friends!
>> Don't trust your sibling!
>> Every sibling is a cheater,
>>> and every friend traffics in slander.
> One cheats the other; no one tells the truth;
>> they train themselves to lie; they wear themselves out by doing wrong.
> You live in a world of deceit,
>> and in their deceit they refuse to know me, declares the LORD. (9:4-6)

To poetic oracles of judgment have been added some prose texts bringing further indictment. For example: "Your wealth and belongings I will deliver as plunder, without a fee, because of all your sins throughout your territory. I will make you serve your enemies in a land you don't know, for my anger blazes like a fire that won't go out" (15:13-14).

In the first half of the book, we encounter some brief passages of promise as well. These are likely postexilic. One wonders whether these notes of hope might have been offered to sustain the fragile covenant relationship for hearers shamed by the preponderance of relentless language of judgment. See, for example, these lyrical passages:

> I will appoint shepherds with whom I'm pleased, and they will lead you with knowledge and understanding. At that time, they will call Jerusalem the LORD's throne, and all nations will gather there to honor the LORD's name. No longer will they follow their own willful and evil hearts. In those days the people of Judah and Israel will leave the north together for the land that I gave their ancestors as an inheritance. (3:15, 17-18)

> But the time is coming, declares the LORD, when no one will say, "As the LORD lives who brought up the Israelites from the land of Egypt"; instead, they will say, "As the LORD lives who brought up the Israelites

from the land of the north and from all the lands where he has banished them." I will bring them back to the land that I gave to their ancestors. (16:14-15; see also the doublet at 23:7-8)

The time is coming, declares the Lord, when I will raise up a righteous descendant from David's line, and he will rule as a wise king. He will do what is just and right in the land. During his lifetime, Judah will be saved and Israel will live in safety. And his name will be The Lord Is Our Righteousness. (23:5-6)

Remarkably, oracles of promise are offered about several enemies as well. While any number of social contexts may have generated such material, one possibility is a postexilic setting in which forging bonds of trust and goodwill between Judah and other nations was a goal of Judah's political leaders. Another possibility is that Judeans living in diaspora in these other nations needed to hear about their own future as being still possible and congruent with God's purposes.

The Lord proclaims: The evil nations have seized the land that I gave my people Israel. I'm going to dig them up from their own lands, and I will dig up the people of Judah from among them. And after I have dug them up, I will again have compassion on them and restore their inheritance and their land. And then, if they will learn the ways of my people, to make a solemn pledge in my name, "As the Lord lives," just as they once taught my people to swear to Baal, then they will be built up in the midst of my people. (12:14-16)

After vivid images of judgment, a series of oracles against Egypt concludes with, "But afterward Egypt will dwell like it did a long time ago" (46:26).

The Lord promises in the future to restore the fortunes of Moab (48:47), the Ammonites (49:6), and Elam (49:39).

Jeremiah 13 gives us the first symbolic "sign-act" performed by the prophet. As you continue to read, look for other sign-acts of the prophet, which constituted a kind of street theater or performance art conveying the word of God to the people in unforgettable images. As Louis Stulman puts it, the prophets "enact the acts of God by the force of artistic expression, especially their body art; they sculpt new configurations of justice and hope by the force of their imagination."[14]

109

Sign-Acts in Jeremiah	
Jeremiah buries a linen undergarment, then digs it up "after a long time." It is ruined, signaling that the LORD "will ruin the brazen pride of Judah and Jerusalem." Jerusalem "will become like this linen garment—good for nothing."	13:1-11
Jeremiah is to have no wife or children, as a sign of a gruesome future: parents and children shall "die of horrible diseases . . . they will die by the sword and by famine, and their corpses will be food for birds and wild animals. . . . There will be no funerals or time of mourning. No one will gash themselves in grief or shave their heads in sorrow."	16:1-9
Jeremiah watches as a potter purposefully ruins and remakes a clay vessel, the process a sign of the LORD's unfettered capacity to destroy or rebuild, depending on whether "a nation or kingdom" turns from evil ways or not.	18:1-11
Jeremiah breaks a jug in the sight of elders and priests at the Potsherd Gate, signifying that the LORD plans to "smash this people and this city. And they will bury the dead . . . until there's no room left."	19:1-13
Jeremiah puts a wooden yoke on his neck, symbolizing that Judah and other nations should willingly submit to the king of Babylon and his invading army.	27:1-15
Hananiah breaks the yoke from Jeremiah's neck as a sign that the LORD will break the political power of Babylon within two years; Hananiah dies within two months, this prophesied by Jeremiah as divine punishment for his false prophesying.	28:1-17
During the Babylonian siege of Jerusalem, Jeremiah buys a field at Anathoth, placing the sealed deed of purchase and an open copy in a clay container, "so they will last a long time," as a sign that "houses, fields, and vineyards will again be bought in this land."	32:1-15
Jeremiah invites the Rechabites to drink wine. Their staunch refusal, in keeping with their ancestral prohibition, is construed as a sign of fidelity that Judah should emulate.	35:1-19
Jeremiah, taken to Egypt against his will, is to bury large stones "in front of Pharaoh's palace at Tahpanhes" to signal the place on which Nebuchadnezzar of Babylon will set his throne when he has conquered and ravaged Egypt.	43:8-13

Jeremiah writes in a scroll "all the disasters that would happen to Babylon." He then orders that Seraiah son of Neriah, who is in a royal delegation that will travel to Babylon, should read the scroll aloud in Babylon, tie a stone to the scroll, and throw it in the Euphrates, proclaiming on behalf of the LORD, "In the same way, Babylon will sink and never rise again because of the disaster I'm bringing against it."	51:59-64

The impossibility of intercession having been asserted in 11:14 and 14:11-12, we see in 15:1-4 how serious the LORD is about the inevitability of doom: "Even if Moses and Samuel stood before me, I wouldn't change my mind about these people" (15:1). Even the two most honored intercessors in Israel's sacred history would not be able to avert the punishment. Here, the parallels with the Exodus are used in a scathingly ironic way. Where Moses pleaded with Pharaoh to let the Israelites go, in this circumstance, even the eloquence of Moses would not avail. The sinful Judeans will be "let go," all right: they'll be released to the scourge of pestilence and the sharp blade of the sword, to gnawing famine, and to captivity. A similarly brutal "release" will be granted by the LORD as punishment for the practice, forbidden in the Torah, of Judeans holding other Judeans in slavery: "Therefore, the LORD proclaims: Since you have defied me by not setting your fellow citizens free, I'm setting you free, declares the LORD, free to die by the sword, disease, and famine! And I will make you an object of horror for all nations on earth" (34:17).

The intractability of Judean sin is expressed through a powerful metaphor in Jeremiah 17: "Judah's sin is engraved with an iron pen. It's etched with a diamond point on the tablets of their hearts and on the horns of their altars. Their children remember their altars and sacred poles by the lush trees and high hills" (17:1-2). This image will be reversed in an oracle of promise in the Book of Consolation, when the Torah will be written on the people's hearts (31:33). In Jeremiah 20, conflict with Pashhur the priest continues the motif of internecine plotting and conflict that is central to the Jeremiah traditions; it is explored in greatest depth in the laments of Jeremiah (see below). Jeremiah 22–23 shows intense interest in

111

two types of community leaders who have led the people astray: Judah's rulers and false prophets.

Speaking Truth to Power

An essential ingredient of Jeremiah's meaning-making map, his tapestry of hope, is truth-telling. From the outset, the prophet names and breaks a surplus of denials and deceptions, and he dares to critique social structures, domain assumptions, and prevailing values that anesthetize the community to its true condition. . . . Impressive sanctuaries, brawny nationalism, urban think tanks, and even trusted doctrines will not avert disaster and fundamental transformations in community life. And so Jeremiah speaks truth to the powerbrokers invested in these systems.

—Louis Stulman and Hyun Chul Paul Kim[15]

The Laments of Jeremiah

To live out a prophetic vocation in ancient Israel or Judah would have been challenging. Prophets were regularly engaged in public confrontations with religious and political authorities. Seers and other intermediaries experienced visions—surely unsettling at best. From what we can glimpse in the literary representations of these events in antiquity, some of these visions were terrifying or wrenchingly sad. Prophets faced threats, beatings, incarceration, public scorn, and the possibility of execution. The Jeremiah traditions reflect in an unusually sustained way on the arduous and demoralizing nature of a life lived in faithfulness to the prophetic vocation.

Six compositions in the book of Jeremiah are considered to be formal laments, also called the "confessions" of Jeremiah. These are found at 11:18–20; 12:1-6; 15:10-21; 17:14-18; 18:18-23; and 20:7-18. These first-person poems represent suffering and struggle as constant companions in Jeremiah's prophetic ministry. Consider these plaintive reflections voiced by Jeremiah:

- "I was like a young lamb led to the slaughter." (11:19)

- "Why do guilty persons enjoy success? Why are evildoers so happy?" (12:1)

- "I wish I had never been born! I have become a source of conflict and dissension in my own country. Even though I haven't lent or borrowed, still everyone curses me." (15:10)

- "Heal me, LORD, and I'll be healed. . . . You know what comes out of my mouth; it's always before you. Don't terrorize me; you are my refuge in time of disaster." (17:14, 16-17)

- "They have dug a pit to capture me, set traps for my feet. But you, LORD, you know all their sinister plots to kill me. Don't overlook their wrongdoing; don't cleanse their sin from before you. May they stumble before you; when you become angry, do something about them." (18:22-23)

- "Whenever I speak, I must cry out, I must shout, 'Violence and destruction!' For the word of the LORD has become for me a reproach and derision all day long. If I say, 'I will not mention him, or speak any more in his name,' then within me there is something like a burning fire shut up in my bones; I am weary with holding it in, and I cannot. . . . Why did I come forth from the womb to see toil and sorrow, and spend my days in shame?" (20:8-9, 18 NRSV)

Themes in this moving material include shame, weariness, the threat posed by antagonists, and the overwhelming nature of the prophetic mission. Jeremiah's struggle with the prophetic vocation has long been used as a resource for spiritual counseling and vocational guidance in Christian tradition. We may consider also the suffering of the prophet as a witness to the duress that the covenant community must endure as a whole. A sociopolitical reading might hear in the fractured voice of the prophet the anguish and rage of a community forced to live under conditions of threat—forced displacement, colonization—while nevertheless being called, as is the Suffering Servant in Isaiah, to make visible the power and holiness of the LORD in a world bent on exploitation and cruelty. Robert Carroll offers an interpretation that recognizes the blurring of the persona of Jeremiah with the scribal circles that honored his legacy and the covenant community writ larger:

> His words and deeds embrace the communities of the sixth and fifth centuries along with all the problems facing them. . . . This is not a real person but a conglomerate of many things, reflecting the fortunes of various Jewish communities during and after the Babylonian period. The "historical" Jeremiah may still be there hidden or weighed down under the additions and interpretations of countless editors and transformed beyond recognition, so that we cannot now rediscover him with any assurance. . . . Hence the figure of Jeremiah which is discerned in the text . . . must be interpreted as . . . a very complex amalgam of social, political, and theological elements which, though lacking consistency or coherence, reflects the hermeneutically rich strands which constitute the book of Jeremiah.[16]

The lamenting prophet cries out not only in the formal lament poems but elsewhere in the book of Jeremiah as well. Particularly powerful is 8:18–9:3, a passage that lifts up a wrenching rhetorical question and a moving image of grief:

> Is there no balm in Gilead?
>> Is there no physician there?
> Why then have my people not been restored to health?
> If only my head were a spring of water,
>> and my eyes a fountain of tears.
>> I would weep day and night for the wounds of my people.
>> (8:22-9:1)

John Bracke underlines the theological significance of a lamenting prophet who speaks for the LORD and whose voice may, at times, become indistinguishable from that of the deity:

> Because in the book so much similarity exists between laments that are the direct speech of God and the laments spoken by the prophet, it seems likely that the laments of Jeremiah need to be heard as reflecting

God's hurt and pain. . . . The laments of the prophet Jeremiah mirror the anguish of God. This concern with God's anguish does not allow us to read in the book a simple retribution theology: Do well and be blessed by God; disobey and be punished by God. To this retribution equation, the book of Jeremiah adds God's anguish. . . . Thus, one of the challenges of studying the book of Jeremiah is to see how the Lord's judgment of and suffering over Israel and Judah are related.[17]

Influenced by trauma studies, Kathleen O'Connor reads Jeremiah as the paradigmatic survivor:

He neither denies nor rejects YHWH, even as he names the bitterness of living with this God. Jeremiah's spiritual candor and perseverance yield a model for ancient audiences to emulate. O'Connor says that the book of Jeremiah creates poetic and symbolic language to help traumatized survivors speak of their suffering and to begin to interpret it, cope with it, and to endure through it until that new day when life might appear again among them. One way it does this is by telling Jeremiah's life story as the story of the "ideal survivor." . . . [Jeremiah's] struggles render visible and human their own sorrow, anger, and contradictions, and in doing so, his life summons them to come to grips with their reality.[18]

Jeremiah endures not only the terror of the Babylonian onslaught but also the virulent disputes and antagonisms roiling his own community. In the history of reception of the laments of Jeremiah, the prophet has been taken as a model for faith communities, a model for individual believers struggling spiritually or theologically toward healing, and a model for leaders called to speak a prophetic word.

"Balm in Gilead," refrain and verse 1

There is a balm in Gilead
to make the wounded whole;
there is a balm in Gilead
to heal the sin-sick soul.

Sometimes I feel discouraged
and think my work's in vain,
but then the Holy Spirit
revives my soul again.

Words: traditional African American spiritual

Jeremiah 26–45

Jeremiah 26 is often spoken of as a "second version" of the temple sermon of Jeremiah 7, and many points of contact with that earlier chapter are evident. But Jeremiah 26 focuses on the political figures who support or oppose Jeremiah, and so the aim of its storytelling is rather different from the point of the sermon in Jeremiah 7. Chapters 27–29 of Jeremiah are considered to have had their own transmission history, not least because of their focused themes of false prophecy and submission to Babylon, as well as the consistent use of *Nebuchadnezzar* for the king of Babylon in these chapters rather than the *Nebuchadrezzar* that we find everywhere else in Jeremiah.

Submission to Babylon

The urgency of submitting to the Babylonian army governs much of the material in the second half of Jeremiah. Contestations abound. Jeremiah 29 and Jeremiah 35 arguably present two radically opposed points of view, related, again, to partisan fighting over the legacy of Jeremiah according to differing theopolitical agendas. There is a fascinating narration of ancient letter-writing in Jeremiah 29. Dueling letters are described as different persons jockey for power in the Babylonian diaspora and back in Jerusalem.

Verse 15 makes it crystal clear that a broad-based attack was being mounted against prophetic authority in the Babylonian diaspora group. We can clearly see a polemical beginning of an indictment, "Yet you say, The LORD has raised up prophets for us in Babylon," and the Babylon group had to head off that political attack. So they added verses 16-20, which have absolutely nothing to do with charges against prophets in Babylon but which, instead, boldly, out of the blue, turn the tables on the resistance group back in Judah:

> This is what the LORD proclaims concerning the king sitting on David's throne and all the people who live in this city, that is, those among you who didn't go into exile: The LORD of heavenly forces proclaims: I'm going to send the sword, famine, and disease against them. I will make them like rotten figs that are too spoiled to eat. I will pursue them with the sword, famine, and disease; and I will make them an object of horror to all nations on earth and an object of cursing, scorn, shock, and disgrace among all the countries where I have scattered them, because they wouldn't listen to my words, declares the LORD, which I sent them time and again through my servants the prophets. They wouldn't listen, declares the LORD. (29:16-19)

The awkwardness of this late interpolation is breathtaking. It constitutes indisputable evidence of the partisan battle going on over which group could claim prophetic authority to validate their own political position. This vitriolic material, just like Jeremiah 24 and Jeremiah 44, is directed at their own compatriots. It has been shoehorned in, late in the development of the Hebrew text tradition (absent in the LXX), in order to deflect an attack on the authority of the Babylonian diaspora and its prophets.

Compare that Jeremiah with the prophet as he is portrayed in Jeremiah 35. Jeremiah gathers officials in a temple conference room and performs a sign-act that lauds the Rechabites, a heroically anti-assimilationist seminomadic group, for their fidelity to the LORD and the traditions of their ancestors. Jeremiah sets out pitchers of wine for the Rechabites. They decline, as he knew they would, because they will not compromise their integrity. Their ancestor commanded them "'never to drink wine; nor . . . to build or own houses or plant gardens and vineyards;' . . . We have obeyed . . . we haven't built houses to live in or had vineyards, fields, or crops. We have lived in tents," and they are living temporarily in Jerusalem only because they are terrified of the Babylonians (35:6-11). Commentators have long wondered: why are the Rechabites saying all this? They needed only to refuse the wine; they didn't need to go into such length about how they don't live in houses and don't plant vineyards and about how frightened they are of the Babylonians unless the point of this scenario is to counter the advice that the Babylonian diaspora traditionists are saying Jeremiah gave them (29:5-7). Here we have the Jeremiah of the resistance, against accommodationism and assimilation, commending the Rechabites for resisting and for staying true to their ancestral heritage. This Jeremiah says outright to the inhabitants of Judah and Jerusalem: "Can you not learn a lesson and obey my words?" (35:13 NRSV).

The prose in Jeremiah 32–45 narrates the events immediately preceding the fall of Jerusalem, the fall of that city, and the aftermath, which involves executions, an assassination, and an attempted coup. Crucially important to the stories here is the political loyalty of the various leaders of the community. This material is unusually rich in personal names of individuals; the narrator takes great care to align people with one group or another in the fierce internecine battle for political control following the devastation of Jerusalem. Unquestionably, it mattered a great deal to the traditionists who preserved this material to be clear about which individuals were allies and which were antagonists. It is my suspicion that in this bitter conflict between the Babylonian diaspora Judeans and those left behind in Judah—and, perhaps more to the point, their descendants fighting for power in reconstruction-era Judah—the historical Jeremiah, who had remained in Judah until he was taken to Egypt (43:6), may have been aligned with the resistance group. Certainly the pro-Babylon group had to work very hard to shape the material toward the alternative possibility. Further, the resistance position is notably closer to the perspective of much of the early poetry in the book. We will never know for sure, and all of the book of Jeremiah, now, is authoritative Scripture for those who honor the biblical canon and hear this text in worship. But it is important to hear polyphony, where multiple voices are singing or speaking. If we give the loudest traditionist voice the final and undisputed say, we might actually lose a substantial portion of the witness of the man who had been the historical Jeremiah. Of course, postcolonial readers would argue that it is no simple thing to "hear" the prophetic voice that is produced from a colonized social space. Creativity and accommodation, resistance and ambivalence, indigeneity and hybridity: all of these must be engaged in our analysis. The prophets' interpretation of lived experience was complex and conflicted. The authority of "Jeremiah" is as much produced by Judean complicity in Babylonian hegemony as it produces discourse against Babylonian hegemony.

The Book of Consolation

The beautiful oracles in Jeremiah 30–31, known as the Book of Consolation, are remarkable for their tenderness and their portrayals of joy. These oracles are unexpected in the book of Jeremiah, which focuses intently on Judah's sin, the raw vulnerability of Judah to the sovereignty of cruel enemy Babylon, and the pernicious failings of the Judean community.

And indeed, some diction and imagery in these chapters sounds much more like Second Isaiah (for example, 31:8-9, 21) and like restoration material in Hosea (e.g., 31:18-20) than like the rest of the book of Jeremiah. These chapters build on artfully expressed reversals that would have delighted an ancient audience. The best known and most powerful example is drawn as a poetic reversal of bereavement in 31:15-17. "A voice is heard in Ramah": this enigmatic opening draws the audience into the unspeakable grief of the loss of children, which is here named and lifted up in a book that has known much horror and little tenderness. Dearly loved matriarch Rachel weeps inconsolably, showing the depth of Judah's anguish at the destruction and exile of its people. The LORD counsels explicit reversal of this grief: "Keep your voice from crying and your eyes from weeping. . . . They will return from the land of their enemy! There's hope for your future, declares the LORD" (31:16-17). Other reversals bring consolation as well:

Yet all who ravage you will be ravaged;

all who oppress you will go into exile.

Those who rob you will be robbed,

and all who plunder you will be plundered. (30:16)

Then the young women will dance for joy;

the young and old men will join in.

I will turn their mourning into laughter and their sadness into joy;

I will comfort them. (31:13)

We've already thought above about 31:22, that anomalous note that promises transformation on a level never before experienced. A reversal of Jeremiah's own prophetic mission (1:10) is promised as well: "Just as I watched over them to dig up and pull down, to overthrow, destroy, and bring harm, so I will watch over them to build and plant, declares the LORD" (31:28).

Stirring material about a new covenant comes near the end of Jeremiah 31. If the book of Isaiah had sung of a second Exodus through the wilderness back to Judah, here, we may imagine a new Sinai event, this time with the LORD inscribing the covenant not on stone tablets but on the hearts of the people: "I will put my Instructions within them and engrave them on their hearts. I will be their God, and they will be my people. They will no longer need to teach each other to say, 'Know the LORD!' because they will all know me, from the least of them to the greatest, declares the LORD" (31:33-34).

This transcendent passage functions as an explicit reversal of the indictment in 17:1-4, where Judah's sin had been said to be engraved upon their hearts: "Because you have committed such sins . . . You will lose the inheritance that I gave you. I will make you slaves of your enemies in a land you don't know, for my anger blazes like a fire that won't go out" (17:3-4). This oracle of eternal punishment is lifted—is rewritten with the pen of grace—in Jeremiah 31. The people will never again break the covenant or forget that they belong to God.

Hope Despite Trauma

Jeremiah's oracles of hope resonate with us even now. In the words of Kathleen O'Connor:

> Jeremiah's little book of consolation enflames possibility and awakens yearning for a better world. It breaks into the frightful aftermath of disaster by insisting on divine power as the enacting agent of new life. The little book invites a kind of wounded alertness to the new world God is about to bring forth. . . . Jeremiah's vision disrupts the inertia of the present time and portrays God as the interrupting energy at [the] heart of the world. . . . In that new world about to break in, old and young, laity and priests eat, rejoice, and dance together in the watered garden of Zion restored.[19]

Jeremiah vividly names the horrors experienced by Judah during the war with Babylon, the siege of Jerusalem, and the exile—Jeremiah "confronts Judah's national catastrophe without flinching."[20] But there are dimensions of hope, including the points that hope is "rooted in suffering," "exists on the margins," and "involves community-building."[21] This honesty plumbs the depths and complexities of Jeremiah without oversimplifying. The interpreter should neither look away from the book's graphic violence and despair nor seek to "solve" the problems of this turbulent text in a superficial or idealistic way. The book of Jeremiah deserves—and demands—that all of its witness be heeded.

Much more could be said about other features of Jeremiah 25–45. Note the powerful theological debate created by the prayer of Jeremiah in 32:16-25, which emerges as a prayer of resistance that boldly calls God to account, with the deity responding with fierce indignation, justifying the terrible catastrophe with which the LORD has purposefully afflicted the people but setting it within a larger picture in which restoration will eventually come. Consider also the commendation of the Ethiopian eunuch, Ebed-melech, in 38:7-13 and 39:15-18, and the similar commendation of Jeremiah's faithful scribe Baruch (45:1-5). These allies may represent daring political support and commitment to the courageous preservation of the Jeremiah traditions, respectively.

Jeremiah 46–52

Ruination of different kinds comes to visceral expression in the final chapters of the book of Jeremiah, which include oracles against enemy nations and a historical appendix detailing the fall of Jerusalem. Oracles against other nations are elegantly structured and beautifully representative of ancient Israelite poetic art. But with their militaristic invective and relishing of images of slaughter, sexual violation, and destruction, these oracles are deeply troubling. They raise a difficult hermeneutical question with which you may have grappled elsewhere in biblical reading, for example with Joshua's narratives of wholesale slaughter of Canaanite indigenes. What do we do with Scripture texts that call gleefully for horrific violence to be enacted upon historical enemies of ancient Israel?

The issue comes up regarding the psalms of imprecation, which call down God's fury on personal enemies of the speaker and on nations that have opposed or harmed Israel. Some interpreters address the ethical problem by suggesting that these psalms reflect all aspects of being human (including our less-appealing characteristics) and thus are descriptive of the range of human affective possibilities rather than prescriptive of direct action. This position cannot easily be maintained in view of the several places in the Psalms where the speaker is none other than the Lord, unabashedly confirming a delight in the slaughter of adversaries. Another proposal is that since the psalms call for God to wreak vengeance, humans are prevented from acting in vengeance themselves, thus this kind of material serves the helpful function of deflecting human aggression. That perspective rests on a misguided notion of how rhetoric of violence works in human communities. Authorizing sacred texts are cited before, during, and after horrific acts of violence by governments, smaller groups, and individuals. It deflects nothing for a biblical text to assign the agency of violence to God; such a move is often interpreted by those bent on violence as signaling that religious fidelity involves participating in divinely sanctioned violence.

Even if you are sympathetic to one or the other of the proposals above for reading psalms of imprecation, they do not work well for prophetic oracles of vengeance. Such oracles clearly delight in the militarized slaughter of enemies throughout villages, capital cities, and even entire regions, this violence to include the violation and killing of noncombatants. So how do we read the oracles against the nations, beyond the basic—and bland—scholarly observation that they are products of an ancient historical context that is not our own? Below are some options chosen by those who have gathered around these texts as sacred Scripture.

(1) Some believers assert that the straightforward meaning of these oracles is indeed God's will, however repugnant their cries for bloodshed and the slaughter of children may be to contemporary sensibilities. We may not domesticate Scripture or "sanitize" it according to modern ethics. These oracles may have served as good news for ancient Israel or Judah and must be respected as such.

(2) Some assert that these oracles are edifying, but not in a simple way. From the earliest days of the Christian church, allegorical or other spiritualizing readings were deployed as powerfully instructive for the believer struggling with malevolent forces on the spiritual plane or "enemies" that do harm from within the psyche. From the perspective of ideology critique, I have argued that Jeremiah 48 uses a sophisticated network of semantic linkages, overt comparisons of Moab and Judah, and tradition-historical freight to create "Moab" as a warning to sinful Judah.[22]

(3) Some bracket the violent rhetoric as appalling but continue to look for interesting themes and images within these oracles, mining the material in ways that are true to the core ethics and theology of a particular faith tradition.

(4) Some reject these oracles completely. These are death-dealing texts that ought not be hallowed in any way. They did not instruct their first audiences well about the loving Creator and that Creator's purposes, and they do not teach us anything valuable today, beyond the obvious fodder they provide for thinking about the intersections of religion and violence.

Whatever your position on rhetorics of punitive shaming and retributive violence in the Bible, I encourage you to take these two steps:

- Acknowledge what these texts express, without rendering the content by means of euphemisms or minimizing the traumatizing horror of these utterances.

- Understand that every hermeneutical framing of the issue is a choice on the part of a reader or reading community. No reading is natural or inevitable. No reading is the only intelligent response or the only faithful way of interpreting these texts.

Jeremiah 46 cries down destruction upon Egypt, whose pride, represented with sarcasm in 46:7-8, will be brought low by the power of the Lord GOD of heavenly forces (46:10). In 46:26, we see one of several unexpected notes of promise in these oracles: after its drastic punishment: "Egypt will dwell like it did a long time ago, declares the LORD." Jeremiah 47, against Philistia, is notable for its direct address of the "sword of the LORD" (47:6), reminiscent of Isaiah's direct address of Assyria as the rod of God's anger (Isa 10:5-11) and a blood-curdling oracle in Ezekiel in which the sword of God virtually takes on a life of its own in a mimetic description of combat (Ezek 21:8-17).

Literary artistry is amply on display in the oracles against Moab collected in Jeremiah 48. We see here bitter sarcasm; dramatic dialogue ("Listen to the cries for help . . . 'Destruction and massive devastation!' Moab is shattered; its young cry for help," 48:3-4); a terrifying proverb that sounds like wisdom literature but is much scarier than what you'd read in Proverbs (48:10); ironic evocations of lament (48:17, 31-32); brutal and repulsive images (48:25-26); woes and images of terror galore. Jeremiah 49 treats Ammon, Edom, Damascus, Kedar, and Elam. Ammon and Elam are given promises of restoration, but the others are not. Perhaps 49:11 may be a bona fide promise to Edom: "Leave me your orphans, and I'll look after them; trust your widows [to] my care," but it is probably better read as a threat veiled in frightening sarcasm.

Jeremiah 50–51 comprises oracles against archenemy Babylon. This poetically artful collection intermingles invective against Babylon with words of hope for Judah. Some of the promise material sounds as if the scribe had studied Second Isaiah. Consider 50:4-5, with its emphasis on return of exiles to Zion and an everlasting covenant; 50:8 ("Now wander far from Babylon. Get out of that country"); and similarly 51:6 (compare Isa 52:11, "Depart, depart! Go out from there!"); 51:15-19, the paean to God the Creator as One who shows up the useless idols of other nations. We have a structurally elegant "sword song" in 50:35-38 and direct address of a weapon of war—the war-club—in 51:20-23. Finally, the dramatic sign-act that Jeremiah commands in 51:59-64 provides a fitting conclusion to these powerful oracles. The coda in 51:64, "Jeremiah's words end here," is a clear indication that the words of the prophet are ended and that Jeremiah 52 is later material of a different kind.

The historical material in Jeremiah 52 is almost identical to material in 2 Kings 24–25. This chapter vividly narrates the trauma of the siege, the resultant famine, and the eventual overpowering of Jerusalem by the Babylonian invaders. The details are horrifying to read. The famine is so severe that there is no food for the people. All the Judean soldiers flee, abandoning their noncombatant friends and family to the predations of the enemy. Zedekiah's officials and sons are executed in front of him; the king's eyes are put out, and he is taken in chains to Babylon, where he will die in prison. The walls of the city are broken down. The temple furnishings and implements are broken and looted, then the temple and other structures are burned. The narrative does not report the screams and sobbing of the inhabitants of Jerusalem, nor are we told of bodies littering streets awash in blood. But it is a scene of horror. The power of the narratology leaves us in the ruins of Jerusalem, pondering the defiling of Judah's sacred heritage and the suffering of the bereaved, maimed, and terrified survivors who have been forced into an arduous journey to Babylon. The implied audiences ancient and contemporary, struggling to process what the Jeremiah traditions make visible, are drawn into the urgent and ongoing work of theology and ethics amid the rubble. The final note about Jehoiachin is read by many scholars as a note of hope, his "elevation" above the status of other captured kings presumably signaling the Babylonian regime's potential favor toward Judah. I believe that is a drastic misreading. Jehoiachin is a prisoner, and the text is careful to say that he dies in prison. No material good comes to Judah from their erstwhile king getting an allowance of daily rations and a place of honor at the table of Evil-merodach. Rather, this text may be a final expression of resistance, an ironic glimpse at what the "submit to Babylon and live" ideology yields: eventually, some nicer garments and daily food as you live out the rest of your life in the fortress of the oppressor. As Stulman and Kim say, "Jeremiah is an artifact of hope. Jeremiah is an artifact of terror."[23] Hope and terror are blended in this remarkable book, even at the last.

For Further Reading

Brueggemann, Walter. *The Theology of the Book of Jeremiah*. Old Testament Theology. New York: Cambridge University Press, 2007.

Diamond, A. R. Pete, Kathleen M. O'Connor, and Louis Stulman, eds. *Troubling Jeremiah*. JSOTS 260. Sheffield: Sheffield Academic Press, 1999.

Kalmanofsky, Amy. *Terror All Around: Horror, Monsters, and Theology in the Book of Jeremiah*. LHBOTS 390. New York: T & T Clark, 2008.

Leuchter, Mark. "Jeremiah: Structures, Themes, and Contested Issues." In *The Oxford Handbook of the Prophets*, 171–89. Edited by Carolyn J. Sharp. Oxford: Oxford University Press, 2016.

Najman, Hindy, and Konrad Schmid, eds. *Jeremiah's Scriptures: Production, Reception, Interaction, and Transformation*. JSJSup 173. Leiden: Brill, 2016.

O'Connor, Kathleen M. *Jeremiah: Pain and Promise*. Minneapolis: Fortress, 2012.

Stulman, Louis. *Jeremiah*. AOTC. Nashville: Abingdon, 2005.

Stulman, Louis, and Hyun Chul Paul Kim. "Jeremiah as a Messenger of Hope in Crisis," "Jeremiah as a Complex Response to Suffering," and "Conflicting Paths to Hope in Jeremiah." In *You Are My People: An Introduction to Prophetic Literature*, 97–141. Nashville: Abingdon, 2010.

Chapter 4

Ezekiel: Prophet of Holiness

What a brilliant and disturbing witness we have in the book of Ezekiel! This fascinating book is, according to ancient rabbinic tradition, the most dangerous book of the Bible, a book that readers shouldn't approach until they are well prepared, wise, and spiritually mature. Ezekiel is represented as a fearless performance artist who experiences spiritual bilocation in his visions; the plot unfolds with boldness. Further, the book of Ezekiel is a work of literary and cultural genius. This ancient priest draws expertly on traditions from his own and other cultures, creating a mysterious and terrifying symbolic universe within which the covenant community's only choice is to yield to a LORD who is wholly Other. Joseph Blenkinsopp characterizes Ezekiel as a "visionary priest who also happened to have an extraordinary breadth of learning seen . . . in his interest in the archaic period of history, his use of mythological themes, and his expertise in the forms and substance of sanctuary law."[1] The book of Ezekiel is different in a number of striking ways from the books of Isaiah and Jeremiah, not least in the dramatic vision of the divine Chariot of YHWH that Ezekiel sees and hears, in the experiences of bilocation that the prophet experiences, in the graphic sexual metaphors it deploys in oracles against Judah, and in the crystalline detail with which the prophet describes the heavenly temple.

As regards the historical provenance of the book of Ezekiel, it seems to present a simpler picture than we see in either Isaiah or Jeremiah.

Both Isaiah and Jeremiah show signs of having had multiple kinds of material worked into their prophetic traditions: many of their poetic oracles likely were delivered orally, then written down by scribes, and then sub-collections and larger versions of each prophet's scroll were further amplified and edited in multiple stages. The composition of Isaiah spanned two and a half centuries, reflecting on history from the time of the Syro-Ephraimite crisis beginning in 735 to the postexilic period, after 515 BCE. In the postexilic period, internecine strife and polemical arguing roiled the community: priests, prophets, and leaders disagreed about the temple, who might serve and worship there, and so on. So the literature of the book of Isaiah reflects diverse political and theological interests related to at least three distinct historical contexts: that of the eighth-century Isaiah of Jerusalem, that of the late exilic or postexilic Second Isaiah, and then a little later on, Third Isaiah in the reconstruction period of the Second Temple. The book of Jeremiah, too, has undergone a complicated process of composition and redaction, including reorganization and significant expansions in the Hebrew text tradition over several generations. A fascinating jumble of discrete poetic oracles, large blocks of prose and smaller prose interpolations, doublets, and possibly independent blocks of material, Jeremiah presents some organization and certainly a coherent trajectory of the plot, but the book reads as polyphony. Volatile differences of politics and theology make different dimensions of the literary heritage of Jeremiah a challenge to read together.

Ezekiel, by contrast, seems considerably simpler in literary and historical terms. The priest and prophet Ezekiel is said to have been deported to Babylon in the first wave of deportations in 597, and he prophesied, according to the dates of his oracles, between 593 and 571 BCE. The explicit dates in Ezekiel run in rough chronological order, the few exceptions perhaps to be taken as evidence of the purposeful way in which the book was crafted. In the date list below, the months are translated into the equivalent modern calendar that contemporary readers will recognize, to give you a transparent sense of the timeline.

July 593	1:1	Ezekiel has a vision of the divine Chariot.
September 592	8:1	Ezekiel has a vision of abominations being committed in the Jerusalem temple.
August 591	20:1	Elders consult Ezekiel and are met with a prophetic diatribe on Israel's history of covenantal faithlessness.
January 588	24:1	The day on which the Babylonian siege of Jerusalem begins.
	24:2	The prophet is commanded by Yhwh to "write down the name of this day, this very day."
587	26:1	On the first day of an unspecified month, Ezekiel delivers oracles against Tyre.
January 587	29:1	Ezekiel delivers oracles against Egypt.
April 571	29:17	Ezekiel delivers an amended oracle against Tyre.
April 587	30:20	Ezekiel prophesies that the military strength of Egypt has been broken.
June 587	31:1	Ezekiel delivers an oracle against Egypt.
March 585	32:1	Ezekiel offers another oracle against Egypt.
April 586 (the month supplied by the LXX)	32:17	Ezekiel offers an extended oracle against Egypt, complete with depiction of the underworld.
January 585	33:21	A fugitive tells Ezekiel that Jerusalem has fallen.
April 571	40:1	Ezekiel sees a vision of the new temple, land boundaries, and gates of the new Jerusalem.

The literary setting within an artistic work ought never be assumed to be the same as the actual time in which the work was written. As a literary production, Ezekiel pays close attention to events in the exilic period. There are not as many anachronisms, literary disruptions, and other clues in Ezekiel as there are in Isaiah and Jeremiah to indicate substantial revisions from a later historical context. Nevertheless, scholarly debates continue about whether Ezekiel is to be dated early or instead expresses theological and political concerns more relevant to a later time. Some doublets do suggest redeployment of received material. There is undated material in Ezekiel; some blocks of material seem to stand independently and could well have been generated long after the exile. This may be the case with the proto-apocalyptic material in Ezekiel 38–39 and the temple material in chapters 40–48. But overall, while the book of Ezekiel is literarily diverse, it is not as complex as Isaiah is in its way and Jeremiah is in a different way. There is a guiding and well-structured sensibility underlying this material, even in lengthy poetic oracles. The carefully crafted coherence of the book suggests that Ezekiel was known as written prophecy from its inception, whether produced mainly in the exilic period or later. A small number of relatively short and confusing oracles may suggest an originally oral performance (see, for example, Ezek 7 and some passages in Ezek 21). But the book is notable for its striking quality of writtenness. Some interpreters have argued that Ezekiel was produced at a liminal moment in the development of Israelite prophecy from oral performance to written representations of prophecy.

The substance of Ezekiel's prophecies is strange indeed. His oracles are mystical and allegorical, and the referents are by no means always clear. In places, Ezekiel's oracles are bizarre, and some clearly were designed to be offensive to the implied audience. What Ezekiel sees in his visions involves supernatural creatures and events that are far from the realm of ordinary experience. Every prophetic book offers memorably dramatic imagery, but Ezekiel's style is more hyperbolic and florid than the styles of other prophetic books, with the exception of Hosea. All of these literary features, taken together, mean that while the book is unified and intelligible on one level, it is nevertheless difficult to read and understand. The witness of the prophet Ezekiel is dazzling but also startling; disturbing theological themes abound.

The book presents a unified literary structure that moves from judgment on Judah (chaps. 1–24), to judgment on enemy nations (chaps. 25–32), to mixed oracles of judgment and promise (chaps. 33–34), then to good news for Judah, albeit articulated in the shaming diction characteristic of Ezekiel, and judgment against mythic enemies (chaps. 35–39), and finally to a vision of the glorious heavenly temple (chaps. 40–48). In the words of Joseph Blenkinsopp, Ezekiel exhibits a "striking architectonic unity" in its literary structure that drives from judgment of Judah to judgment of the nations to hope for Judah.[2] Ezekiel's theology shows strong affinities with priestly tradition. There is much interest in Ezekiel in the presence, movement, and power of the *kāvôd* of the LORD, the "glory," a technical term in ancient Israelite priestly parlance that signifies the mysterious presence of YHWH. Much language and imagery in Ezekiel has to do with cultic practices or their flouting, and with the defilement of the land and the temple because of Judah's sinful idolatrous practices. Moral and cultic sins are often called *tô'ēvôt*, "abominations," in Ezekiel (see e.g., 6:11; 8:6, 9, 13, 15, 17; 9:4; 16:2; 18:13, 24)—a powerfully pejorative term drawn from priestly diction. Also indicative of a priestly sensibility is Ezekiel's interest in the dimensions of a new temple and the functions of its cultic personnel (chaps. 40–48).

Theological Themes

Two general points may help orient you to Ezekiel's prophesying before we turn to specific themes.

First: Ezekiel's mortality is stressed over against the insuperable power and awe-inspiring transcendence of the LORD. Ezekiel is addressed throughout the book as "human one" (CEB) or "O mortal" (NRSV). The phrase used to be translated in androcentric language as "son of man" (KJV), which is not a more literal translation but instead is based on an overemphasis on the "son" relationship in the Hebrew syntax, where the relevant Hebrew term in a construct chain simply designates a member of a group. (Compare *bene' yisrael*, which means "Israelites.") In this case, the group of which Ezekiel is a member is the group of human beings. The NRSV interpretation "mortal" is a better translation for several reasons. The precise nuance may involve a projection of the finite capacities, humility, or mortality of Ezekiel's humanness over against the power and transcendence of God. Per the priestly theological understanding of the book of Ezekiel, there is a vast chasm between the holiness of God and the sinfulness and humility of the human being before God, something that is articulated in various ways throughout the book.

Second: Ezekiel is to act as a sentinel to the "house of Israel" (3:17), the identity of Judah poetically expressed here in a way that anticipates the prophet's hopes for eventual restoration of the northern kingdom to unity with Judah (see 37:15-28). This role is emphasized in the commissioning of the prophet in Ezekiel 2 and 3. Ezekiel is to speak the LORD's words to the people "whether they listen or whether they refuse, since they are a household of rebels, they will know that a prophet has been among them" (Ezek 2:5). His vocation is to warn them of the wrath to come. This is significant, not only for understanding the role of the prophet, but also for thinking theologically about the larger rhetorical purposes of the book of Ezekiel. All of the rhetoric of Ezekiel, including the florid invective and blaming of his people for the trauma that they have suffered, is meant to warn. Sentinels warn in order that those who hear will take action to protect their community. Ezekiel's warnings, harsh and even cruel, are meant to catalyze repentance in the hearts and minds of his audience. His role as sentinel is to reform the distorted and sinful practices of the covenant community, so that they might live.

We will explore three themes that are central to the diction and theology of Ezekiel. The first theme is expressed through a repeated refrain in Ezekiel that underlines the sovereignty of YHWH throughout history and in all circumstances. The second theme has to do with the significance of the divine Chariot moving from the Jerusalem temple eastward in several carefully delineated stages. The third theme involves the power dynamics enacted through the graphically sexualized imagery Ezekiel uses for Samaria and Judah.

"Then They Shall Know That I Am the LORD"

A refrain we encounter over sixty times in the book of Ezekiel is that when X or Y happens for good or ill, then Israel or other nations shall know—God says—"that I am the LORD." You will notice this theological claim after gruesome oracles of judgment:

Say:

Hear the Lord GOD's word, mountains of Israel!
The Lord GOD proclaims to the mountains and hills,
to the valleys and their deepest ravines:

I'm about to bring a sword against you and destroy your shrines.

Your altars will be destroyed,

> your incense altars broken.

> And I'll make your slain fall in front of your idols.

I'll throw the Israelites' corpses in front of their idols,

> and I'll scatter your bones all around your altars.

Wherever you live, cities will be in ruins, shrines made desolate,

> turned into utter ruin.

Your altars will be punished and then broken down.

Your idols will be demolished,

> your incense altars shattered,

> and all your works wiped out.

The slain will fall among you,

> and you will know that I am the LORD. (6:3-7)

When I turn the land of Egypt into a wasteland and the land is deprived of all that fills it, and when I strike down those who live there, then they will know that I am the LORD. (32:15)

You'll see that the refrain also comes up in oracles of salvation.

The Lord GOD proclaims: When I gather the house of Israel from the peoples among whom they've scattered, and I demonstrate my holiness through them in the sight of the nations, they will live on their fertile land, which I gave to my servant Jacob. They will live on it in safety. They will build houses, plant vineyards, and live in safety. When I execute judgments against all who hold them in contempt on every side, they will know that I, the LORD, am their God. (28:25-26)

I will make my great name holy, which was degraded among the nations when you dishonored it among them. Then the nations will know that I am the LORD. This is what the Lord GOD says. When I make myself holy among you in their sight, I will take you from the nations, I will gather you from all the countries, and I will bring you to your own fertile land. (36:23-24)

There are several ways we might read the underlying theological freight of the refrain. All of the below are possible, and you may think of other nuances as well. The unspoken significance may differ from passage to passage in Ezekiel; each occurrence should be considered with exegetical care.

- God may be saying, I am the one who is your LORD. *Unspoken:* Your god is not Marduk of Babylon, who may seem to have been victorious over me, nor some other false god nor one of your idols. I am the one with power. I am the one whom you are called to obey.

- The refrain may be underlining that Israel's LORD has power to destroy and power to restore. *Unspoken:* These events that Judah has undergone are examples of divine performative power. They may look like human decisions within political history; it may seem that they should be understood in human terms, rather than theologically; but that would be a mistake.

- Over against a posture of theological indifference on the part of the sinful people, the refrain may be contesting their lack of interest in the LORD. In 9:9 we see an explanation why the LORD will be shortly pouring out wrath against Jerusalem so that the streets and courtyards will be filled with the bodies of the slain. God says, "The land is full of bloodshed and the city full of perversity; for they say, 'The LORD has forsaken the land, and the LORD does not see'" (NRSV). The people have taken God to be irrelevant to their current circumstances. The refrain, "Then they shall know that I am the LORD," would be staking a powerful counterclaim. *Unspoken:* The LORD is indeed omniscient, engaged, and deeply relevant to what the people are experiencing.

Ezekiel teaches his audience that the LORD does everything to safeguard the LORD's holy name and to display the LORD's holiness to Judah and the surrounding nations. This note is struck again and again throughout the book. From the opening vision of the thunderous divine Chariot to the stunning vision of the new temple, it is clear that the holiness of God is of paramount importance to the priest Ezekiel. It is in the LORD's holiness and unsurpassed might that the hope and resilience of God's people are rooted—there and nowhere else.

The Moveable Presence of God

A second major theme is that the holy presence or glory of the LORD, expressed by the Zion theology as eternally enthroned in Jerusalem (see Isa 6), is in fact moveable and is abandoning Jerusalem because of the loathsome sins of the people. The glory of the LORD is shown to the prophet in "visions of God" (Ezek 1:1); for more on the Chariot, see below the discussion of Ezekiel 1. The Chariot arrives at the river Chebar in Babylon, and Ezekiel receives his commissioning as a prophet to his people. Then the LORD directs Ezekiel to go out into a nearby valley; when he arrives, the Chariot is there, as it had been at the river Chebar (3:22-23), and the LORD gives him detailed instructions.

The next time we hear about the divine Chariot is in Ezekiel 8. Ezekiel has been lifted up by the hair of his head and transported "in visions of God to Jerusalem" (8:3 NRSV). He sees that the "glory of Israel's God" is already there (8:4). He is shown the sinful idolatry of elders in an inner room of the temple. After this, twice it is said that the glory of the LORD rises "from above the winged creatures" to the threshold of the temple (9:3 and 10:4). This suggests that the presence of the LORD is preparing to depart from the temple. The text brilliantly calls attention to this movement with compelling signals of auditory and visual dimensions of the vision, as the reader ponders the new positioning of the Chariot:

> Then the LORD's glory rose from above the winged creatures and moved toward the temple's threshold. The temple was filled with the cloud, and the courtyard was filled with the brightness of the LORD's glory. The sound of the winged creatures' wings could be heard as far as the outer courtyard. It was like the sound of God Almighty when he speaks. (10:4-5)

In a second artful way of drawing the reader's attention to the Chariot, the text recapitulates in 9:9-17 some of the description of the Chariot and the living creatures from Ezekiel 1. At this point, the reader is transfixed by the image, and here another move of the Chariot, detailed in slow motion for enhanced drama, makes the route of divine travel clear:

> Then the LORD's glory went out from above the temple's threshold and it stood over the winged creatures. While I watched, the winged creatures raised their wings and rose from the ground to leave, with their wheels beside them. They stopped at the entrance to the East Gate of the temple, and the glory of Israel's God was up above them. (10:18-19)

Eastward: the Chariot seems to be moving in the direction of Babylon. The decisive trajectory is traced beyond any shadow of a doubt in 11:23, where it is said that the Chariot moves farther in an eastward direction, out of the temple complex entirely, the LORD's glory ascending from Jerusalem and stopping "at the mountain east of the city." Immediately after that, the spirit of God lifts Ezekiel up and brings him in a vision back to Chaldea, "to the exiles" (11:24). With this vision, the Presence of God has implicitly made the journey all the way eastward, to Babylon.

The challenge here to the Zion theology espoused by Isaiah is forceful indeed. Ezekiel insists that Jerusalem has been abandoned to destruction because of its abominations. The Presence of God, preserving the LORD's own power and holiness in this time of crisis, has relocated to Babylon with the first diaspora group, those deported in 597. A strong acknowledgment of this is articulated in a fascinating phrase in 11:16: "Though I removed them far away among the nations . . . yet I have been a sanctuary to them for a little while in the countries where they have gone" (NRSV). The crucial phrase, "sanctuary for a little while," could be translated as "some sanctuary" (CEB) or as "a miniature sanctuary" or, by implication, a "portable shrine," which might subtly echo Israel's time in the wilderness after the escape from Egypt under Moses's leadership. The NJPS translation, "a diminished sanctity," is interesting, but in view of Ezekiel's emphasis on the incomparable power of the LORD, I myself would not choose that translation. Whatever the precise nuance of the phrase, Jerusalem is no longer the enduring and always-protected residence of God's glory.

Upon reflection, you may decide to interpret the mobility of the divine Chariot as signaling power or vulnerability. For the first possibility—mobility as an expression of power—the reader might well focus on the ways in which Ezekiel's theology teaches his audience about the might of the LORD. In this prophetic book, God's purposes and sovereignty are on display for Judah and its enemies, which is to say, for all the world: "then they will know that I am the LORD" in catastrophes and acts of redemption alike. This omnipotent deity will not stand for the insult of despicably sinful worship practices in Jerusalem, need not endure the spectacle of the covenant people filling "the land with violence" (8:17), and certainly cannot be constrained by mere humans regarding where the divine Presence chooses to go. On the second possibility—mobility as an expression of vulnerability—one could focus on the rage and loss experienced by a God who has to vacate the once-magnificent and holy Jerusalem: "Human one, do you see what they are doing, the terribly detestable practices that the house of Israel is doing here that drive me far from my sanctuary?" (8:6). Stulman and Kim suggest that the movement of the divine Chariot is a sign that the LORD is willing to be vulnerable with the covenant people:

> YHWH eventually becomes fully immersed in Israel's pain and alienation. This metamorphosis is most clearly evident in the three vision reports that organize the book of Ezekiel. There we discover that the sovereign God is susceptible to the anguish of war and displacement. . . . YHWH is drawn into Israel's fractured world as a wounded participant. In solidarity with traumatized Israel, YHWH astonishingly becomes a displaced God, and in so doing identifies with the endangered refugee community, even to the point of humiliation.[3]

Ezekiel's God rages at the covenant people, shaming Judeans and their leaders in oracle after oracle that underlines their loathsomeness and the persistence of their sin since the time of Moses. So it may be counterintuitive to read the LORD as purposefully choosing a position of suffering solidarity with traumatized Judah. Yet it cannot be denied that for Ezekiel, the glorious residence of the LORD in Jerusalem has been defiled and the LORD cannot viably be worshipped there any longer. As regards the mobility of the LORD's Chariot, then, it may be productive for the reader of Ezekiel to reflect on three possibilities playing through this exquisite ancient literature. First, we may consider the book's robust claims for the matchless power of the LORD, this including the capacity to move easily, unimpeded, across the ancient Near East. Second, we may consider the clear implication in Ezekiel 8 and 11 that the gravity of Judah's sin effectively has expelled the LORD from the Jerusalem temple. Third, we may consider that even though the LORD rages at the people, nevertheless (with Stulman and Kim) the LORD's presence with the diaspora community in Babylon may be read as divine solidarity with a wounded people.

Sexualized Shaming of Israel

A third major theme in Ezekiel has to do with how power is understood in the book. Pervasive are hyperbolically graphic metaphors of sin as women's promiscuous sexuality, construed as a source of shame to Judean males, to the whole community, and to God, and further construed as worthy of extremely violent punishment that includes public torture and summary execution by a mob. Interpreters across the hermeneutical spectrum have balked at this language, worried about its reception in faith communities, and generally struggled with it. Those who insist that these are "merely metaphors" possess a superficial understanding of how metaphors work. It has been shown over and over again that metaphors have extraordinary power to structure perceptions in keeping with contextualized cultural norms and practices. Among those who engage in a sustained way with the aggression of Ezekiel's rhetoric, feminist interpreters have been particularly bold, calling the language not just violent but pornographic or fetishistic because of the way in which the narratological gaze lingers on details of objectified female bodies imagined as alluring, wanton, and vulnerable, and the way in which it seems to relish males' economic power and their unbridled capacity to strip, torture, and violate the female. The two chapters notorious in this regard are Ezekiel 16 and 23.

In Ezekiel 16, the prophet describes a story in which the Lord GOD sees newborn Jerusalem, already suspect in the cultural codes of the time because of Canaanite parentage ("Your father was an Amorite, your mother a Hittite," v. 3), flailing about on the brink of death as an exposed and unwanted female child. God speaks a word—it's fascinating that the LORD gives a performative command, "Live!" instead of actually caring for the child—and the child grows up, still exposed ("completely naked," 16:7). She is betrothed to the LORD and is decked in splendid clothing ("fit for royalty," v. 13). But she trusts in her own beauty—an odd expression that makes visible the analogy with Judah trusting in its own military strength—and publicly proclaims her sexual availability in a brazen way, an analogy to political alliance-making and the threat of worship of other gods that was perceived as accompanying ties with other groups. Ezekiel continues the story, ranting in extremely graphic language about her sexual promiscuity and describing a detailed fantasy of her brutal punishment at the hands of the very lovers she had enjoyed (16:5-43). According to any humane understanding, the punishment is stunningly disproportionate in nature, but Ezekiel construes it as justice given her sexual immorality and ingratitude: "I have returned your deeds upon your head, says the Lord GOD" (NRSV; CEB: "I will hold you accountable for what you've done"; v. 43). This would have been entirely intelligible in a society based on patriarchal notions of honor and shame and constructed around regulation of kinship ties as a way of guarding the integrity of the community.

Phallocentric constructions of women's sexuality served as markers of those boundaries, which were to be zealously guarded by the males of the group—guarded not only from external threat but also from internal rebellion against those norms. The laws in the Hebrew Bible that prescribed stoning for various sexual infractions were quite in earnest, as is the ongoing criminal tragedy of the stoning of women for perceived sexual immorality, with judicial and extrajudicial executions taking place in the Middle East and in some African and South Asian countries to this day. Ezekiel is not the first prophet to use female-gendered images of shame to represent the spiritual sins of an entire people, but his oracles are unquestionably the most graphic. Ezekiel's florid and offensive sexualized language would certainly have shocked his audience and may have been perceived as imputing gendered shame to the male hearers. There is no prophet in the Bible so skilled at shaming his listeners than Ezekiel, nor another so dedicated to that task. Ezekiel 23 reenacts many of the same verbal assaults of shaming and indictments for hypersexualized behavior that we see in Ezekiel 16. The northern kingdom, Samaria, is described in detailed sexual language as engaging in unconstrained sexual activity with "her lovers the Assyrians" (23:5), then Jerusalem is indicted for even more flagrantly immoral behavior. In this elaborate metaphor, the two characters are "executed" in vivid and gruesome ways, this, again, being portrayed as an understandable and proportionate "repayment" for their sins (v. 49 NRSV).

On the "Rebellious Sister" Motif

Like Victorian literature, the Hebrew Bible concentrates and represents patriarchal anxieties in the figure of the sister. In the Bible, as in Victorian literature, the interpersonal relationship among sisters creates a sister-bond that threatens the authority of the patriarch. . . . The prophetic texts intentionally evoke and develop dangerous sisters as an effective part of [a] rhetoric of horror. By bonding together and pursuing their lovers, these sisters help convey Israel's vulnerability and depravity. Sisters Israel and Judah welcome their violent lovers into God's metaphorical family. The prophets use these sisters as warnings to their audience how not to behave.

—Amy Kalmanofsky[4]

At the end of the blistering polemic in Ezekiel 16 come surprising words of promise:

The Lord GOD proclaims: I will do to you just as you have done, despising solemn pledges and breaking covenants. Nevertheless, I will remember my covenant with you when you were young, and I will establish an everlasting covenant with you. I myself will establish my covenant with you, and you will know that I am the LORD. Then you will remember and be ashamed, and you won't even open your mouth because of your shame, after I've forgiven you for all that you've done. (16:59-60, 62-63)

Alarming? To be sure. Feminist interpreters have heard strong echoes in Ezekiel and Hosea of the cycle of battering and wooing that is prevalent in relationships between batterers and those who endure domestic violence. Nevertheless, this is the kind of oracle of "promise" of which the book of Ezekiel seems capable. It is likely that reform of the covenantal people is one chief goal: Judeans need to understand how deeply they have insulted their God, so that they will turn to the LORD and live.

One dimension of the problem with Ezekiel's venomous and violent rhetoric may have to do with the prophet's own mental state. Ezekiel has been imagined by a number of interpreters as having suffered from post-traumatic stress disorder. We will never know the extent to which emotional or mental illness might have played a role in the case of Ezekiel or, indeed, any other prophet. The book describes a time of numbness that seems to approximate catatonia (3:15b), and the prophet's description of visionary bilocation has points of contact with dissociative episodes. Pretending clinical analysis of the prophet would be irresponsible, but no less irresponsible is the reactionary dismissal of these embodied and perceptual challenges in Ezekiel as if they were not significant. Ezekiel's dramatic visions, his experiences of sitting without communicating and of being mute and bound with cords, and his perceptions of being separated from his body are integral to his prophetic witness and need to be taken seriously in the interpretive endeavor. For believers who read Ezekiel as sacred scripture, emotional woundedness and even pathology need not be seen as compromising the integrity of Ezekiel's prophecies. If your theology allows for God to speak through humans at all, well, there is no one who has not endured some sort of emotional injury in life; there is no one who has not struggled in communication; there is no one who sees everything with clear and undistorted perception. The harm done to Jeremiah and Ezekiel may simply be more visible, because it is narrated as part of the literary plot in each of those books, than trauma or other challenges that may have been experienced by other biblical prophets.

Trauma and the Witness of Ezekiel

More recent interpretive perspectives tend to view Ezekiel's behavior—or rather the literary portrayal of the "disordered" personality—as more indicative of trauma and posttraumatic stress than psychosis or paranoid schizophrenia. First, like those who suffer unmanageable violence, Ezekiel appears detached and disconnected, often vacillating between worlds. Although Ezekiel resides in Babylon, he takes imaginative journeys to Jerusalem; these alterations in consciousness blur his cultural and symbolic boundaries and leave his loyalties, vested interests, and constructed audience conflicted. Second, Ezekiel manifests a certain fixation with violence and death, even when imagining future hope. . . . In response to . . . dire conditions, Ezekiel seeks to establish well-defined lines between purity and pollution. . . . Ezekiel is hypervigilant about such matters. . . . In addition, it is not difficult to discern in the persona of Ezekiel dissociative episodes, constriction, paralysis, hyperarousal, helplessness, and the loss of control (as perhaps indicated by the phrase "the hand of the LORD").

—Louis Stulman and Hyun Chul Paul Kim[5]

A second way we might engage the violently misogynistic rhetoric of Ezekiel is to consider implications of the fact that the implied audience for the book was male. The scribal elites, political leaders, and religious officials who would have had any idea about what Ezekiel was doing would all have been men. Some interpreters have wondered whether addressing Ezekiel 16 and 23 to a male audience was less about actual women than about cultural emasculation of male hearers, the shameful kind of disempowerment that results when a male is compared to an impure or sexually uncontrollable female. In the ancient Near East, male honor and the honor of males' entire kinship groups is predicated on strict male control of access to female bodies. So-called honor killings are metaphorized in Ezekiel, and some have suggested that the rhetorical violence is being done to the implied male hearers. The point is cogent. Nevertheless, the social values on which misogynistic violence is predicated still fatally disadvantage and harm girls, women, and others who are not normative male subjects.

Anomalous Note: Ezekiel 34:1-16

For each major prophet in the Latter Prophets, we are considering an anomalous note: a passage that gestures toward the irreducible complexity of these texts and can serve as a resource for the reader who wishes to interrogate a narrow or difficult perspective in that book. In Ezekiel, our anomalous note is one of radiant hope and tender care. In Ezekiel 34 is a passage so unlike the rest of Ezekiel for its diction of compassion, one wonders whether it might have come from Second Isaiah or might even be ironic rather than earnest. The chapter opens with an extended indictment of "Israel's shepherds"—that is, the rulers of Judah—for brutally exploiting their flock and callously ignoring their people's needs. The LORD's anguish for the people is heartwarming:

> The Lord GOD proclaims to the shepherds: Doom to Israel's shepherds who tended themselves! Shouldn't shepherds tend the flock? You drink the milk, you wear the wool, and you slaughter the fat animals, but you don't tend the flock. You don't strengthen the weak, heal the sick, bind up the injured, bring back the strays, or seek out the lost; but instead you use force to rule them with injustice. Without a shepherd, my flock was scattered; and when it was scattered, it became food for all the wild animals. My flock strayed on all the mountains and on every high hill throughout all the earth. My flock was scattered, and there was no one to look for them or find them. So now shepherds, hear the LORD's word! (34:2-7)

In an astonishing move, Ezekiel waxes lyrical about pastoral gentleness. The LORD will step in and serve as a compassionate tender of the sheep: "I myself will feed my flock and make them lie down. This is what the Lord GOD says. I will seek out the lost, bring back the strays, bind up the wounded, and strengthen the weak. But the fat and the strong I will destroy, because I will tend my sheep with justice" (34:15-16).

Nowhere else in Ezekiel do we see a compassionate God healing the injured. Ezekiel's rhetoric otherwise seems to relish the prospect of the LORD's maiming and destruction of that same flock. Nowhere else in Ezekiel do we see a loving God searching for the lost. Ezekiel's rhetoric otherwise has fugitives from diaspora staggering home unaided, grim in the knowledge of just how loathsome they are (see, for example, 20:42-43 and 36:28-31). Return to these and other images of mercy in Ezekiel 34 when you are worn down from engaging the vituperative shaming rhetoric that is more characteristic of the book. You may wish to remember 34:31 and read it against the backdrop of Psalm 23: "You are my sheep, the sheep of my pasture and I am your God, says the Lord GOD" (NRSV).

Ezekiel 1–24

Ezekiel presents us with stirring oracles and dramatic visions unlike anything else in the Hebrew Scriptures, with the possible exception of visions related in Daniel 7–12 and Zechariah 1–6. Ezekiel is a major source for the dramatic imagery offered in the New Testament book of Revelation. The book opens with a beautifully detailed description of the prophet's vision of the Presence of the LORD in a heavenly Chariot that descends, in storm, flashing fire, and thunder, to the prophet at the river Chebar. This is something impossible to describe, but perhaps best imagined as a moveable throne of the Most High God. It is powered by four living creatures, each with four faces (human, lion, ox, eagle) and four wings. Hybrid creatures are featured in the iconography of a number of ancient cultures across the world; these impossible beings may connote unusual capacities, deep wisdom, and the dangerous "otherness" of the Holy. Beside each of the creatures is a wheel in which resides the spirit of the living creature and by means of which they can move in any direction without turning or veering. Details about the wheels, and especially the note that each rim is "full of eyes all around" (1:18 NRSV), have fascinated artists and preachers for millennia. Through the first millennium of the Common Era, Jewish sages developed an elaborate series of esoteric teachings, "Merkabah mysticism," centered on the divine Chariot of Ezekiel and the rich possibilities offered by this text for spiritualizing interpretations of lightning details, such as "a great cloud flashing fire, with brightness all around" (1:4) and the appearance of "gleaming amber" in the figure on the throne (1:27 NRSV).

"Ezekiel Saw the Wheel," refrain

Ezekiel saw the wheel,
way up in the middle of the air,
Ezekiel saw the wheel,
way in the middle of the air.
The big wheel run by faith,
the little wheel run by the grace of God.
A wheel in a wheel,
way in the middle of the air.

Words: traditional African American spiritual

In Ezekiel 2–3, the role of sentinel is given to the prophet: his job will be to warn the people, whether they heed or not. This stands in some tension with a sign-act in which the prophet is isolated and rendered mute by the LORD (see 3:24-26). Nevertheless, Ezekiel 3 goes on to say that in particular moments, the LORD will make speech possible for the prophet in order that he may fulfill his sentinel role:

> I'll make your tongue stick to the roof of your mouth and take away your ability to speak. You won't be able to correct them, because they are a household of rebels. But whenever I speak to you, I'll open your mouth, and you will say to them: The Lord GOD proclaims. Those who hear will understand, but those who refuse will not. They are just a household of rebels. (3:26-27)

This prophet's sign-acts are similar to those of Jeremiah, except that those Ezekiel is commanded to perform seem more strenuous and odd. Rhiannon Graybill links the silencing of Ezekiel's speech from chapter 1 onward to the duress affecting his body:

> From the beginning, the text suggests the futility, even the impossibility, of prophecy. This disaster is at once political and cosmological. To live in the exile is unthinkable, to worship properly in the exile impossible. Ezekiel's dumbness . . . is a bodily manifestation of the impossibility of prophecy. This impossibility of prophecy is bound up in a crisis of

language. . . . It is not only language that suffers from the positioning of prophecy in disaster—the body of the prophet also suffers, and horribly.[6]

Sign-Acts in Ezekiel

Ezekiel is bound with cords inside his house and rendered mute, so he cannot go out among the people and "reprove them."	3:24-26
Ezekiel is to make a model of Jerusalem under siege, using a brick with siegeworks, battering rams, a ramp, and camps all around, plus an iron plate as a "wall" between his face and the city.	4:1-3
Bound with cords, Ezekiel is to lie on his left side for 390 days and on his right side for 40 days, each day representing a year of the divine punishment of Israel and Judah respectively.	4:4-8
Ezekiel is to make mixed-grain bread baked on dung and ration his food and water, symbolizing the impurity and deprivation that Judeans will experience in diaspora.	4:9-15
Ezekiel is to cut off the hair of his head and his beard, divide the hair into thirds, and destroy the thirds in three different ways to represent the impending punishment of Israel: one third is to be burned, one third is to be struck with the sword, and one third is to be scattered to the wind.	5:1-4
Ezekiel prepares "an exile's baggage" (NRSV) and enacts going into exile. He brings the baggage out in the daytime, then in the evening he digs through the wall with his hands, lifts his baggage onto his shoulder, and carries it away with his face covered.	12:1-16
Ezekiel is to eat bread and drink water with a perceptible affect of fearfulness, a sign to his compatriots that they will soon be doing the same, for the "land will be stripped of all it contains" (NRSV).	12:17-20
Ezekiel is to refrain from public mourning at the sudden death of his cherished wife. His perplexing stoicism is to be a sign of the impending destruction of the Jerusalem temple, the deaths of many in the city, and the exile of survivors.	24:15-27

The oracles in Ezekiel 4–7 give full voice to divine indictments against the people for persistent sin, which involves orienting their religious and social practices according to the influence of other cultures rather than observing the Torah. The LORD describes the problem: "Therefore, the Lord GOD proclaims: You have become more turbulent than these nations around you because you haven't obeyed my regulations or followed my case laws. You haven't even followed the case laws of the nations around you!" (5:7). There is also brief mention of violence ("The earth is full of perverted justice, the city full of violence," 7:23), but Ezekiel is most focused on idolatry and political failures. Divine punishment will be effected through the gruesome realities of siege, famine, disease, diaspora, and the attacks of wild animals, that last threat obliquely alluding to the breaking down of city walls and other structures of protection. Ezekiel gives us a LORD raging uncontrollably, in a fit of fury mustering every kind of horror that could be named:

> Because of you, I will do what I've never done before and will never do again—all because of your detestable practices. Therefore, parents among you will eat their children, and children will eat their parents. . . . I myself will shave you. I will not shed a tear. You will have no compassion, even from me. One-third of you will die of plague and waste away by famine among you. One-third will fall by the sword all around you. And one-third I will scatter to all the winds, letting loose a sword to pursue them. You will become an object of ridicule, a mockery, and a horrifying lesson to the nations all around you, when I impose penalties from case laws against you in anger, wrath, and overflowing fury. I, the LORD, have spoken. When I launch my deadly arrows of famine against you, I have released them for your destruction! I will add to your famine and completely cut off your food supply. I will send famine and wild animals against you, and they will leave you childless. Plague and bloodshed will come to you, and I will bring the sword against you. I, the LORD, have spoken. (5:9-12, 15-17)

The theology of an enraged God seeks to torment, wound, and destroy the covenant people with every terrifying weapon conceivable. If the book of Ezekiel is a text forged in trauma, we must also acknowledge that it is a text that performs trauma, repeatedly and with intense aggression, on its implied audience.

Ezekiel 8–11 shows the Chariot of the LORD's Presence moving out of the sinful city of Jerusalem eastward (toward Babylon). The leadership of Judah is brazenly and irredeemably corrupt, something signaled by the dramatic scene in Ezekiel 8 that has seventy elders offering illicit incense in a temple chamber, where "every form of loathsome beasts and creeping things and all the idols of the house of Israel [are] engraved on the walls all around (8:10). Ezekiel 12–15 contains diverse materials: sign-acts (packing an exile's backpack, eating fearfully); a prophecy that an unnamed "prince" of Judah—Zedekiah—will be forcibly taken to Babylon, where he will die (12:10-13); oracles against false prophets; a call to Judean elders to repent of their idolatry (14:1-8); and prophecies of Jerusalem's impending doom. Noteworthy are the prophet's fulminations against false prophecy in Ezekiel 13, including this representative indictment:

> The LORD's word came to me: Human one, prophesy to Israel's prophets who prophesy from their own imaginations. Say, Hear the LORD's word! The Lord GOD proclaims: Doom to the foolish prophets who follow their own whims but see nothing. Israel, your prophets have been like jackals among ruins. You haven't gone up into the breach or reinforced the wall of the house of Israel, so that it might withstand the battle on the day of the LORD. They saw worthless visions and performed deceptive divinations. Even though the LORD didn't send them, they said, "This is what the LORD says" and expected their word to stand. (13:1-6)

In Jeremiah, we saw the motif that prophetic intercession would not avail: the punishment of Judah is approaching inexorably, and Jeremiah is repeatedly forbidden to intercede. So too Ezekiel cannot intercede effectively. As the LORD makes clear, the sin of Judah is so egregious that even an exceptionally righteous person would save only their own life. Take a look at this excerpt from a longer passage that makes the point relentlessly, over and over:

> Human one, suppose a land sins against me by acting faithlessly, so that I use my power against it, break off its food supply, let famine run rampant, and eliminate both humans and animals. If these three men, Noah, Daniel, and Job, lived there, their lives alone would be saved because they were righteous. This is what the Lord GOD says. Or suppose I allow wild animals to roam through the land, and it becomes so wild that no one can live there or even travel through it on account of the wild animals. If these three men lived there, as surely as I live,

proclaims the Lord GOD, they wouldn't be able to rescue even their sons or daughters. They alone would be rescued, but the land would become a ruin. (14:13-16)

This is reminiscent of the LORD's statement in Jeremiah 15:1 that even Moses and Samuel would not be able to intercede successfully on behalf of doomed Judah. Here in his artful and disturbing rhetoric, Ezekiel is cutting off all avenues of escape, showing his implied audience that the only possible way to survive is to repent.

Ezekiel 17 and 19 present symbolic interpretations of events in the Judean monarchy during the time of Babylon's ascendancy; scholars continue to argue about some of the referents of these artfully elusive texts. Ezekiel 18 stresses the prophet's interest in personal responsibility for sin. Of central importance for the larger purposes of the book is 18:32: "I most certainly don't want anyone to die! This is what the Lord GOD says. Change your ways, and live!" The sentinel function of the prophet is directed toward the goal of inviting, haranguing, and shaming Ezekiel's audience into "turning" so that they—and subsequent audiences—may live. The book has the LORD flagging a stance in the metanarrative, as it were, in this crucial verse: God neither delights in nor commands the actual maiming, sexual assault, or slaughter of anyone, whether adversaries within one's community or other groups that are to be considered political or religious enemies. Here we see, stated robustly by the Lord GOD, that the purpose of Ezekiel is to reform the hearts and minds of the audience so that they will repent and live in congruence with God's purposes for *shalom.*

Ezekiel 20 presents a pejorative rereading of the Exodus tradition. Note well the differences between Ezekiel's fascinating negative appropriation of Exodus themes and Second Isaiah's lyrical deployment of Exodus imagery. According to Ezekiel 20, a harsh revisionist narrative of Israel's early history, Israel had been devoted to the worship of "disgusting things" (20:7) even when Israel was still enslaved in Egypt. Far from rejoicing to serve YHWH, the Israelites rebelled from the first moment of their emancipation:

> On that day I swore that I would lead them out of the land of Egypt to a land that I would show them, a land full of milk and honey, the most splendid of all lands. And I said to them, Every one of you must cast

149

away your disgusting things. Don't let yourselves be defiled by Egypt's idols. I am the LORD your God. But they rebelled against me and refused to listen to me. No one cast off their disgusting things or abandoned their Egyptian idols. So I declared that I would pour out my wrath on them and satisfy my anger against them in the land of Egypt. (20:6-8)

Note the characteristic hyperbole with which Ezekiel paints this dramatic picture. The LORD was on the verge of destroying them while they were still in Egypt but held back "for my name's sake" (20:9) and led them into the wilderness. The story continues: the LORD gave them the Law and the most precious gift of all, "my sabbaths as a sign between us that I, the LORD, have set them apart for my purpose" (20:12). Yet the people continued to rebel. God again withholds punishment, not out of love for the chosen people, nor out of divine mercy, but for the sake of the divine Name. Episode after episode offers occasion for divine wrath, as the people sin repeatedly—according to Ezekiel 20, every step of the journey from Egypt into Canaan. We finally see a note of promise toward the end of Ezekiel 20, but as always with Ezekiel, redemption and forgiveness are about the protection and display of God's holiness (20:41). Ezekiel will not give an inch in his rhetoric: even his salvation oracles are designed to bring his people to their knees in abject recognition of the unutterable power of God's holiness and their own unworthiness.

Ezekiel 21 continues oracles of judgment against Judah and Jerusalem with a terrifying focus on the drawn and flashing sword. Ezekiel 22–23 give us more of Ezekiel's shocking and graphic language, emblematic of the disgust the prophet feels for the sinfulness of his people. Ezekiel 24 narrates the sign-act of Ezekiel losing his wife, a symbol of the terrible loss Jerusalem will experience. One may compare Jeremiah's being told not to marry (Jer 16:1-4). Here, as in some other passages, Ezekiel seems to be reflecting on similar motifs and traditional expectations as we see in the book of Jeremiah, but in some instances, Ezekiel renders them with considerably more drama and force.

Ezekiel 25–39

The latter half of the book of Ezekiel brims with vivid depictions of the impending fate of Israel's enemies. In this material, the prophet gestures toward the plan of YHWH unfolding—or being about to unfold—in terms that are enacted beyond the boundaries of human historical time and beyond the constraints of biological laws that govern creaturely life and death on earth. Some of these oracles, particularly Ezekiel 38–39, may fairly be characterized as "proto-apocalyptic." That is to say, they seem to express an early stream of thinking that came to be elaborated in full and rich detail in Jewish and Christian apocalyptic literature.

Elaborate oracles against other nations in Ezekiel 25–32 hand down polemical indictments against Ammon, Moab, Edom, Philistia, Tyre, Sidon, and Egypt. These oracles are replete with elegant allusions to biblical traditions, artful metaphors, compelling descriptions, dramatic apostrophizing of enemies, and other skillful rhetorical moves. Material in 32:17-32 offers us a tantalizing glimpse into ancient Israelite traditions of the underworld. Unlike Isaiah and Jeremiah, the book of Ezekiel contains no extended oracle directed against Babylon. This is a surprising fact that might subtly acknowledge the grave risk to a prophet who rails publicly against his captor from a position (at least in the setting of the book) in Babylon in the exilic period. Andrew Mein observes:

> The one human king who is never explicitly challenged in the book is Nebuchadnezzar, but the overthrow of Babylonian power must at least be implicit in Ezekiel's oracles of restoration, which from the outset establish YHWH's kingship with the royal claim that "I myself will be the shepherd of my sheep" (34:15). Kingship must also be at the heart of the book's final vision, since in the ancient Near East, temple building is a royal task.[7]

Ezekiel 33 rearticulates the role of sentinel, underlining its importance for the larger rhetorical and theological purposes of this book. Ezekiel receives the news that Jerusalem has finally fallen to the Babylonians (33:21). Ezekiel 34 holds the leaders of Israel responsible for the terrible fate that has befallen the people. An oracle of judgment against Edom (Ezek 35) expresses bitter enmity for the local antagonist, which had aided the Babylonians and gloated at the fall of Jerusalem. In Ezekiel 36 we find restoration material that seems much more like Ezekiel than had the unexpectedly bucolic Ezekiel 34. Here in chapter 36, passages about Israel's restoration and healing are shot through with Ezekielian barbs about his people having defiled their land (36:17), having profaned the Lord's name (36:22-23), and needing to remember their evil deeds and see clearly their own loathsomeness (36:31).

The Valley of Dry Bones and Apocalyptic Warfare

The traditions of the Hebrew Bible were written, for the most part, before the stream of theological tradition known as apocalypticism flourished in Judaism. But a few texts in the prophetic corpus do seem to participate in apocalyptic ideation. The visions in Zechariah 1–6 and Daniel 7–12 may constitute the latest such material in the Hebrew Scriptures. John J. Collins explains the defining features of apocalyptic literature:

> The classic Jewish and Christian apocalypses are characterized not only by the theme of revelation but by the prominence of the supernatural world and of eschatology. Eschatology is not only concerned with the end of the world or history in the manner of the historical apocalypses, but also with the fate of the dead. . . . Most crucially, the apocalypses are distinguished by the belief in the resurrection and judgment of the individual dead. . . . The ancient apocalypses . . . are prone to dualism, to the division of the world between the elect and the damned, and are often gleeful in their anticipation of eschatological vindication.[8]

Ezekiel 37–39 gives us dramatic oracles that seem to constitute an early reflex in the stream of thinking that developed into full-blown apocalyptic.

Ezekiel 37:1-14 describes the prophet's vision of what happens in a valley of dry bones, and the interpretation of the event offered by the Lord. This passage offers a remarkable enactment of hope for Israel that is nevertheless viscerally graphic and terrifying: a slow-motion revivification of bones into skeletons and then into standing corpses, and—only after receiving "breath" through Ezekiel's prophesying—finally into living

152

beings. This is the reconstitution of the Judean exilic community: people of God who had been defeated and exiled by the Babylonians and who had been rhetorically slaughtered by the words of their harshest prophet, Ezekiel. The story in Ezekiel 37 is told with breathtaking vividness in ten short verses, a vision that has drawn the attention of countless artists over the centuries. Ezekiel is transported by the hand of the LORD to a valley—in fact, "the valley," the definite article in the Hebrew suggesting to many interpreters that this known place would be the valley mentioned in 3:22, which according to that narrative seems to be walking distance from the river Chebar in Babylon. So Ezekiel is placed in the middle of a Babylonian valley near the settlement of his community of diaspora Judeans. The valley is filled with bones that are very dry: these corpses have lain on the ground, unburied and unmourned, for a long time indeed. One recalls a passage in Jeremiah in which a wrathful LORD pursues vengeance in a terrifying scope, upon Judah and Jerusalem (25:18, 29) and upon all the nations of the earth: "At that time, those struck down by the LORD will fill the earth. And no one will mourn for them or prepare their bodies for burial. They will become like refuse lying on the ground" (Jer 25:33).

The picture in Ezekiel's valley of dry bones is chilling: death, defilement, and abandonment as far as the eye can see, with no one left to remember who these dead had been. Ezekiel is then told to prophesy to the bones in the name of the Lord GOD: "I am about to put breath in you, and you will live again. I will put sinews on you, place flesh on you, and cover you with skin. When I put breath in you, and you come to life, you will know that I am the LORD" (37:5-6). We know well from the disturbing Ezekiel 16 that the divine word saying, "Live!" will perform that which it desires. And indeed, spectacular and horrifying results unfold. There is no better voice in the Latter Prophets to describe this vision than the voice of Ezekiel, this prophet who has so terrified his audience with graphic and violent language, one who himself had been rendered speechless by the LORD at the beginning of his prophetic ministry (3:26), one who had been stunned into silence when he first encountered the thunderous and brilliant holiness of God (3:15). Ezekiel speaks, now, the unspeakable: "There was a great noise as I was prophesying, then a great quaking, and the bones came together, bone by bone" (37:7). Remember that these are countless bones filling an entire valley: the sound would have been deafening. "I looked"—the self-consciousness of the prophet's gaze is Ezekiel's equivalent of slow-motion horror unfolding, step by step: "When I looked, suddenly there were sinews on them. The flesh appeared, and then they were covered over with skin. But there was still no breath in them" (37:8). Here you must banish from your mind any later images of glorious resurrection in art or hymnody, any idea of the children of Judah leaping and dancing for joy. What we have now, in this narrative moment, is a valley filled with enfleshed corpses. The bones had leaped and rolled and rattled toward each other; sinews had entwined around them; raw human tissue had formed and thickened upon them; skin had stretched itself taut across the bodies; but there was no breath in them. This was only a reversal of the process of decomposition. The bodies are not yet standing. At this fraught and powerfully suspenseful moment in the narrative, we are gazing upon heaps of corpses, as far as the eye can see. One wonders that there could have been breath in Ezekiel himself at the visioning of it—this dramatic visualizing of slaughtered bodies.

The prophet is commanded to prophesy again: "Prophesy to the breath; prophesy, human one! Say to the breath, The LORD God proclaims: Come from the four winds, breath! Breathe into these dead bodies and let them live" (37:9). What choice does Ezekiel have? Which terror would be worse, seeing these corpses reanimated or refusing to do what the LORD has commanded? He does as he has been commanded: "When the breath entered them, they came to life and stood on their feet, an extraordinarily large company" (37:10). The Hebrew is *ḥayil gādôl məʾōd-məʾōd*: not just a crowd of people, but a massive army. Ezekiel has just prophesied life, bone by bone, inch by gruesome inch, back into the forgotten armies of Israel and Judah, those who had been slain in battle not only in the war with Babylon but in all the battles going back as far as anyone could remember. These warriors had lain so long unburied, defiling the ground and unable to rest, that all hope had been lost in the diaspora settlement. "Our bones are dried up, and our hope has perished. We are completely finished" (37:11) had been the cry of the exiles in Babylon: utter despair.

And Ezekiel the prophet had answered their cry. Compelled to warn them as if his own life depended on it (3:17-18), he had warned them by the harshest of rebukes, by elaborate allegories, and by hyperbolic language of sexual shaming that would have insulted them to the core of their being. Ezekiel had taken their most sacred tradition of liberation and turned it into a shameful revisionist history of their narrow escapes from well-deserved destruction (Ezek 20), ranting that whether good or ill happened to them, finally, one day, they would realize that God is the LORD, and they would turn and live (18:32). So: now the LORD has resurrected an exceedingly great army in the middle of Babylon. Where will this army go? "I will bring you back to Israel's fertile land," promises this God of terror and resurrection (37:12); "I will put my breath in you, and you will live. I will plant you on your fertile land, and you will know that I am the LORD. I've spoken, and I will do it. This is what the LORD says" (37:14).

This will involve an eschatological battle against Gog of the land of Magog (chaps. 38–39). With Israel reconstituted, brought back to its land, and allowed to live in safety once again (38:8), the LORD must secure Israel's *shalom* for all time, defeating all of the hordes, primordial and mythical and terrifyingly real, that ever thundered down from the north against God's people. The LORD will act, in this as in all things in the book of Ezekiel, for the sake of the LORD's holy name: "I will make known my holy name among my people Israel. They will never again degrade my holy name, and the nations will know that I, the LORD, am holy in Israel" (39:7). The holiness of God has always been Israel's most powerful weapon against all who would enslave or destroy the people of God. The political leaders had forgotten, ever since the time of the first king, Saul—but Israel's priests had always known that Israel's power was only in their God. Ezekiel's extraordinary vision of the divine Chariot is meant to teach this truth. His prophesying that the divine Chariot was leaving Jerusalem made the point in the negative: where the LORD's holiness could no longer dwell because of the corruption of the people and their leaders, great would be the ruin of that place. Ezekiel's prophetic word now revivifies a hopeless and abandoned people. The implied audience can finally see, chapter after chapter of the LORD's rage, having endured oracle after oracle built around offensive images, that Ezekiel's prophesying has been intended to revivify this people, to awaken them to the presence of God in their midst. The LORD has been a "miniature sanctuary" to this people in a foreign land (11:16), and perhaps now they will understand that the LORD had always intended to gather this chastened and traumatized people and bring them home (11:17). The dramatic visions of Ezekiel 37–39 prepare the way literarily and theologically for the reestablishment of Jerusalem as the LORD's own habitation, something Ezekiel expresses in a unique and transcendent vision of the new temple in Ezekiel 40–48.

Ezekiel 40–48

Ezekiel's vision of the new temple shows how crucially important the cultic center of Judah's life will be for the reformed community of believers. The prophet is given a heavenly guide in his vision, "a man standing in the gate. He appeared to be bronze, and he had a linen cord and a measuring rod in his hand" (40:3), who shows Ezekiel the features of the temple, exhorting him to pay close attention and then to declare to "the house of Israel" all he has seen (40:4). In loving detail, Ezekiel 40–42 shows us the architectural proportions and features of the wall, thresholds, gates, and windows; vestibules and columns; outer courts, inner courts, galleries, and chambers; doors, tables, an altar, and more. The glory of the LORD enters the temple, and the prophet once more hears the voice of the LORD, this time affirming that here is where the divine Presence will reside. Israel will have learned, finally, to be "ashamed of its iniquities" (43:10 NRSV)—the lesson that had been taught with such terrible force in the preceding chapters of the book of Ezekiel. "Now let them remove their disloyalties and their kings' corpses from me, and I will dwell among them forever" (43:9). The rest of Ezekiel 43 and 44–46 review ordinances for sacrifices, the service of the levitical priests, allotment of land in the holy district around the temple, ethical trade, practices related to liturgical festivals and sabbaths, and more. Note a political tension in what Ezekiel says about the Israelite priesthood in 44:10-16, in which the Levites are rebuked for idolatry and the "family of Zadok" is commended for faithfulness. The Zadokite priestly line is privileged in Ezekiel; the Levites are summarily demoted to the status of lower-level temple servants ("They won't approach me to officiate for me as priests or approach any of my holy things or the most holy place. Though they will bear their humiliation and the consequences of their detestable practices," 44:13). Where the presence of the LORD dwells, there will be the portions of the tribes of Israel, there offerings will be made morning by morning, and from there will come all that is needed for Israel's life and flourishing.

Ezekiel's vision of the river of life flowing from the temple (47:1-12) is water streaming from below the temple threshold on the south side, flowing east. As Ezekiel and his guide walk away from the temple, the water is ankle-deep, then knee-deep, then waist-deep; finally it has become a river so deep that it cannot be crossed. Its miraculous capacity to turn stagnant water into fresh water opens up an expansive utopian vista with countless creatures rejoicing in a renewed world:

> Wherever the river flows, every living thing that moves will thrive. There will be great schools of fish, because when these waters enter the sea, it will be fresh. Wherever the river flows, everything will live. People will stand fishing beside it, from En-gedi to En-eglayim, and it will become a place for spreading nets. It will be like the Mediterranean Sea, having all kinds of fish in it. Its marshes and swamps won't be made fresh (they are left for salt), but on both banks of the river will grow up all kinds of fruit-bearing trees. Their leaves won't wither, and their fruitfulness won't wane. They will produce fruit in every month, because their water comes from the sanctuary. Their fruit will be for eating, their leaves for healing. (47:9-12)

Moshe Greenberg notes, "This vision specifically connects temple and fertility and singles out for transformation the most barren tract of land—the wilderness of Judah—and the body of water most inhospitable to life, the Dead Sea, a dramatic exhibition of God's beneficent presence in the temple."[9]

The eschatological vision of the new temple did not need to come true in the lifetime of Ezekiel—scholars have made much of the fact that the Second Temple was not actually built or operated according to his specifications—because it was already true. The power of God was present in the diaspora community, in that revivified, exceedingly great army that had learned to stand on its feet in hope instead of languishing in the dryness of despair. "Then they will know that I am the LORD," thunders Ezekiel's God over and over again, and the people do learn it, according the promise inscribed at the end of the scroll of Ezekiel: the name of their new city is no longer to be Jerusalem but "The LORD is There" (48:35). Through Ezekiel's intermediation, dramatic and violent and unsettling though it be, his people will have learned to recognize that the LORD is in their midst.

The biblical prophets inhabit a dangerously liminal or "threshold" space, poised between the overpowering purposes of God and the sinful realities of human life in community. Ezekiel inhabits this liminality in three different ways. Ezekiel witnesses from this liminal place because of his vocation as prophet. He also inhabits and witnesses from this liminal place because of his priestly role with his people (at least before his deportation) and his priestly sensibility: it had been his job to stand in the breach between divine and human in the place governed by holiness. Standing at the altar is risky under the best of circumstances. If God is indescribably powerful, and if God's holiness is profoundly other than the profanities and corruptions of everyday life, then the risks of intermediation are quite real. Ezekiel witnesses from a liminal place, thirdly, because of his actual physical and psychic location in diaspora, traumatized and culturally emasculated. The hyperbolic and graphic and violent nature of his rhetoric may have to do with his struggling to mediate the disruption that has wreaked such havoc on his people and their cultural institutions. After reading Ezekiel closely, we can no longer be complacent in our social bodies as if they were neutral sites for living faithful lives, and we can no longer be complacent with our own or false prophets' "whitewashing" (chap. 13) of political and spiritual crises. Through Ezekiel's eyes, we glimpse the terrible ways in which human moral and religious practices fall short of true fidelity to God. That may not be a comfortable recognition. Resistance is possible, and we may wrestle mightily with some of the ways in which Ezekiel expresses his prophetic vision. But in Ezekiel 1, 34, and 40–48, we have robust and visionary assurances of the presence of God as we negotiate these challenges.

Stulman and Kim characterize the importance of Ezekiel's witness: "This literature heralds that the God of Israel is not found in safe and familiar places but in brokenness and at the margins."[10] Some of the difficult dimensions of this book may have been produced not out of unexamined woundedness but as part of an overarching rhetorical strategy:

> For hope to bloom, Ezekiel must deal a deathblow to the entrenched power arrangements associated with Jerusalem and its temple. The old world must be exposed as a failed system, a stranglehold of injustice and idolatry that can no longer provide security and protection. Although counterintuitive, death and destruction are an integral part of Ezekiel's calculus of hope.[11]

Communities gathered around Scripture can learn from the book of Ezekiel, in all its intensity, notwithstanding its violent rhetoric and its tactics of shaming. After Ezekiel, readers surely will learn to see more clearly the desperation to which some may be driven when they have suffered the loss of everything they had held dear. And we may learn that "visions of God" are possible for refugees, fugitives, and exiles—even in times of crisis, even amid the ruins.

For Further Reading

Block, Daniel I. *The Book of Ezekiel, Chapters 1–24* and *The Book of Ezekiel, Chapter 25–48*. NICOT. Grand Rapids: Eerdmans, 1997, 1998.

Mein, Andrew. "Ezekiel: Structures, Themes, and Contested Issues." In *The Oxford Handbook of the Prophets*, 190–206. Edited by Carolyn J. Sharp. Oxford: Oxford University Press, 2016.

Stulman, Louis, and Hyun Chul Paul Kim. "Ezekiel as Disaster Literature" and "Ezekiel as Survival Literature." In *You Are My People: An Introduction to Prophetic Literature*, 145–81. Nashville: Abingdon, 2010.

Chapter 5

The Book of the Twelve: Prophetic Polyphony

The twelve Minor Prophets made up a single scroll in antiquity. Some scholars argue that the books having been written on a single scroll does not necessarily mean they were read together as one composition. But there is evidence that these short prophetic writings were considered, at least by some, as a unified literary composition in canonical terms since the very earliest times. The intertestamental wisdom book Sirach, dated to the second century BCE, refers to "the bones of the Twelve Prophets": "May the bones of the twelve prophets sprout new life from their burial places, because they comforted Jacob and rescued them with hopeful confidence" (Sir 49:10).

Thus well before the dawn of the Common Era, the Minor Prophets were thought of as a distinct and recognizable group with their own coherence in the traditions of ancient Israel. Early church theologians Hilary of Poitiers (310–368), Jerome (c. 347–420), and Augustine (354–430) spoke of these twelve biblical books as a collection. The Twelve appear in different orders in the Hebrew text tradition (the MT) and the early Greek translation (the LXX).

Masoretic Text	Septuagint
MT Order and LXX Order of the Twelve	
Hosea	Hosea
Joel	Amos
Amos	Micah
Obadiah	Joel
Jonah	Obadiah
Micah	Jonah
Nahum	Nahum
Habakkuk	Habakkuk
Zephaniah	Zephaniah
Haggai	Haggai
Zechariah	Zechariah
Malachi	Malachi

The LXX version seems to be concerned first with judgment on the northern kingdom of Israel, which we see in Hosea, Amos, and Micah, three prophets who level oracles of judgment against Ephraim, the northern sanctuary of Bethel, and Samaria. Then the LXX order seems to move to prophetic books that deal with Judah, Jerusalem, and the nations. Micah may serve as a "hinge" in that regard because it focuses indictments on the north but also talks about Judah and Jerusalem, helping reorient the implied audience of the Twelve to Judah as the history of Israel unfolds. Joel then emphasizes the fate of Jerusalem and the nations. The next three books in the LXX order focus entirely on enemy nations (Obadiah versus Edom, Jonah versus capital city Nineveh in Assyria, and Nahum also versus Nineveh). The last four books, Zephaniah, Haggai, Zechariah, and Malachi, could be said to focus on Jerusalem. Zephaniah treats dimensions of communal life that have corrupted Jerusalem and made the city vulnerable; Haggai addresses the rebuilding of the temple and governance of Judah; Zechariah presents visions and oracles related to Jerusalem's glorious restoration; and Malachi discusses covenantal obedience and ritual practices centered on the altar of the Jerusalem temple.

In the Masoretic (Hebrew) order, there is not such a clear progression from judgment of the north to judgment of the south. Marvin Sweeney has argued that each subsequent book in the Twelve in the MT is responding to some crucial matter raised in the preceding book, so that we see more of an organic ordering according to theological issues.[1] For example, Sweeney argues that Joel comes after Hosea in the MT order because once Hosea has clarified the threat that existed against the northern kingdom, Joel steps in to make it clear that Jerusalem has always been at risk as well. In Amos we see mention of Edom at the end (Amos 9:12); then in the MT order, Obadiah follows, which further develops the indictment of Edom. "Insofar as Obadiah takes up the condemnation of Edom and its submission to Zion on the Day of Yhwh, it constitutes a projected fulfillment of the scenarios laid out in both Joel and Amos," Sweeney offers.[2] Micah, Sweeney says, stresses the universal peace that will come at the reign of the messianic king; then Nahum rejoices over Nineveh's downfall. Habakkuk claims that God is bringing the Babylonians against Judah but that the enemy will be punished; Zephaniah calls for a purification of Jerusalem; Haggai focuses further on the temple and the law, Zechariah offers visions about the rebuilding of the temple, and Malachi finally speaks of the return of the LORD as an opportunity for purification and a chance for the people to return to reading the Law. Sweeney suggests that in both narrative trajectories—that of the MT and that of the LXX—we see an arc related to the covenant of Yhwh and people imagined as a marriage. This arc moves from a focus on the marriage covenant broken at the beginning (Hos 1–3) to a note that the LORD hates divorce (Mal 1:14-16). Sweeney reads this trajectory as signaling encouragement for the people to read the Torah and learn to obey God.[3]

Many interpreters will find fruitful the search for thematic continuities and artful cross-references in the Book of the Twelve. Just remember this caveat: when we juxtapose literary works of any depth of complexity, we can discern—or create—points of contact and literary resonances in a wide variety of ways. Here is a counterexample that goes in a different direction than the trajectory proposed by Sweeney. We could read Hosea and Malachi as making the same point, but amplifying it with different dictions and different foci. Hosea uses the story of the prophet and Gomer and vivid metaphors of female infidelity to make a theological

163

point, whereas Malachi speaks in concrete legal terms about male infidelity to make a point about reform of social relations at the heart of the covenant community. Rather than reversing the picture painted in Hosea 1–3, Malachi 2 could be construed as filling in a gap. Where Hosea rages against idolatry imaged as ingratitude and uncontrolled sexual behavior on the part of the woman, Malachi urges that the husband, too, be held accountable, for both spouses need to be faithful to each other if the community of believers is to honor the God to whom they offer sacrifices. I muster this counterexample simply to underline that the creativity and perspective of the exegete are always involved in making choices about which literary and historical evidence to privilege and how to construe significance. I hope you will delight in exploring connections among different prophetic books within the Twelve. It can be intellectually enlivening to study congruences, shifts of emphasis, and polyphonic difference as significant in this multifaceted prophetic book.

Intertextual resonances within the Book of the Twelve suggest two things. First, some of the books of the Twelve seem to have known other books within that group. Second, redactors may have shaped subgroups purposefully into a more unified document. Scholars are fascinated by the question of how ancient Israelite prophetic traditions may have drawn on each other as a larger "book" (scroll) consciousness developed. Several literary connections reach across individual books and subgroups within the Book of the Twelve. For example, the refrain that the LORD is "slow to anger and [*something*]" (NRSV) occurs in Jonah 4, Joel 2, and Nahum 1. All three prophets are utilizing a traditional refrain that occurs in its fullest form in the dramatic narrative of Moses's encounter with YHWH in Exodus 34. Further, there is an allusion to the tradition in Micah 7:18-19, which uses a key phrase and several nouns from our refrain, though the verses do not constitute verbatim quotation. One or two of these books of the Minor Prophets might be reflecting on the refrain as a response to its occurrence in another book within the Twelve. The connection among them is observable, though the direction of influence and full import of this intertextual conversation may never be known.

An Ancient Refrain: "The LORD Is Slow to Anger"

Exod 34:6-8: The LORD passed before him [Moses], and proclaimed, "The LORD, the LORD, a God <u>merciful and gracious, slow to anger, and abounding in steadfast love and faithfulness, keeping steadfast love for the thousandth generation, forgiving iniquity and transgression and sin, yet by no means clearing the guilty</u>, but visiting the iniquity of the parents upon the children and the children's children. . . ." And Moses quickly bowed his head toward the earth, and worshiped. (NRSV)

Joel 2:11-13	Jonah 4:1-3	Nah 1:2-3
Truly the day of the LORD is great; terrible indeed— who can endure it? . . . Rend your hearts and not your clothing. Return to the LORD, your God, for <u>he is gracious and merciful, slow to anger, and abiding in steadfast love, and relents from punishing</u>. (NRSV)	But this was very displeasing to Jonah, and he became angry. He prayed to the LORD and said, "O LORD! . . . That is why I fled to Tarshish at the beginning; for I knew that <u>you are a gracious God and merciful, slow to anger, and abounding in steadfast love, and ready to relent from punishing</u>. And now, O LORD, please take my life from me, for it is better for me to die than to live." (NRSV)	A jealous and avenging God is the LORD . . . ; the LORD takes vengeance on his adversaries and rages against his enemies. <u>The LORD is slow to anger but great in power, and the LORD will by no means clear the guilty</u>. (NRSV)

Mic 7:18-19: Who is a God like you, <u>pardoning iniquity</u> and passing over the <u>transgression</u> of the remnant of [his] possession? He does not retain his <u>anger</u> forever, because he delights in showing <u>clemency</u>. He will again have <u>compassion</u> on us; he will tread our iniquities underfoot.

Many interpreters have noticed what are called "catchwords"— repeated language or specific motifs—connecting the ends of some books in the Twelve with the beginnings of the books that come after them.[4] Other linkages that do not involve beginnings and endings have been spotted as well.

Linkages within the Twelve	
Joel 3:16 The LORD roars from Zion, and utters his voice from Jerusalem; the heavens and the earth quake. But the LORD is a refuge for his people, a shelter for the people of Israel.	Amos 1:2 The LORD roars from Zion. He shouts from Jerusalem; the pastures of the shepherds wither, and the top of Carmel dries up.
Joel 3:10 Beat the iron tips of your plows into swords and your pruning tools into spears; let the weakling say, "I am mighty."	Mic 4:3 They will beat their swords into iron plows and their spears into pruning tools. Nation will not take up sword against nation; they will no longer learn how to make war. (// Isa 2:4)
Amos 9:12 So that they may possess what is left of Edom, as well as all the nations who are called by my name.	Obad 17 The house of Jacob shall take possession of those who dispossessed them (NRSV).
Mic 4:6-7 On that day, says the LORD, I will gather the lame; I will assemble those who were driven away and those whom I have harmed. I will make the lame into survivors, those driven away into a mighty nation.	Zeph 3:19 I will deliver the lame; I will gather the outcast. I will change their shame into praise and fame throughout the earth.

Those are just a few of the inner-biblical quotations and allusions in the Book of the Twelve. Some may simply be evidence of a common heritage of shared linguistic elements and traditional tropes, but others point to artful intention in the scribal shaping of the final form of the Book of the Twelve. Sweeney notes that Joel shows "extensive citation" of Obadiah and thematic contacts with Amos.[5] Habakkuk 2:13-14 quotes Jeremiah 51:58 and Isaiah 11:9. Zechariah 9:9 may be alluding to Micah 4:8. Thus, while the scroll of the Twelve comprises individual books, each with its own historical setting and focused prophetic message, the scroll has long been seen as a witness of significance read as a thoughtfully shaped whole.

The Twelve as Prism of Biblical Prophecy

The Twelve presents thematic tensions and complexities—distinctive voices, even divergent and clashing voices—held together by towering motifs that are common to the prophetic corpus as a whole, such as judgment and salvation; divine absence and divine presence; tradition and hope; war and restoration. . . . The first three books—Hosea, Joel, and Amos—reenact the ravaging forces of war, to pluck up and pull down, whereas the last three books—Haggai, Zechariah, and Malachi—imagine restoration, to build and plant. In between these pillars, the remaining six books expose the betrayal, abuse, and demise of the nations (OAN), in which Jonah and Nahum as a core depict two conflicting interpretive perspectives. . . . The year 587 shattered the community's long-standing renderings of Yhwh, its understandings of the universe, [and] its cherished narrative. The year 540 opened the door to newness and hope when exile and captivity appeared to be normative. Together these pivotal moments organize the Twelve and propel ongoing interpretive communities to ponder the wreckage of war, exile, and colonization, as well as justice, liberation, and hope.

—Louis Stulman and Hyun Chul Paul Kim[6]

Theological Themes

Because the Book of the Twelve contains twelve unique compositions from different historical periods, you'll see many different emphases as you read these ancient texts. We will consider three major themes that run like gold threads through two, three, or more books within the larger scroll of the Twelve: explorations of the relationship between divine judgment and redemption, the motif of the Day of Yhwh, and the importance of authentic worship in the covenant community.

Relationship between Judgment and Redemption

In the Book of the Twelve, the relationship between prophecies of doom and prophecies of redemption is a complex thing, a dialogical relationship rather than an overarching story line moving from judgment to restoration. It is not the case that we see simple progression from more oracles of dire judgment against Israel and Judah to more oracles of hope for rebuilding, even though historically, the nations of Israel and Judah did survive crises (the Syro-Ephraimite War in 735–732, the fall of the northern kingdom in 721, and the fall of Jerusalem and Judah in 587) and then did rebuild, beginning with the repatriation of the exiles under the decree of Cyrus of Persia in 538, then the rebuilding of the temple (520 to 515), and finally the rebuilding of the wall of Jerusalem in the fifth century BCE (see Ezra–Nehemiah, which, again, was a single book in antiquity). In the Twelve, there is no simple arc from catastrophe to restoration. Rather, in individual prophetic books and in the larger scope of the Book of the Twelve, we see a dynamic interplay between judgment and promise. God is both a God of wrath and a God of tender mercy and compassion, from the beginning (Hosea) to the end (Malachi) of the scroll of the Twelve.

Admittedly, it is clear that later redaction added promise oracles at the ends of prophetic books. Amos is judgment, judgment, judgment—or better, intensifying from judgment to more alarming judgment to absolutely terrifying judgment—right up until the last few verses of Amos 9, where there are words of promise. Hosea is brutal: ravaging metaphors are piled up one after the other until Hosea 14, where the language changes to pacific and nurturing images. So within some books, that literary movement from doom to promise does hold. But judgment and redemption belong together theologically in the witness of the prophets; they are articulated as twinned qualities of the people's identity. The prophets urge their audiences to understand the dynamic as dialectical, as moving back and forth in every historical time between the grim persistence of Israel's sin, the Lord's extreme displeasure with that sin, and the Lord's infinite capacity for mercy.

The role of the nations has always been a vexed and complicated matter in Israel's prophetic witness, and this is certainly true in the Book of the Twelve. The nations are never simply antagonists and adversaries, although they are that, and there are venomous oracles crying out for the destruction of the nations in many prophetic books. The call for vengeance is brought out acutely with the presence of Obadiah and Nahum in the Book of the Twelve, two prophetic books that constitute bloodcurdling oracles against other nations. But we also have the surprising Amos 9:7, where Amos, en route to destroying his audience's confidence in the election traditions of Israel, sarcastically mentions that God brought not only Israel up out of Egypt but the Philistines from Caphtor and the Arameans from Kir. Multiple exoduses: an astonishing claim! Even if the reader wishes to characterize this as a rhetorical flourish designed to shame and destabilize Amos's audience, still, we have a claim that the God of Israel is a God who delivers other nations. Further, we have the book of Jonah, with its scandalous claim that God plans to show mercy on Nineveh, the capital city of Israel's most brutal enemy. In the expansive vision of Micah 4, many peoples and nations will stream to Zion to learn the ways of Torah, eager to become peacemakers and no longer train in the ways of war (Mic 4:3). Without question, the overwhelming posture in the Book of the Twelve regarding other nations is a posture of desire for their destruction. But it is important to keep in mind the notes of resistance and new possibility for those international relationships as well. Recall the universalist moments in Isaiah that include the nations in God's promises, albeit in a subjugated position; recall also in Jeremiah the brief promises of restoration to Egypt, Moab, Ammon, and Elam. So too in the Book of the Twelve, the nations are swept up into the dialectic of divine judgment and redemption, at the mercy—in every sense—of the Holy One who roars from Zion (Amos 1:2, Joel 3:16, Hos 11:10) and who also "delights in showing clemency" (Mic 7:18 NRSV).

The Day of YHWH

The theme of the coming "Day of YHWH" is important for the Book of the Twelve and serves as a broad basis for literary interrelationships in the book. The idea, expressed both in historical terms and in eschatological terms that anticipate the end of history, is this: the LORD is coming to vindicate the righteous and punish those who have been exploiting and harming others with apparent impunity. The motif occurs no fewer than thirteen times in the Book of the Twelve, in four different prophets: Joel (1:15; 2:1, 11; 3:4, 14), Amos (5:18, 20), Obadiah (v. 15), and

Zephaniah (1:7, 14). The motif occurs only twice otherwise in the entire corpus of the Latter Prophets (Isa 13:6, 9). From this we may surmise that the motif of the Day of YHWH was worked through the Twelve with intention and forethought. The Book of the Twelve spans historical contexts from the eighth century BCE to the late Second Temple period, and the motif surely would have been seen as relevant for every age, though it is likely that the motif developed late in the flourishing of Israel's prophetic traditions. The image of an avenging God coming to destroy Israel's enemies would have offered powerful theological consolation during the many times when Judah was harassed by local adversaries such as Ammon, Edom, and Moab, and when Israel and Judah were militarily subjugated by the larger empires that strode the battlefields of the ancient Near East (Egypt, Assyria, Babylon, Persia). Note that the motif of the Day of the LORD is turned against God's own people, too, when they are indicted for social injustice and idolatry by the prophets who serve as their moral conscience and theological compass.

Below are two paradigmatic examples. The devastation of the entire earth is in view in Isaiah's oracle against Babylon. This usage of the motif highlights the cosmic power of YHWH:

> Wail, for the day of the LORD is near.
>> Like destruction from the Almighty it will come.
> Then all hands will fall limp;
>> every human heart will melt,
>> and they will be terrified. . . .
> Look, the day of the LORD is coming with cruel rage and burning anger,
>> making the earth a ruin, and wiping out its sinners.
> Heaven's stars and constellations won't show their light.
> The sun will be dark when it rises;
>> the moon will no longer shine.
> I will bring disaster upon the world for its evil,
>> and bring their own sin upon the wicked.
> I will end the pride of the insolent,
>> and the conceit of tyrants I will lay low. (Isa 13:6-11)

By contrast, Amos uses the tradition of the Day of Y<small>HWH</small> to undermine the complacency of those within the covenant community who "trample on the poor" and "afflict the righteous" (5:11, 12). This catastrophic expression of divine justice will take them by surprise:

> Doom to those who desire the day of the L<small>ORD</small>!
>
>   Why do you want the day of the L<small>ORD</small>?
>
> It is darkness, not light;
>
>   as if someone fled from a lion, and was met by a bear;
>
>   or sought refuge in a house, rested a hand against the wall,
>
>   and was bitten by a snake.
>
> Isn't the day of the L<small>ORD</small> darkness, not light;
>
>   all dark with no brightness in it? (Amos 5:18-20)

Even where the phrase "the day of Y<small>HWH</small>" does not occur, related themes may be being expressed in passages in which God is implored to avenge wrongs or is envisaged as approaching miscreants—whether individuals or entire nations—with judgment in mind. Reading the Latter Prophets, you may have noticed how fervent and pervasive is the hope for divine recompense against malefactors.

The Importance of Authentic Worship

The central role of ancient Israel's rituals and festivals, along with the observance of the Torah more generally, ought not be divorced from prophetic witness. I say this against an older position, seen before the work of Julius Wellhausen (1844–1918) but formulated in an influential way in Wellhausen's 1883 work, *Prolegomena to the History of Israel*, that the prophets came before the codification of Israel's laws and cultic practices. Wellhausen interpreted this "late" focus on the Law pejoratively, as a descent into legalism that compromised the inspired witness of the prophets. On Joseph Blenkinsopp's reading, it was, "according to Wellhausen, precisely the codification of the laws that created a situation fatal to the exercise of prophecy."[7] Wellhausen's position yielded a distorted view that underestimates the importance of halakhic and ritual observance for the Latter Prophets. In many passages in the Twelve, we can see a passionate interest in right worship and in the restoration and appropriate use of the temple. To press their implied audiences toward those goals, the prophets sometimes use scathing critique of inauthentic worship separated from the practice of justice within the covenant community—but that should not be read as rejection of the system of worship. It is precisely because faithfulness is lived through love of neighbor and love of God, interwoven and inseparable, that the prophets excoriate their communities when either of those two dimensions has been disregarded. Fidelity is expressed through justice and through observance of the Torah. Right worship and a commitment to justice are lived together in the reformed community.

Below are two passages that press their hearers toward justice. Each uses terms that suggest that the gestures of worship are empty without attention to the demands of righteousness before God and justice for the neighbor:

> Yet even now, says the LORD,
>> return to me with all your hearts,
>>> with fasting, with weeping, and with sorrow;
>> tear your hearts and not your clothing.
>>> Return to the LORD your God,
>>> for he is merciful and compassionate, very patient, full of faithful love,
>>> and ready to forgive.
>> Who knows whether he will have a change of heart
>>> and leave a blessing behind him,
>>> a grain offering and a drink offering for the LORD your God?
>>> (Joel 2:12-14)

I hate, I reject your festivals;

I don't enjoy your joyous assemblies.

If you bring me your entirely burned offerings and gifts of food—

I won't be pleased; I won't even look at your offerings of well-fed
animals.

Take away the noise of your songs;

I won't listen to the melody of your harps.

But let justice roll down like waters,

and righteousness like an ever-flowing stream. (Amos 5:21-24)

Now consider these passages about the centrality of temple worship
and halakhic observance (i.e., obedience to ritual instructions):

You expect a surplus, but look how it shrinks. You bring it home, and
I blow it away, says the LORD of heavenly forces, because my house
lies in ruins. But all of you hurry to your own houses. Therefore, the
skies above you have withheld the dew, and the earth has withheld its
produce because of you. I have called for drought on the earth, on the
mountains, on the grain, on the wine, on the olive oil, on that which
comes forth from the fertile ground, on humanity, on beasts, and upon
everything that handles produce. (Hag 1:9-11)

Nevertheless, from sunrise to sunset, my name will be great among the
nations. Incense and a pure grain offering will be offered everywhere in
my name, because my name is great among the nations, says the LORD
of heavenly forces. But you make my name impure when you say, "The
table of the LORD is polluted. Its fruit, its food, is despised." But you
say, "How tedious!" and you groan about it, says the LORD of heavenly
forces. You permit what is stolen, lame, or sick to be brought for a sacrifice, and you bring the grain offering. Should I accept such from your
hands? says the LORD. I will curse the cheater who has a healthy male
in his flock, but who promises and sacrifices to the LORD that which is
corrupt. I am truly a great king, says the LORD of heavenly forces, and
my name is feared among the nations. (Mal 1:11-14)

The temple, liturgical practices, and Torah observance are vitally
important for reestablishing the covenant community after the crisis of
the Babylonian exile. We see this not just in the Book of the Twelve, but

also in the beautiful temple vision in Ezekiel 40–48 and in oracles promoting inclusive worship and halakhic observance in Isaiah 56:

> The immigrants who have joined me,
>> serving me and loving my name,
>>> becoming my servants,
>> everyone who keeps the Sabbath
>>> without making it impure,
>> and those who hold fast
>>> to my covenant:
> I will bring them
>> to my holy mountain,
> and bring them joy
>> in my house of prayer.
> I will accept their entirely burned
>> offerings and sacrifices on my altar.
> My house will be known as a house
>> of prayer for all peoples. (Isa 56:6-7)

Hosea

Hosea prophesied during a time of dangerous political instability in the northern kingdom. Israel had six monarchs in about twenty-five years (Jeroboam II, Zechariah, Shallum, Menahem, Pekahiah, and Pekah), enduring crisis after crisis, with four assassinations between 747 and 732. If you look at a chronological table of rulers in an annotated Bible, you'll see how short the rules of some of these kings were: three years, two years, less than one year. Several passages reflect on the political arrogance and lawlessness that characterized the time.

> They approach like a hot oven,
>> their hearts burning.
>>> Throughout the night,
>>>> their anger smolders;
>>> in the morning,
>>>> it continues to burn like a flaming fire.

All of them are hot as an oven;

>they devour their rulers.

All their kings have fallen;

>none of them call upon me. (7:6-7)

For now they will say:

>"We have no king,

>because we don't love the LORD.

>>What then could a king do for us?"

They have spoken empty words,

>swearing falsely

>>when making covenants;

so judgment springs up

>like poisonous weeds

>>in the furrows of the field. (10:3-4)

Instability is reflected also in 13:10-11:

Where is your king now,

>so that he can save you?

>Where in all your cities are your judges,

>>of whom you said,

>>"Give me a king and rulers"?

I gave you a king in my anger,

>and I took him away in my wrath.

It is not surprising, given the political context, that the book of Hosea is itself volatile. In a number of places, Hosea's diction is virtually unintelligible. The Hebrew text of Hosea is among the most difficult texts to read in the Hebrew Bible. Hosea is best known for an extended metaphor of Israel as an unfaithful wife. The book explores this theme in its opening chapters by means of two narratives about the LORD commanding Hosea to marry, or be in a loving relationship with, a sexually promiscuous woman (chaps. 1–3). Commentators throughout the centuries have found the LORD's command shocking on moral grounds. There has been less attention in the interpretive history of Hosea to the gendered shaming language that is characteristic of this book, which comes up immediately in the book and is rearticulated in subsequent chapters. Feminist interpreters have called attention to the pathology underlying the metaphorical ideation that God might appropriately batter and kill unfaithful "wife" Israel. Because men's violence against women has been considered appropriate in many social groups and cultural contexts over the centuries, and has even been advocated as biblically sanctioned in some deeply distorted interpretations, this aspect of Hosea had not drawn enough critique in the history of interpretation. The advent of feminist criticism in the scholarly guild has helped to bring ethical and theological dimensions of this problem more to the fore, but the violent language of Hosea is still sometimes explained away as "just" a metaphor, a position in need of more analytical rigor regarding the powerful ways metaphors work on the social imaginations of those who use them. Here are some of the relevant passages:

> Level a charge against your mother;
>> plead with her!
>> She is not my wife,
>>> and I am not her husband.
>> Let her remove prostitution
>>> from her presence,
>>> and adultery from between
>>>> her breasts,
>> or else I will strip her naked
>>> and expose her
>>>> as on the day she was born.
>> I will make her like a desert,
>>> and turn her into a dry land,
>>> and make her die of thirst. (2:2-3)

They will eat but not be satisfied;

> they will have sex like prostitutes,

>> but they will not have children,

because they have rejected the LORD

> to devote themselves

>> to false religious practices.

> Wine and new wine

>> destroy understanding. (4:10-11)

Don't rejoice, Israel!

> Don't celebrate as other nations do;

> for as whores you have gone away

>> from your God.

> You have loved a prostitute's pay

>> on all threshing floors of grain. (9:1)

Hosea is deeply concerned about his people's worship of the Canaanite god Baal. He also fulminates against worship involving the calves of Samaria, statuary and related cultic practices involving either illegitimate representations of YHWH or other gods (see 8:5-6; 10:5; 13:2). A central point of Hosea's prophesying is that the people have forsaken or misdirected the fidelity that belongs rightfully to the LORD.

The book of Hosea is an extraordinarily artful text, even though readers may be hard-pressed to track the themes and sudden shifts of oracles as they tumble over one another in the literary sequence of this book. As you read, stay alert for the rich density of metaphors concerning these motifs and metaphors:

- mothers
- conception, pregnancy, childbirth, and miscarriage
- children, children born out of wedlock, and orphans
- adultery and sexual promiscuity
- parental compassion and nurturing

Many of the oracles of Hosea evoke these images. The prophet comes back to them again and again.

Divine Wrath and Mercy in Hosea

God's will to punish and his will to pardon do not neutralize each other. Rather they are expressed together in the strongest terms, savage and tender. This gives the speeches a turbulence, a seeming incoherence, in which we reach the limits of language for talking about the goodness and severity of God.

—Francis Andersen and David Noel Freedman[8]

Hosea is permeated with dense reflection on earlier biblical traditions. We see occasional oblique references to the patriarchs and to the Exodus—for example, 12:12-13:

> Jacob fled to the land of Aram;
>> there Israel served for a wife,
>> and for a wife he kept watch
>>> over livestock.
> By a prophet the LORD
>> brought Israel up from Egypt,
>> and by a prophet he was guarded.

But more prominent than references to the Exodus are place-names that create a kind of "map" of who Israel has been in the past. The audience is compelled to reconstruct historical events and their significance for the present through Hosea's repeated references to earlier events in the Valley of Jezreel, the Valley of Achor, Gilgal, Beth-Aven, Mizpah, Tabor, Shittim, Gibeah, Ramah, Adam, Gilead, Shechem, Baal-Peor, Beth-Arbel, Bethel, Admah, and Zeboiim. The reader who looks all of these up will find narratives of sin and fractured cultural identity, stories that show precisely who Israel should not be. Each of the place-names in Hosea is being used metonymically to signal a past instance of rebellion. Each one involves an embodied kind of unfaithfulness involving desire or consumption, an appetite for illegitimate plunder, illegitimate sex, or illegitimate food. The references to place in Hosea are saturated with allusions to transgressive desire and death from stories in the Pentateuch and the Deuteronomistic History.[9] Working through the geography in Hosea, the implied audience is compelled to remember:

- the fatal sin of Achan in the matter of purloined spoil (Valley of Achor in Hos 2:15; see Josh 7:26)

- the LORD's rejection of the disobedient Saul as king, with Samuel hewing the Amalekite king Agag in pieces, reminiscent of eviscerations that are described in Hosea (Gilgal in Hos 4:15, 9:15, 12:11; see 1 Sam 15)

- the horrific events after the rape and dismemberment of the Levite's concubine in Judges, with internecine warfare almost destroying the tribe of Benjamin, and the subsequent abduction and sexual enslavement of virgins of Jabesh-gilead and Shiloh (Mizpah in Hos 5:1; see Judg 19–21)

- the catastrophic sexual mixing of Israelite men with Moabite women during the wilderness journey, with a wrathful LORD commanding the impalement of Israelite leaders and killing twenty-four thousand Israelites by a plague (Shittim in Hos 5:2 and Baal-Peor in Hos 9:10; see Num 25)

By means of these and many other geographical references, Hosea creates a web of allusions to places where Israel was shown to have been unfaithful with devastating consequences. The pedagogy of place-names in Hosea constructs a grim history of sin. In order for the hearers to figure out what Hosea is saying, they have to reconstruct their own identity, historically and geographically, as an identity based on story after story of sexual harm, cultic infractions, eating-related boundary transgressions, and terrible internecine violence. The ancient hearers who deciphered these allusions would have had to uncover some of the most shameful and blood-drenched episodes in Israel's history. Hosea is earlier than Ezekiel, so it's interesting to consider Hosea's reflection on Israel's ancient traditions as a forerunner of the way in which Ezekiel 20 uses the Exodus as a tradition of shame that reveals how close Israel kept coming to being destroyed by God's wrath.

Hosea 4 shows the prophet's concern about failure to observe the Torah. In 4:2, some of the covenantal stipulations in the Ten Commandments seem to be in view (see Exod 20 and Deut 5): Hosea charges that "swearing, lying, murder, together with stealing and adultery are common; bloody crime followed by bloody crime." As we saw with Isaiah 24, so also here, sin has cosmic consequences. The land or "the earth itself becomes sick [the word in Hebrew is the same as in Isaiah], and all who live on it grow weak" (4:3). The priest, whose job it is to guide the people into halakhic obedience, has abdicated his role: "you have forgotten the Instruction of your God" (4:6). In Hosea 5 are some metaphors for God designed not only to frighten the audience but also to evoke revulsion: the LORD is "like maggots" (NRSV) and "like decay" (5:12), as well as "like a lion" (5:14) to those who disobey. Hosea 6 offers a deftly sarcastic portrayal of insincere repentance. Many interpreters seem to take 6:1-3 as earnest, but verses 4 and 5 clearly signal that the confession in the preceding verses is to be considered unreliable; a similar rhetorical move is made in 8:2-3. The beautiful opening of Hosea 11 alludes to the Exodus tradition, portraying Israel's liberation from slavery in Egypt as an expression of the LORD's nurturing care. Some interpreters have discerned that the image of a caregiver bending down and feeding an infant (11:4) is likely an image of maternal breastfeeding. The prophet then moves swiftly to an oracle of judgment (11:5-7), and then to a stirring promise of divine love:

> How can I give you up, Ephraim?
>> How can I hand you over, Israel?
> How can I make you like Admah?
>> How can I treat you like Zeboiim?
> My heart winces within me;
>> my compassion
>>> grows warm and tender.

> I won't act on the heat of my anger;
>
> > I won't return to destroy Ephraim;
>
> > for I am God and not a human being,
>
> > > the holy one in your midst;
>
> I won't come in harsh judgment. (11:8-9)

The verses above would serve well as a countertext for a reader seeking biblical grounds on which to resist the many oracles of horrific punishment in the Latter Prophets. Hosea then moves again into judgment oracles that suggest a reversal of the Exodus, with God bringing the people back into the wilderness: "I am the LORD your God from the land of Egypt; I will make you live in tents again, as in former days" (12:9).

In Hosea 13 we encounter some of the most terrifying divine images in the entire Bible. The LORD will be to Israel like:

- a lion

- a leopard lurking by the road

- a bear robbed of her cubs who tears open the covering of Israel's heart

- a wild animal who mangles Israel

- plagues as of Death itself

- destruction as of Sheol itself

Some translations hear words of promise here, but they do not fit in the context, and no emendation is necessary on syntactical grounds. Hosea 13 is judgment all the way through. The Hebrew verb in "*I will become like a lion*" (13:7, emphasis added) is the same word we see in 13:14; it need not be read as an interrogative particle, as many translations propose. The first two rhetorical questions are the sort that expect an answer in the negative. Here is my translation:

Shall I ransom them from the power of Sheol? [*no*]

Shall I redeem them from Death? [*certainly not*]

O Death, I myself will function as your plagues!

O Sheol, I myself will function as your destruction!

Compassion is hidden from my eyes.

In Hosea 13, the motif of mothers and children comes to a close with gruesome images: Ephraim as a stillborn child (13:13), the little children of Samaria dashed in pieces and pregnant women of Samaria ripped open (13:16). This virulent polemic yields in Hosea 14 to gracious promises of protection and flourishing for Israel. God's people have been made "orphans" through the violent rhetoric of Hosea—the prophet has destroyed their "mother" (2:2; 4:5). But the purpose all along, as with the extremity of Ezekiel's oracles seen in light of Ezekiel 18:32, has been to catalyze repentance so that the people may return to the LORD and live (14:2-3). The closing images of the book are lyrical and soothing. Having experienced the trauma of the prophesying of Hosea, the reader is restored by images of dew, lily, cedar forests, olive trees, gardens, blossoming vines, and a nurturing God who murmurs, "I am like a green cypress tree; your fruit comes from me" (14:8). God is the source of shade, the source of stability, the source of fidelity.

Whoever is wise

understands these things.

Whoever observes

carefully knows them.

Truly, the LORD's ways are right,

and the righteous will walk in them,

but evildoers will stumble in them. (14:9)

Now that the implied audience has been compelled to look closely at their history of transgressions, now that their misunderstandings have been attacked and eviscerated, they are finally ready to respond.

Joel

The book of Joel reflects on numerous traditions from other biblical books. Joel's drawing of phrases and images from all over the Bible, one commentator says, "gives Joel the appearance of a learned interpreter."[10] The list of phrases drawn from other biblical books includes material from Ezekiel, Isaiah, Amos, Nahum, Obadiah, the Psalms, and other books as well. This impressive artistic reflection on truths spoken by other voices and in other times has been woven deftly into three short chapters in Joel. As with Ezekiel before him, Joel demonstrates that the prophets were not only visionaries who communicated prayerfully with their God. But also they were gifted with discernment and literary skill to mine the sacred traditions of Israel for words that could be applied to powerful effect in their own contexts.

Joel 1 begins with a call to attention directed to the elders and all the people. The prophet urges lamentation and repentance as appropriate responses to the divine judgment enacted in a devastating plague of locusts. The swarming of the insects is graphically depicted in Joel 2, spoken of as the Day of the LORD. Joel offers us several unforgettable images. One is of the ruthless destructive power of the locusts experienced in his time:

> What the cutting locust left,
>
> > the swarming locust has eaten.
>
> What the swarming locust left,
>
> > the hopping locust has eaten.
>
> And what the hopping locust left,
>
> > the devouring locust has eaten. . . .
>
> > because a nation,
>
> > > powerful and beyond number,
> >
> > > has invaded my land.
>
> Its teeth are like lions' teeth;
>
> > its fangs are like those of a lioness.
>
> It has destroyed my vines,
>
> > splintered my fig trees,

> stripped off their bark
>> and thrown it down;
> their branches have turned white. (1:4, 6-7)

Famine could result from such plagues of locusts in the ancient Near East. What's more, without crops to make cereal offerings and to feed the animals needed for sacrifice, worship would be severely compromised in Judah. Agricultural produce were essential for honoring the Lord with the blessings of life. Floods, droughts, earthquakes, failures of crops, and other natural disasters were seen as acts of divine judgment.

Joel 2:13 gives us the prophet's most famous exhortation, "Rend your hearts and not [just] your clothing!" (NRSV). Another unforgettable passage, much cherished in the history of reception, is Joel's lyrical poem about God's spirit being poured out upon all in the community:

> After that I will pour out my spirit
>> upon everyone;
>>> your sons and your daughters
>>>> will prophesy,
>>> your old men will dream dreams,
>>> and your young men will see visions.
>> In those days, I will also pour out my
>>> spirit on the male and female slaves. (2:28-29)

This passage moves into eschatological images:

> I will give signs in the heavens and on the earth—blood and fire and columns of smoke. The sun will be turned to darkness, and the moon to blood before the great and dreadful day of the Lord comes (2:30-31).

Yet another dramatic image in Joel is the image in Joel 3 of God gathering all of the nations into the dread Jehoshaphat Valley, which means the Valley of Yhwh-judges. This rebuke to the nations lays out the grounds for their destruction by the Lord: the enemy nations "have divided my land, and have cast lots for my people. They have traded boys for prostitutes, and sold girls for wine, which they drank down" (3:2-3).

To other enemies: "You have taken my silver and my gold, and have carried my rich treasures into your temples. You have sold the people of Judah and Jerusalem to the Greeks, removing them far from their own border" (3:5-6).

So the Lord will now turn the tables by selling the nations' children into slavery in Judah. Brutal stuff, and it grows more frightening when we read the vengeful ironic reversal of the Isaiah 2 // Micah 4 passage promising universal peace. Here in Joel, the nations are to arm themselves for a battle in which they will be slaughtered:

> Announce this among the nations:
>> Prepare a holy war,
>>> wake up the warriors;
>> let all the soldiers draw near,
>>> let them come up!
> Beat the iron tips of your plows into swords
>> and your pruning tools into spears;
>>> let the weakling say, "I am mighty."
> Cut with the sickle,
>> for the harvest is ripe.
> Go and crush grapes,
>> for the winepress is full. (3:9-10, 13)

Joel promises that the Lord will protect Zion and restore the covenant people who have suffered so much at the hands of enemies. In the liminal place where historical time comes to an end, the Lord will be seated as judge in this terrible valley and will destroy the nations for what they have done over the centuries to God's dearly loved people.

Amos

Amos has been cherished in the history of interpretation as the paradigmatic social-justice prophet. The beginning of the book is unique in the prophetic corpus: the reader is startled to encounter oracles against other nations, which are normally in the middle or at the end of prophetic books. Amos leads off with oracles of judgment against other nations in

Amos 1–2, only to turn his indictment against Judah and Israel in what literary critic Robert Alter has called a "rhetoric of entrapment." Notice the rehearsal of God's saving deeds in 2:9-11 toward the end of putting increasing pressure on the unfaithful within Israel. Amos is skilled at using ambiguity, rhetorical questions, sarcasm, and irony.

Artful Ambiguity in Amos

The enigmatic Hebrew phrase "I will not cause it [or him] to return" occurs eight times in Amos 1–2. It is translated in the NRSV as "I will not revoke the punishment" and in the CEB as "I will not hold back the punishment." It functions as a refrain in the poetic rhetoric of entrapment by means of which Amos weaves his opening oracles against other nations into a snare that catches Judah and Israel (2:4-8). James Linville reviews the variety of scholarly proposals, which are multiplied in light of the fact that in biblical Hebrew questions can be unmarked, so something might be a declarative statement or a rhetorical question expecting precisely the converse as the expected answer. Possibilities for the mysterious phrase in Amos include these:

- I will certainly requite him
- I will not intervene
- I will not pass it by
- I will not turn back *or* turn it back [thus NRSV, "I will not revoke"]
- I will not bring him back [from exile]
- Shall I not stop him?
- I will not withdraw it
- Shall I not withdraw it?
- I will not remove it [viz. "the yoke," via revocalizing another word]

Linville writes,

"One must ask to what purpose is the entrapment in Amos. . . . I am of the opinion that such games served a very serious purpose in the religious life of the interpretative community. I hold that such games served to provide focal points for reflection on seemingly contradictory facets of their beliefs about God and Israel's history and destiny. . . . In the attempts to interpret it, to know how to read it, the reader becomes engaged in an exploration of multiple contexts of meaning, as if Yahweh will not be constrained by any single meaning attached to his own words. The problem of manifesting the divine word in human language causes one to suffer the discourse, to explore in detail its intricacies, its impasses and potentials."[11]

Amos 3 is worthy of attention for the way in which this prophet uses the Exodus tradition to stress that Israel's chosenness means that the covenant people are all the more accountable for sin. Notice in 3:12 Amos's gruesome representation of what a hoped-for "rescue" would look like: "two legs or the piece of an ear." In Amos 4, the LORD remembers a series of divine punishments that have failed to effect the people's repentance. If one wanted to muster a deconstructive reading of the notion of retributive justice, one could argue that here the LORD seems to admit powerlessness to change the heart of God's people. The divine speech serves to confirm the ineffectiveness of divine punishment as a means to coerce covenant loyalty. A resistant reader might argue that this text opens up a subversive space in which one can argue against the notion that retributive justice works.

Many, including myself, would argue that the heart of Amos's theology can be found in Amos 5, where we see three powerful exhortations that express well the prophetic hope to catalyze repentance in the hearers. The first is, of course, spoken by the LORD.

- "Seek me and live." (5:4)
- "Seek the LORD and live." (5:6)
- "Seek good and not evil,
   that you may live;
         and so the LORD, the God of heaven forces,
   will be with you just as you have said." (5:14)

Amos 5:21-24 gives us the prophet's well-known critique of worship without a commitment to justice in the worshipping community, and his stirring call for social justice, "Let justice roll down like waters, and righteousness like an ever-flowing stream" (5:24). What Amos has in mind here is no bucolic creek but, instead, a dry riverbed overwhelmed with the roiling waters of a flash flood. God's justice will be a torrent sweeping away every act of injustice, every scheme against the disadvantaged, every gesture of brutality toward the marginalized, every posture of callous indifference to the suffering of the poor. The power of Amos 5:24 was highlighted during the U.S. civil rights movement, when it was deployed many times by Martin Luther King Jr., including in his "I Have a Dream" speech in August 1963 in Washington, DC, and in a March 1965 essay for *The Nation*.

Brilliant ironic reversals are effected in Amos that ironize many aspects of Israel's self-understanding.[12] Amos draws his audience in with deceptively simple rhetorical questions such as "Does a lion roar in the forest when it has no prey?" and "Will a bird fall into a trap on the ground when there is no bait for it?" (3:4-5), these building in a crescendo of threat as the audience slowly realizes they are assenting to a series of signs that judgment is coming upon them. Punishments that the LORD has sent, per Amos 4 (famine, drought, blight, mildew, locust, pestilence, war), have not had the effect of driving sinful believers back to the One who is powerful to destroy and redeem. The expert hearer gradually realizes that these afflictions are named in almost the same order in Solomon's prayer in 1 Kings 8:35-40 (drought, famine, pestilence, blight, mildew, locust, war), where the point of the prayer is that the people can save themselves only if they "pray toward this place [the Jerusalem temple], give thanks to your name, and turn away from their sin."[13] The Day of the LORD (5:18-20) will be a day of inescapable entrapment: here Amos ironizes the audience's hope that they might be able to flee from the LORD's wrath. Irony may be found also in the confrontation between Amos and Amaziah in Amos 7. In this dialogue, Amos skillfully understates his authority: he is no professional guild prophet but simply a "trimmer of sycamore trees" who has been commissioned by the LORD to prophesy (7:14-15). The disclaimer, of course, subtly emphasizes that the true power in this conflictual situation is wielded neither by the king whom Amaziah seeks to protect nor by Amos himself, but by the LORD.

Amos offers three hymns to the LORD that are designed to intimidate the implied audience. The first hymn is the shortest; the second is longer and its imagery is more frightening, and the third is the longest and most alarming. The series grows in intensity, heightening the audience's perception of the Creator's power and the inescapability of doom.

First doxology:

> The one who forms the mountains,
>
>> creates the wind,

> makes known his thoughts
>> to humankind,
> makes the morning darkness,
>> and moves over the heights of the earth—
>> the Lord, the God of heavenly forces is his name! (4:13)

Second doxology:

> The one who made
>> the Pleiades and Orion,
> and turns deep darkness
>>> into the morning,
> and darkens the day into night;
> who summons the waters of the sea,
>> and pours them out
>>> on the surface of the earth—
> this one's name is the Lord—
> who causes destruction to flash out
>> against the strong,
>> so that destruction comes
>>> upon the fortress. (5:8-9)

Third doxology:

> The Lord, God of heavenly forces,
>> touches the earth and it melts,
>> and all who live in it are sick to death.
> All of it rises up like the Nile
>> and sinks again,
>>> like the Nile of Egypt.
> It is the Lord who builds
>> his upper rooms in the heavens
>> and establishes his residence
>>> upon the earth;

189

> who summons the waters of the sea,
>
>> and pours them out
>>
>>> upon the face of the earth—
>>>
>>> the LORD is his name. (9:5-6)

With these hymns, Amos's implied audience finds itself in an impossible position. They dare not dissent from these celebrations of God's might. Yet standing with Amos in the posture of doxology requires them to perceive the destructive power of a God who advances precisely in order to punish them. Francis Andersen and David Noel Freedman observe that in these hymns, "the most ominous threat of all is that every act of creation can be canceled, the work reversed and undone."[14] Even more ominous may be the implication that Israel itself, the people chosen to be God's "treasured possession" (Deut 7:6 NRSV), whom the LORD had "formed and made" (Isa 43:7), can be unmade in a moment by the One who commands darkness, floods, lightning, and earthquakes.

Amos twists and reverses the Exodus traditions, using subtle word-play and reconfigurations of the significance of the Exodus as a way to attack the complacency of his audience, undermining their confidence in Israel's election as God's chosen people. When Amos cites the Exodus, he does not celebrate the LORD's deliverance of Israel from slavery or miraculous provision for Israel in the wilderness. In Amos's caustic prophesying, Israel's deliverance from Egypt serves as forensic evidence that proves their accountability for sin: "Hear this word that the LORD has spoken against you, people of Israel, against the whole family that I brought out of the land of Egypt: You only have I loved so deeply of all the families of the earth. Therefore, I will punish you for all your wrongdoing" (3:1-2).

In 5:17 and 8:2, the LORD proclaims imminent judgment against Israel: "In all the vineyards there will be bitter crying because I will pass through your midst [to destroy], says the LORD" (5:17), and "The end has come upon my people Israel; I will never again pass them by" (NRSV, in the sense of sparing them from punishment). In both passages, the verb used is the same verb as that in Exodus 12:12 describing the LORD's passing through to strike down the firstborn of Egypt. Here the unspoken meaning reverses the security Israel enjoyed during the ancient first Passover of the messenger of death in Egypt. A few verses further on, Amos alludes obliquely to two of the ten plagues that the LORD had inflicted on Egypt in the time of the Exodus:

> On that day, says the Lord GOD,
>> I will make the sun go down at noon,
>> and I will darken the earth
>>> in broad daylight. (8:9; compare Exod 10:21-23)

> I will make it like the mourning for an only son,
>> and the end of it like a bitter day. (8:10 NRSV; compare Exod 12:29-30)

Finally, Amos shocks his audience by suggesting that their deliverance from Egypt had, after all, been just one of many acts of redemption that the LORD had performed for peoples of the earth: "Haven't I brought Israel up from the land of Egypt, and the Philistines from Caphtor and the Arameans from Kir?" (9:7). Amos will not let his audience rely on anything other than earnest—indeed desperate—repentance. By the time the book of Amos has concluded, the prophet has left not a scrap of complacency or pride with which his people might cover themselves. Exposed and vulnerable, they seek the LORD, that they might live.

Obadiah

Obadiah is an oracle against Edom. Its historical setting is uncertain. The shortest book in the Hebrew Scriptures, Obadiah packs quite a punch in its invective against Edom for assisting the Babylonians when they sacked Jerusalem. Obadiah calls to mind the close fraternal ties between Israel and Edom, represented in the Genesis stories of origin in twin brothers Jacob and Esau. Obadiah gives us a vivid picture of Judah's venomous response to betrayal by a close neighbor:

191

Because of the slaughter and violence

    done to your brother Jacob,

        shame will cover you,

        and you will be destroyed forever.

You stood nearby,

        strangers carried off his wealth,

    and foreigners entered his gates

        and cast lots for Jerusalem;

    you too were like one of them.

You shouldn't have waited on the roads

        to destroy his escapees;

    you shouldn't have handed over

        his survivors on the day of defeat. (Obad 10-11, 14)

Jonah

Many narratives in the Hebrew Scriptures have been written with a degree of literary skill that goes underappreciated. Even brief stories show hallmarks of scribal sophistication: attention to salient details of character, subtly revealed; freighted silences in which the reader is meant to connect seemingly disparate pieces of information; gradual unfolding of the particular significance of matters through dialogue between characters; and more. In the Hebrew Scriptures, we find several longer prose pieces that have been crafted with exquisite artfulness. The authors responsible for these exemplars of ancient scribal genius show an unusual depth of insight into human character, exceptional skill at designing plot elements and suspenseful pacing, and a gift for chiseled yet revelatory dialogue that can leave a contemporary literary critic agape in admiration. These gem-like longer pieces include the Joseph material in Genesis 37–50, the books of Ruth and Esther, and the prophetic book of Jonah.

Narrative Artistry in Biblical Hebrew Prose

"An essential aim of the innovative technique of fiction worked out by the ancient Hebrew writers was to produce a certain indeterminacy of meaning, especially in regard to motive, moral character, and psychology. . . . Meaning, perhaps for the first time in narrative history, was conceived as a *process*, requiring continual revision—both in the ordinary sense and in the etymological sense of seeing-again—continual suspension of judgment, weighing of multiple possibilities, brooding over gaps in the information provided."

—Robert Alter[15]

"The depth with which human nature is imagined in the Bible is a function of its being conceived as caught in the powerful interplay of this double dialectic between design and disorder, providence and freedom."

—Robert Alter[16]

"The Bible's verbal artistry, without precedent in literary history and unrivaled since, operates by passing off its art for artlessness, its sequential linkages and supra-sequential echoes for unadorned parataxis, its density of evocation for chronicle-like thinness and transparency."

—Meir Sternberg[17]

"[Consider] the general strategy of disclosure whereby the given does not suffice and the sufficient is not given in time or at all. In its application to character portrayal, this strategy manifests itself in a distributed, often oblique and tortuous unfolding of features. So reading a character becomes a process of discovery, attended by all the biblical hallmarks: progressive reconstruction, tentative closure of discontinuities, frequent and sometimes painful reshaping in face of the unexpected, and intractable pockets of darkness to the very end."

—Meir Sternberg[18]

The story of Jonah is one in which plot twists and unexpected developments leave the reader pondering whether what one had been thinking earlier could still hold true. The subtleties of characterization here are marvelous. Far from the wrenching struggles of the earnest and overwhelmed Jeremiah in the grip of the prophetic vocation, equally far from the bold agency of the priest Ezekiel in his authoritative pronouncements and dramatic sign-acts to lay bare the sinfulness of his compatriots, Jonah is a reluctant prophet who offers almost nothing for the prophetic task. When the Lord commissions Jonah to deliver an indictment against Nineveh, capital of Assyria and home of the king of one of Israel's most relentless enemies, Jonah wordlessly takes off in the opposite direction.

All that transpires in the plot, then, is refracted through the planes and sharp angles of Jonah's recalcitrant personality. Through what is said and what is left unspoken, we are invited to consider his emotions, his integrity, his understanding of prophetic vocation, his perspicacity, and his reliability as speaker. That last is a notion from literary criticism. In literatures throughout the centuries and across cultures, storytellers have known how to create characters that are heroic and characters that are weak, or perhaps appealing but with a fatal flaw; characters whose voices are rendered as utterly reliable, characters who clearly are responding from self-interest or woundedness or one of an infinite number of other generative problems sketched or hinted at in their backstories, and characters whom the discerning reader is meant to understand as unreliable. Interpreters also inquire into the character of the Lord in this compelling short story. Some pay particular attention—as the story itself seems to directs us, through its narrative art—to the question of why the Lord pursues Jonah so relentlessly. Many characters in the Bible, whether protagonists or foils, are represented as at least partially unreliable in particular narrative moments. Perhaps the narrator has made clear that they lack necessary information, or the reader can see that they withhold information, or we are led to believe that they don't understand what is at stake. Perhaps a character is undermined by their own flaws even though trying to do right. Then there are those who indeed are sketched as evil, motivated by ignoble aims, and so on. As you read this story, be aware that Jonah is not necessarily being represented by the ancient author as a hero, as beloved by God, as an effective prophet, or as an example to be emulated by believers. In Jonah 1, with the disobedient Jonah making for Tarshish aboard ship, the narrator gives us a strong cue that Jonah is less faithful than others. A "great storm" is created by the LORD, and the narrator shows Jonah deep in slumber in the hold even as giant waves threaten to capsize the boat. Jonah is oblivious to the LORD's will and to these dramatic signs of divine displeasure, while by contrast, each of the sailors appeals to his own deity. When it has become clear that Jonah is the cause of their straits, the sailors have misgivings about throwing him into the sea and pray fervently before acceding to his wishes. They are good and faithful men, these sailors. Many alert readers have seen their strength of character as designed to show Jonah in a poor light by comparison.

The narrative arc of Jonah is delightfully complex. After the initial exposition, our protagonist undergoes two major conflicts, and there are two separate resolutions or "endings" to the book. His time spent in the briny deep constitutes the first conflict to which Jonah must respond—and respond he does, with an elaborate psalm (Jon 2) that he prays from the belly of the fish that has swallowed him. Many readers over the centuries have heard the psalm as earnest in tone, reading it as a turning point for Jonah spiritually, the dark moment in which he realizes his dependence on the LORD and begs for divine assistance with a repentant heart. An alternative: with some other scholars, I hear the psalm as devastatingly ironic, and in that way fully congruent with its larger literary context. Jonah uses metaphors from the Psalms in a literal way that is meant to be taken perhaps as simply hilarious, but more likely as evidence that he has no clue about the real force of his sacred traditions or that he is willfully manipulating sacred tropes. For example, "You had cast me into the depths in the heart of the seas, and the flood surrounds me" (2:3) would normally be spoken as metaphor in a liturgical psalm (see Ps 42:7: "Deep called to deep at the noise of your waterfalls; all your massive waves surged over me"), but Jonah means it literally. It's as if Jonah were to mouth piously, "You drew me up from the desolate pit, out of the miry bog" (Ps 40:2 NRSV), just after he, through his own fault, had fallen into an actual swamp and needed someone to throw him a line. Jonah prays, "Deliverance belongs to the LORD!"(2:9)—a true statement, but surely ironic in the mouth of this prophet who wants nothing to do with the task the Lord has set before him. A venerable line of interpretation with which I agree is that the fish, hearing pieties from a character who is so transparently unreliable and manipulative, regurgitates him onto the shore in a paroxysm of disgust (2:10).

Jonah trudges to Nineveh and shouts one short clause of admonishment, and all of Nineveh falls to its knees in repentance. Those attentive to irony in Jonah may not be able to concur with the position of some that Jonah is about mercy for Assyria. Within the plot, the Lord does choose to withhold punishment on this notorious city. But consider the absurdly prompt and comprehensive repentance of all in Nineveh upon hearing a few surly words from a bedraggled stranger. This hyperbolic repentance of every single creature, down to the animals wearing sackcloth and enduring an enforced fast from food and water, surely flags that it is not the earnest faithfulness of the worthy Assyrians that is cueing the Lord's mercy. A historical aside: Nineveh was destroyed in 612 by the Babylonians. If Jonah was composed later than that, which many scholars believe, then the audience would have known well that Nineveh had been destroyed. In light of this, some scholars argue that God's grace to a brutal enemy nation could never have been the central point of the story, since the audience in real life knew that Nineveh had been obliterated already. Divine mercy is about something else, in the unspoken message of this dazzling ironic text. It may be about the Lord's sovereignty, or about the woeful lack of mercy God has shown God's own people by comparison, or about the stubborn malfeasance of even Israel's prophets compared to the instantaneous repentance of the cruelest enemy Israel had ever known. Mercy in Jonah is no simple thing.

So what is the point of the Jonah story? Many different interpretations have been offered in the rich history of reception of this book. Here are three views that have strong proponents in the scholarship on Jonah:

(1) the book aims to demonstrate the Lord's sovereignty over all nations;

(2) the book celebrates the Lord's unexpected grace to the least worthy;

(3) the book is an ironic protest about the LORD's not having been merciful to Israel.

As you reflect on Jonah, you may find that your own view of the book changes mercurially as you hold first one narrative element, then another to the light. One thing is certain: the book of Jonah is a brilliant piece of ancient narrative. With Jonah, we may muse on the notion of prophetic vocation with a deeper understanding of the potentially razor-sharp ironies involved.

Micah

Micah prophesied toward the end of the eighth century BCE, so he was likely a younger contemporary of Hosea and Amos and a peer of Isaiah of Jerusalem. Micah 1–3 comprises the first section, which many scholars consider to go back to the original prophet Micah, with the exception of 2:12-13. Micah 4–5 is replete with exilic and postexilic themes, including an eschatological view of the nations streaming to Zion and a hope for a messianic Davidic ruler, so this material is considered by most scholars to have been composed centuries later, as faithful scribes reflected on and amplified the earlier material. Micah opens with searing oracles of judgment in Micah 1–3. In Micah 1, notice the compelling downward trajectory in the opening images: the LORD comes down to "tread on the shrines of the earth" (1:3), mountains and valleys are reduced to rubble pouring down steep slopes (1:4), Samaria is then broken down into rubble in the valley (1:6), and its images are pulverized into dust left on the ground (1:7). Note the gendered imagery of Judah as female sex worker (1:7) and bereaved mother (1:16; the imperatives there are in the feminine singular). You may enjoy the way in which Micah characterizes his opponents with blistering sarcasm in 2:6-11. We can almost see the prophet rolling his eyes in aggravation:

> "They mustn't preach!" so they preach.
>> "They mustn't preach of such things!
>> Disgrace won't overtake us."

(Should this be said, house of Jacob?)

"Is the LORD's patience cut short?

Are these his deeds?"

Don't my words help

the one who behaves righteously?

If someone were to go about inspired

and say deceitfully:

"I will preach to you

for wine and liquor,"

such a one would be

the preacher for this people! (2:6-7, 11)

Elsewhere in the Latter Prophets, too, is reported discourse that reveals traces of communal opposition to the prophetic word. The prophets ventriloquize the antagonists who have dismissed them as wrong, misguided, or irrelevant.

Opposition to the Biblical Prophets

Isaiah's adversaries mock: "Whom will he teach knowledge, and to whom will he explain the message? Those who are weaned from milk, those taken from the breast? For it is 'tsav letsav, tsav letsav; qav leqav, qav leqav,' here a little, there a little." (Isa 28:9-10 NRSV)

Jeremiah's adversaries connive: "But I was like a gentle lamb led to the slaughter. And I did not know it was against me that they devised schemes, saying, 'Let us destroy the tree with its fruit, let us cut him off from the land of the living, so that his name will no longer be remembered.'" (Jer 11:19 NRSV)

Ezekiel's adversaries flatter: "As for you, human one, your people talk about you beside the walls and in their doorways. One by one, they say to each other, 'Let's go hear what sort of message has come from the LORD.' So they come to you as people do, and they sit before you as my people. They listen to your words, but they refuse to do them. Though they speak of their longing for me, they act out of their own interests and opinions. To them you are like a singer of love songs with a lovely voice and skilled technique. They listen to your words, but no one does them." (Ezek 33:30-32)

Hosea's adversaries taunt: "The days of punishment have come; the days of judgment have arrived; Israel cries, 'The prophet is a fool, the spiritual man is mad!' Because of your great wickedness, your rejection of me is great." (Hos 9:7)

Micah's adversaries scold: "'They mustn't preach!' so they preach. 'They mustn't preach of such things! Disgrace won't overtake us.'" (Mic 2:6)

Micah 3 offers several memorable moments of prophetic rhetorical art. First, in a viscerally powerful image, Micah indicts unjust Judean leaders for cannibalizing their people: "But I said: Hear, leaders of Jacob, rulers of the house of Israel! Isn't it your job to know justice?—you who hate good and love evil, who tear the skin off them, and the flesh off their bones, who devour the flesh of my people, tear off their skin, break their bones in pieces, and spread them out as if in a pot, like meat in a kettle" (3:1-3).

Micah proceeds by denigrating the false prophets and claiming his own prophetic charism as given by the LORD. Then comes his prophecy that Zion will be levelled by enemies, an oracle that would come to play an important role in the dramatic narrative of conflict in Jeremiah 26:

> But me! I am filled with power,
>> with the spirit of the LORD,
>> with justice and might,
>> to declare to Jacob his wrongdoing
>> and to Israel his sin! (3:8)

> Hear this, leaders of the house of Jacob,
>> rulers of the house of Israel,
> you who reject justice
>> and make crooked all that is straight,
> who build Zion with bloodshed
>> and Jerusalem with injustice!
> Her officials give justice for a bribe,
>> and her priests teach for hire.
> Her prophets offer divination for silver,

> yet they rely on the LORD, saying,
> > "Isn't the LORD in our midst?
> > Evil won't come upon us!"
> Therefore, because of you,
> > Zion will be plowed like a field,
> > > Jerusalem will become piles of rubble,
> > > > and the temple mount will become
> > > > an overgrown mound. (3:9-12)

Micah 4:1-7 presents an eschatological vision of Zion being recognized by all nations as the cosmic center of the universe. Jerusalem is the seat of Torah instruction, and the nations yearn to know the LORD. (You may recall that this prophecy appears almost verbatim in Isaiah 2.) Micah 5 is well known for its promise that a messianic ruler is to come from Bethlehem to inaugurate a reign of peace (5:2-5), a prophecy reflected in early Christian traditions about Jesus. Micah 5:2 is the source for the Phillips Brooks hymn, "O Little Town of Bethlehem." One of the most beloved passages in the Latter Prophets is Micah 6:1-8, a poem framed as a legal dispute between the LORD and Israel, the so-called covenant lawsuit form that had analogues in other ancient Near Eastern cultures. Micah calls the mountains and hills—the "ancient foundations of the earth" (NRSV)—as witnesses against Israel. The case is presented: recital of the LORD's holy deeds on behalf of Israel, with special emphasis on the opportunities they'd had to heed the Torah and the prophets. As you've already seen with Ezekiel and Amos, so too Micah is dexterous and innovative in his mining of Israel's sacred traditions: Aaron and Miriam are mentioned only here in the Latter Prophets, and one wonders whether they are ambiguous figures here—Aaron having taking initiative in the golden calf debacle (Exod 32) and Miriam having contested Moses's authority (Num 12)—or are cited simply as a trio of venerable leaders. The evocative formulation in 6:5, "Remember everything from Shittim to Gilgal," has occasioned much scholarly dialogue about the precise nuance of meaning. The mention of Balaam and Shittim draws the audience's attention to Numbers 22–25, Shittim being a featured site in Hosea's cartography of Israel's sin as well.

Thus it may be that this recital in 6:4-5 is intended to underline that the LORD has saved Israel repeatedly even despite Israel's own malfeasance. There is artistic heightening in the poetry, with the rhetorical questions in 6:6-7 moving from animal sacrifice to hyperbolic quantities of offerings ("thousands of rams" and "ten thousands of rivers of oil") to the suggested sacrifice of the speaker's oldest male child. This progressive elevation of the stakes yields a stirring answer as to what is incalculably more precious than any of the other offerings. To "do justice, embrace faithful love, and walk humbly with your God" (6:8) is all the LORD has ever asked, and it constitutes the pinnacle of right ethics and right worship. Micah 6:8 has long been appreciated as an excellent grounding for theologies of social justice. It has been interpreted as a summary of the entire Torah and as a prism through which the life of faith may be viewed.

Micah 7 moves from a psalm-like lament over the dissolute and violent state of human relationships to a claim that the speaker will be vindicated by God and that God's people will once again know God's power for healing and victory. The lament in Micah 7 works beautifully to create an *inclusio*, an envelope structure where something is introduced at the beginning and then revoiced at the end. There are two elements in chiastic or "mirroring" order, as you'd see in the structure of a poem built on an ABB'A' rhyme scheme. In Micah 1 we have imagery of the LORD coming in judgment, then the lament of the prophet in 1:8. Mirroring that, in Micah 7 you have these themes in reverse order: the lament of Zion and the prophet's assurance that the LORD will save. This structure is an artful way to show the hoped-for reversal of the dynamic of judgment.

> **1:2-7** The peoples and earth are called to listen as YHWH appears in mighty judgment

> **1:8** "On account of this, I will cry out and howl;
>
> I will go about barefoot and stripped.
>
> I will cry out like the jackals,
>
> and mourn like the ostriches."

7:1-7 "I'm doomed! I've become like one who, even after the summer fruit has been gathered, after the ripened fruits have been collected, has no cluster of grapes to eat, no ripe fig that I might desire." (7:1).

7:14-20 The ears of the nations "will be deaf" as Yʜᴡʜ appears in mighty compassion

Lamentation is featured more fully in the opening chapters of Micah as well. In 1:10-16, Micah bids a series of towns—some of them obscure—to lament. The first imperative, "In Gath tell it not," is interesting because it is a direct quotation drawn from 2 Samuel 1, where David laments the deaths of Saul and Jonathan and sings, "Oh, no, Israel! Your prince lies dead on your heights. Look how the mighty warriors have fallen! Don't talk about it in Gath; don't bring news of it to Ashkelon's streets, or else the Philistines' daughters will rejoice" (2 Sam 1:19-20). Francis Andersen and David Noel Freedman note that Micah here is evoking "one of the worst disasters to befall the monarchical institution of Israel, nothing less than the termination of a dynasty."[19] The audience hears "no need to weep there" (1:10) because the tragedy is too grave. In subsequent verses, the implicit addressees are adjured to "roll yourself in the dust," "pass by . . . in nakedness and shame," "wail," and "make yourselves bald and cut off your hair because of your cherished children . . . for they have gone from you into exile." The coming disaster is inescapable, "an evil against this family from which you will not be able to remove your necks" (2:3). Those whom Micah indicts will "wail bitterly: 'We are utterly destroyed!'" (2:4). By this point, it has become clear that the prophet is evoking the idea of lament as a way of indicting rich oppressors for their practices that disempower others.

Finally, I draw your attention to the way in which the prophet and God are voiced in the opening of the book. In Jeremiah, there are places where the prophet's voice and the voice of God seem to blur, and then places where the prophet's voice stands over against God. Hermeneutically, we may say that the prophet utters both God's voice and his own voice, offers both God and not-God in his speech. Theologically, we glimpse the prophet standing in that excruciating liminal place between the divine and the human, seeing all with agonizing clarity, speaking sometimes on behalf of the one, and sometimes on behalf of the other. We may see this discursive liminality in Micah too, this blurring of voices. The lamenting in 1:8-9 comes from the prophet. On one level, that seems clear enough. In the ancient scribal imagination, Micah is the only one who could go barefoot; that would not be likely predicated of the deity even metaphorically. But also, because the "I" of the preceding verses is the LORD, the prophet's voice blends with the divine voice. Timothy Beal argues that the voice we hear in Micah 1:8-9 is God's voice. He presses the case that the text is purposefully ambiguous and argues that there are clues to the speaker's identity as God. For example, he notes that the phrase "my people" (1:9) is used in the Hebrew Bible overwhelmingly with the LORD as the speaker (104 times) and only five times with the prophet as speaker. On Beal's reading of Micah, "We find YHWH making radical shifts between devastating wrath on the one hand and wild dirge-like lament on the other"; this reveals a "profound divine ambivalence" about God's own punishing of the people. Beal says Micah gives us the remarkable image of God lamenting "like the jackals . . . roam[ing] through the cities, among the piles of unclean corpses, his howls echoing through the barren buildings."[20] He suggests that we see here the "very character of God unraveling,"[21] something that we might postulate of the fractured and raging character of God in Hosea as well.

On the strength of the chiastic structure of Micah 1 and 7, we might consider Micah 7 to reconstitute this LORD who had become wild with grief, who had become unraveled in this text. In Micah 7, the prophet reminds God who God had been and who God should be again: "Shepherd your people with your staff, the sheep of your inheritance, those dwelling alone in a forest in the midst of Carmel. Let them graze in Bashan and Gilead, as a long time ago. As in the days when you came out of the land of Egypt, I will show Israel wonderful things" (Mic 7:14-15). Micah prophesies in the name of a God who has come down (Mic 1) and perhaps even become grief-stricken in the trauma of judging the covenant people. Micah prophesies also to that God, calling God back to the divine compassion that constitutes who God is.

Nahum

The prophet Nahum directs oracles of doom against Nineveh, the capital of Assyria. Its images are vivid and dramatic. The tone of unbridled vengeance in this short book is intense, presenting a challenge for the contemporary interpreter concerned with ethics and biblical authority. Verses that describe the LORD bellowing at adversaries, "I will make your grave, for you are worthless" (1:14), violently exposing their nakedness in a public shaming gesture that invites sexual violation (3:5), and throwing filth upon them (3:5) will be repugnant for many readers of Scripture who are dedicated to peace-making ("Happy are people who make peace, because they will be called God's children," Matt 5:9) and those who take seriously the command to love one's enemies ("Love your enemies. Do good to those who hate you. Bless those who curse you. Pray for those who mistreat you," Luke 6:27-28).

Nahum is assuredly artful in evoking battle scenes. Nahum 2:3-4 and 3:2-3 depict the Divine Warrior, the LORD, besieging Nineveh. The images of the overwhelmed city are hypnotically terrifying:

> The shields of his warriors are red;
>> his soldiers are dressed in crimson.
> The ironwork of the chariots
>> flashes like fire
>>> on the day he has prepared;
>>>> the horses quiver.
> The chariots race wildly
>> through the streets;
>>> they rush back and forth
>>>> through the squares.
> They look like flaming torches;
>> they dart like bolts of lightning. . . .

Cracking whip and rumbling wheel,
    galloping horse and careening chariot!
Charging cavalry, flashing sword,
    and glittering spear;
      countless slain, masses of corpses,
        endless dead bodies—they stumble
          over their dead bodies! (Nah 2:3-4; 3:2-3)

Some scholars justify this kind of poetry by noting how cruel Assyria was, and indeed, the ancient nation was infamous for torturing captives. But the besieging of a city would have captured everyone there in a net of horror. As you consider this poetry's sustained focus on vengeance and bloodshed, remember that such military onslaughts caused the suffering and deaths of countless noncombatants. Some interpreters take the more abstract view that this florid rhetoric was designed to bolster the Judean audience and would not necessarily have been enacted against flesh-and-blood enemies. But history has shown that violent rhetoric can do terrible damage to intended targets, unintended victims, and even those who have set themselves up as the ones with power to harm. Such rhetoric perpetuates a culture of brutality with pernicious effects that can distort the views of religious communities for generations or even centuries. So if you are a reader who honors this scriptural text and the many other prophetic texts that relish the slaughter of enemies, I encourage you to consider how you might adopt a posture of resistance to this language, which is certainly the product of trauma but enacts new harm in its own way.

If you're searching for something relevant for transformative work against oppressive structures, you might note in Nahum 3:18-19 the prophet's sarcastic baiting of the king of Assyria. One could read those lines to imply that no earthly malevolent power can stand against God's justice. The unusual move of ending the book with a rhetorical question (3:19) is reminiscent of the ending of Jonah. Given that both Jonah and Nahum are intensely concerned with Nineveh, this literary similarity may not be coincidental. Finally, to Nahum's pointed question, "For who has ever escaped your endless cruelty?" (NRSV) the implied audience may be spurred to answer that they themselves have escaped the grip of Assyria. They have survived to read or hear the book of Nahum, and to celebrate the invincible might of YHWH over those who would subjugate the covenant people.

Habakkuk

Habakkuk 1 opens with a striking dialogue between the prophet and God. The prophet laments the violence and unrighteousness he sees all around him:

> LORD, how long will I call for help and you not listen? I cry out to you, "Violence!" but you don't deliver us. Why do you show me injustice and look at anguish so that devastation and violence are before me? There is strife, and conflict abounds. (1:2-3)

The LORD answers in a way that would strike terror into the implied audience:

> Look among the nations and watch! Be astonished and stare because something is happening in your days that you wouldn't believe even if told. I am about to rouse the Chaldeans, that bitter and impetuous nation. . . . The Chaldean is dreadful and fearful. He makes his own justice and dignity. His horses are faster than leopards; they are quicker than wolves of the evening. (1:5-8)

As in Isaiah and Jeremiah, so here God plans to deploy an enemy nation, the Babylonians, to serve the divine purposes. How is this a response to the prophet's initial lament? It seems to be of the genre, "I'll give you something to cry about": the violence scourging the prophet's community currently is as nothing compared with the horrors that will be wreaked by the Chaldean invaders. The prophet begs for mercy, affirming YHWH's power as the Holy One from primordial time who cannot abide injustice and will not abandon this righteous covenant people to destruction.

In Habakkuk 2 the prophet resolves to stand as sentinel (see Ezek 3), waiting watchfully for YHWH's response. The LORD then addresses the

206

powerful among the people with a series of woes, quoting other sacred traditions in these indictments. We hear an echo of Jeremiah 51:58 ("People labor in vain; nations toil for nothing but ashes!"), the theme of the cup of wrath (Jer 25 and elsewhere), and an echo of Second Isaiah's polemic against useless idols. In Habakkuk 2:20 is a striking admonition that has been used in liturgical traditions as a call to worship: "But the LORD is in his holy temple. Let all the earth be silent before him."

"Let All Mortal Flesh Keep Silence," verse 1

Let all mortal flesh keep silence,
and with fear and trembling stand;
ponder nothing earthly-minded,
for with blessing in his hand
Christ our God to earth descendeth,
our full homage to demand.

Words: Liturgy of St. James, paraphrased by Gerard Moultrie (1829–1885)
Tune: Picardy, seventeenth-century French carol

Habakkuk 3 is presented as a prayer of the prophet, reinforcing the sense we had at the beginning of the book of a psalm-like form. It raises for us the interesting question of psalm-like material perhaps having been added later to prophetic books. Some scholars argue that the psalm-like material in Jonah 2, Micah 7, and Habakkuk 3 was all added later to their books. The effects of interpolations raise fascinating questions about how biblical books signify through shifts of style and new voicings. Habakkuk 3 opens up the discourse of Habakkuk again after the powerful closing verse at the end of chapter 2 had exhorted all to bow in silence before the might of the Holy One. The move to reopen dialogue amplifies the possibility of resistance. Habakkuk, it would seem, is deeply divided in the prophetic vocation. He says in one breath, "the LORD is in his holy temple. Let all the earth be silent before him" (2:20), and then in the next breath, he cannot keep silence despite what he has just prophesied, so he bursts forth with,

> Lord, I have heard your reputation.
>> I have seen your work.
> Over time, revive it.
>> Over time, make it known.
> Though angry, remember compassion. (3:2)

The prophet cannot contain his urgent pleading on behalf of his people. Standing in that threshold place, he sees the holiness of God and bids all to keep silence before the majesty of the Lord—yet he himself must cry out, reminding the Lord of the divine redemptive deeds of old and insisting that the Lord show mercy to the covenant people "over time." A courageous witness indeed! Habakkuk offers a beautiful recital of the Lord's saving deeds (3:3-15), offering a Scripture lesson for the implied audience about what they believe even as he calls the Lord to act as the Divine Warrior once again. Note that this extended mythopoetic portrayal manages to evoke primordial Israelite traditions, the Lord's defeat of the Egyptians at the Red Sea, and the miraculous victory of Joshua against a Canaanite coalition (3:10-11; Josh 10:1-14). Immediately following a stirring image of the Lord "churning the mighty waters" (NRSV), the voice of the prophet becomes subdued as he reminds the Lord what is (still) at stake for a people trembling at the approach of calamity. The concluding notes of praise seem virtually to sing the desired presence of a delivering God into the midst of the worshipping community. As Amos had prophesied, it is especially in times of deprivation and threat that Israel must "Seek the Lord and live" (5:6). Habakkuk knows this truth, and so he sings for all he is worth: "though the olive crop withers, and the fields don't provide food . . . I will rejoice in the Lord. I will rejoice in the God of my deliverance" (3:17-18). He sings, and his community is strengthened to survive another day.

Zephaniah

Zephaniah seethes with oracles of judgment against Judah and Jerusalem. It opens with a broad lens on the Lord's coming judgment of the earth ("I will wipe out everything from the earth, says the Lord," 1:2), then focuses in on idolatrous priests and people. The LORD will find the miscreants wherever they may hide. The dread of a wrathful deity coming to find and destroy, portrayed powerfully in Amos 9 and subtly hinted at in Psalm 139, can also be seen here in Zephaniah 1:12, which has the deity ruthlessly "searching Jerusalem with lamps" to root out evildoers.

God as Relentless Pursuer	
The LORD speaking to Amos: I saw the LORD standing beside the altar, and the LORD said: Strike the pillars until the foundations shake, shatter them on the heads of all the people. With the sword, I will kill the last of them; not one of them will flee, not one of them will escape. If they dig through into the underworld, from there my hand will take them. If they climb up to the heavens, from there I will bring them down. If they hide themselves on the top of Carmel, I will search for them there and remove them. If they hide from my sight at the bottom of the sea, I will give an order to the sea serpent, and it will bite them. If they are forced from their homes before their enemies, there I will give an order to the sword, and it will kill them. (Amos 9:1-4)	Amos 9
Job speaking to God: What are human beings, that you exalt them, that you take note of them, visit them each morning, test them every moment? Why not look away from me; let me alone until I swallow my spit? (Job 7:17-19)	Job 7
The psalmist speaking to God: Where could I go to get away from your spirit? Where could I go to escape your presence? If I went up to heaven, you would be there. If I went down to the grave, you would be there too! If I could fly on the wings of dawn, stopping to rest only on the far side of the ocean—even there your hand would guide me; even there your strong hand would hold me tight! If I said, "The darkness will definitely hide me; the light will become night around me," even then the darkness isn't too dark for you! Nighttime would shine bright as day, because darkness is the same as light to you! (Ps 139:7-12)	Psalm 139

The theme of the Day of the LORD is in view here (1:14-16). In Zephaniah 2, the prophet's rhetoric broadens its scope to include punishment of Philistia, Moab, Ammon, and Assyria; the Ethiopians, not usually a target of biblical prophets' wrath, face judgment as well (2:12). Zephaniah envisions the Day of the LORD as a terrifying sacrifice, with the offering to be none other than the guests whom the LORD has consecrated (1:7). We see here an amplification of Amos's insight that the Day of the LORD will be darkness: Zephaniah thunders that it will be "a day of fury, a day of distress and anxiety, a day of desolation and devastation, a day of darkness and gloominess, a day of clouds and deep darkness. . . . Their blood will be poured out like dust and their intestines like manure. . . . His jealousy will devour the entire land with fire" (1:15, 17-18).

Zephaniah 3 indicts Jerusalem for injustice, its leaders depicted as "roaring lions" and "wolves of the evening," terrors to their own people (3:3). They have failed to recognize the LORD's correcting hand in their disaster (3:7), just as in Amos 4; the LORD complains that the people have failed to interpret the significance of crisis after crisis as a spur to repent and return to the LORD. In Zephaniah 3:9 is an intriguing promise: God will "change the speech of the peoples into pure speech, that all of them will call on the name of the LORD and will serve him as one." Some interpreters take this to mean that people will no longer speak the false speech of idolatry,[22] while others see it as a reversal of the curse laid on humankind at the dawn of human culture, in the Tower of Babel story (see Gen 11). The latter reading might be supported by the emphasis, two verses further, on the LORD planning to "remove from your midst those boasting with pride. No longer will you be haughty on my holy mountain" (3:11). This might seem to show that the arrogance and presumption of those akin to those who had been building the Tower of Babel would be removed from the community of the faithful. The book ends with robust oracles of hope and gladness for Zion.

Haggai

Haggai, dated to 520 BCE, concerns itself with the rebuilding of the Jerusalem temple. The completion of that monumental project in 515 would inaugurate what scholars call the Second Temple period in the history of Judaism. While God's house is not cared for, the people also cannot prosper: "Because my house lies in ruins, while all of you hurry off to your own houses. Therefore the heavens above you have withheld the dew, and the earth has withheld its produce" (1:9-10 NRSV). Failure to revere the holiness of God in God's dwelling place has devastating consequences.

Haggai is interested in matters of cultic practice and in the political leadership of the postexilic community. The story of the response of Zerubbabel and Joshua to God's word (1:12-15) sounds much like the kind of story we see in Ezra–Nehemiah. Haggai 2 offers divine reassurances that, through God's intervention, economic support will be secured to prosper the building project ("I will shake all the nations, so that the treasure of all nations shall come," 2:7 NRSV). The remainder of the chapter may be concerned, in part, with a delay in fulfillment of that vision. In 2:17, we can hear an echo of Amos 4: Israel has been struck by the LORD as punishment for sin, "but you didn't return to me." Expansive notes of promise are struck in the concluding verses of the book that include blessing for Judah ("From this day forward, I will bless you," 2:19), destruction of Judah's enemies (2:21-22), and reestablishment of divinely appointed governance for God's holy people (2:23).

Zechariah

With Zechariah, we have moved into the Persian period fully. The Persians governed their far-flung territories by means of a system of provinces—satrapies—wherein were placed local governors loyal to their Persian overlords. Within this system, indigenous cultures and religions were permitted to flourish, so long as their political ideologies and religious praxes did not interfere with the Persians' regular extraction of heavy taxes and other material resources.

We see in this period a reestablished Jerusalem temple, the increasing power of high priest, and a hope for the restoration of the Davidic monarchy that is becoming increasingly eschatological in nature.

The book of Zechariah has two distinct parts. In Zechariah 1–8, the prophet receives a stunning series of eight visions that dramatize prophetic

211

and proto-apocalyptic themes of judgment and restoration. Together, these visions narrate a story line in which the ancient audience is expected to discern the truths of recent history. As you read, note the visions and the interpretations offered by the prophet's angelic guide:

- a rider on a red horse, in front of red, sorrel, and white horses (1:8-17)
- four horns and four blacksmiths (1:18-21)
- a man with a measuring line (2:1-5)
- the high priest and the Adversary standing before the LORD (3:1-10)
- a gold lampstand with a bowl and seven lamps, flanked by two olive trees (4:1-14)
- a flying scroll (5:1-4)
- a basket containing Wickedness, flown to Shinar (Babylon; 5:5-11)
- four chariots with red, black, white, and gray horses respectively (6:1-8)

In Zechariah we see reflection, not unlike that in the book of Jeremiah, on the prophets as having been an authoritative cultural institution in the ongoing life of Israel and Judah. In Zechariah 1, the prophets, as in Jeremiah, are closely connected with the authority of the Torah:

> But you must say to the people, The LORD of heavenly forces proclaims: Return to me, says the LORD of heavenly forces, and I will return to you, says the LORD of heavenly forces. Don't be like your ancestors to whom the former prophets preached: The LORD of heavenly forces proclaims: Turn from your evil ways and your evil deeds. But they didn't listen; they didn't draw near to me. So where are your ancestors? Do the prophets live forever? In fact, didn't my words and laws, which I gave to my servants, the prophets, pursue your ancestors? And then the people changed their hearts, and they said, The LORD of heavenly forces has treated us according to what we have done, exactly as he planned. (1:3-6)

Zechariah 7 notes the importance of authentic spiritual orientation when the people perform ritual practices (7:5-6). Polemical attention is given to the witness of the former prophets, the stubborn disobedience of the people, and the catastrophic consequences of their disobedience, material surely intended to instruct, and shame, the implied audience about their history. The narrative moves to language about the LORD's jealous protection of Zion and plans to establish the *shalom* of Jerusalem once again (8:1-17). This section of Zechariah ends with a vivid description of joy and gladness for Judah and the streaming of nations to Jerusalem to seek the LORD of heavenly forces (8:18-23).

Zechariah 9–14 is markedly different in tone and style from what precedes. In Zechariah 9–10, oracles against other nations mingle with words of promise to Zion and Judah, and we encounter the image of a humble but victorious king "riding on a donkey" (9:9 NRSV), an oracle that proved to be a rich theological resource for New Testament traditions about the triumphal entry of Jesus into Jerusalem (see Matt 21:1-11, Mark 11:1-11, Luke 19:29-40, and John 12:12-19). Zechariah 11 offers a baffling multilayered story that seems to have much in common with a prophetic sign-act. Mixing symbolic language and concrete language, it presents the speaker becoming a "shepherd," engaging in conflict with other leaders, being paid for overseeing a "flock intended for slaughter," performing a rupture between Judah and Israel, then indicting an emerging leader as "foolish" ("worthless" in NRSV) and uttering a curse on him. The oracles in Zechariah 12–14 go in a different direction, promising the victory of Israel over its enemies, cleansing and restoration for Israel and the Davidic line, an end to idolatry and false prophecy, a gruesome description of a divinely ordained plague on Jerusalem's enemies (14:12), and images of the transformation of life on earth when the LORD comes to reign.

Malachi

Malachi contains diverse traditions that reflect concerns of the postexilic period. Malachi 1 briefly slams Edom and then reflects on the problem of believers offering blemished or inappropriate sacrifices. Malachi 2 chastises the levitical priests for a lack of integrity in their teaching function and holds the people to a high moral standard for marital fidelity. Malachi 3 speaks in eschatological terms of the LORD's punishment of sinners as a refiner's fire purifies crude metals, detailing a number of offenses of the people and, finally, discussing a "book of remembrance" in which are written the names of those who fear the LORD. Malachi 4 offers a beautiful eschatological vision of restoration, an admonition to adhere to the Torah, and a promise to send Elijah to unify the people in righteousness.

In Malachi occur two famous and beautiful passages, the first about the LORD's coming "as a refiner and a purifier of silver. He will purify the Levites and refine them like gold and silver. They will belong to the LORD, presenting a righteous offering" (Mal 3:3), showing even late in the literature of Scripture the crucial importance of the right practice of the sacrificial cult. The second is the gorgeous promise in 4:2, rich with imagery that will be refracted in the Christian hymn, "Hark! The Herald Angels Sing": "But the sun of righteousness will rise on those revering my name; healing will be in its wings so that you will go forth and jump about like calves in the stall." Marvin Sweeney notes, "Psalm 19 is especially clear in associating the imagery of the sun or light with YHWH's Torah," and says that this allusion to the Torah as a source of instruction and healing "seems to underlie the references [in Malachi 4:2] to the righteousness and healing capacities of the sun."[23]

"Hark! The Herald Angels Sing," verse 3

Mild he lays his glory by,
born that we no more may die,
born to raise us from the earth,
born to give us second birth.
Risen with healing in his wings,
light and life to all he brings,
hail, the Sun of Righteousness!
hail, the heaven-born Prince of Peace!
Hark! the herald angels sing
glory to the newborn King!

Words: Charles Wesley (1707–1788), alt.
Tune: Mendelssohn, Felix Mendelssohn (1809–1847);
adapt. William H. Cummings (1831–1915)

For Further Reading

Kessler, Rainer. "The Twelve: Structure, Themes, and Contested Issues." In *The Oxford Handbook of the Prophets*, 207–23. Edited by Carolyn J. Sharp. Oxford: Oxford University Press, 2016.

Stulman, Louis, and Hyun Chul Paul Kim. "An Anthology of Dispersion and Diagnosis (Hosea–Micah)" and "An Anthology of Debate and Rebuilding (Nahum–Malachi)." In *You Are My People: An Introduction to Prophetic Literature*, 185–249. Nashville: Abingdon, 2010.

The Prophets and Radical Change

The prophets of ancient Israel and Judah have bequeathed an extraordinary inheritance to all who are committed to transformative change, "repair of the world" (*tîkkûn 'ôlām*), or renewal of vision in their communities. First, the heritage of the biblical prophets is valuable for those who locate themselves actively within Jewish, Christian, and Muslim faith communities. Such folk reflect on scriptural witness regularly in liturgy and learn to understand the ancient prophets within a deepening sense of their communities' formation and reformation as participants in the radical purposes of God. Second, the prophets are of significance for those who inhabit other communities of conviction, as well. Prophetic vision and rhetoric can be a vital resource for those involved in social advocacy traditions, political reform movements, and intentional communities committed to shared ethical norms. Third, the Latter Prophets are essential reading for all those involved in the ongoing work of reflecting on history from antiquity to the present. This includes not just academic historians and archivists but also those who wish to understand and preserve personal, family, institutional, or communal history, for example, through oral history projects or the crafting of memoirs, biographical works, or fiction that imagines the history of a community through time. Fourth, the biblical prophets can be a marvelous source of inspiration for those who work on visionary expression through the arts: in music; drawing, painting, and other graphic arts; sculpture; spoken word or other performance art; textile or ceramic art; the writing of prose essays, poetry, short stories, or novels; and other modes of artistic truth-telling.

As you've read the Latter Prophets, you've seen the diversity of skillful ways in which they secure the attention of their implied audiences. One key prophetic technique is to hold up contrasts, excoriating one possibility and affirming the other. This rhetorical move invites the audience to stand in solidarity with the prophetic perspective, rejecting that which is unfaithful or unethical and striving to meet the expectations for behavior worthy of the visionary community. The prophets use line and shadow, word and action, oracle and story artfully to delineate many kinds of dramatic contrasts. Through these contrasts and the implicit invitations they extend, the prophets are teaching their communities how to draw on their history, how to understand the present moment, and how to discern their communal vocation for the future.

Since the prophetic witness has been written down in scrolls and preserved for future generations, we have the opportunity to read the Latter Prophets and learn afresh in our own contexts about how to effect radical changes that will enhance justice and equity. Interpreting the prophets can constitute a pedagogy through which each reader learns how to speak to their own community about what has been, what is now, and what is emerging. Of course, there are also things we learn *not* to do by studying the prophets. Much has changed over the centuries since the prophets tended their sycamore trees in the countryside and walked barefoot through the streets of Jerusalem. Ways of reading have changed. Diverse indeed are the hermeneutical approaches with which readers explore, embrace, and deconstruct theological and ethical positions in the Bible. But that diversity, too, is true to the polyphony of Scripture and the pedagogical practices of the ancient prophets.

In these closing pages, it may be instructive to reflect on some of the ancient alternatives sketched out by the prophets in their dramatic diction, as we ponder our contemporary challenges and possibilities. Below, we will consider three striking contrasts that come up over and over again in the prophetic literature: arrogance versus humility, desert versus garden, and ruination versus rebuilding.

1. Arrogance versus humility. The prophets contrast the arrogance of oppressors with the humility of those who understand that their power lies not in themselves but in the One who created them. Brutal imperialists who use military power to plunder the material resources of other nations will see that their power is only temporary. In the centuries during which the books of the Latter Prophets were composed, imperialism involved the march of armies across the landscape of the ancient Near East. Sieges of walled cities, hand-to-hand combat, and—once a region was subjugated—the extraction of huge payments of tribute were means by which the arrogant controlled and oppressed other groups. The power of such regimes will be brought low by the LORD. The prophets also convict those whose arrogance fuels their desire to exploit their own people—they will be held accountable. The prophets call those who seek the LORD to walk in humility, with a clear-eyed awareness of their own sin and an earnest desire to reform their lives, living instead by the precepts of Torah and governed by compassion for the poor and the marginalized.

Arrogance	Humility
But when the LORD has finished all this work on Mount Zion and in Jerusalem, he will punish the Assyrian king's arrogant actions and the boasting of his haughty eyes. He said, "By my own strength I have achieved it, and by my wisdom, since I'm so clever. I disregarded national boundaries; I raided their treasures; I knocked down their rulers like a bull. Will the ax glorify itself over the one who chops with it? Or will the saw magnify itself over its user? As if a rod could wave the one who lifts it! As if a staff could lift up the one not made of wood!" (Isa 10:12-13, 15)	He has told you, human one, what is good and what the LORD requires from you: to do justice, embrace faithful love, and walk humbly with your God. (Mic 6:8)
The LORD proclaims: the learned should not boast of their knowledge, nor warriors boast of their might, nor the rich boast of their wealth. No, those who boast should boast in this: that they understand and know me. I am the LORD who acts with kindness, justice, and righteousness in the world, and I delight in these things, declares the LORD. (Jer 9:23-24).	The one who is high and lifted up, who lives forever, whose name is holy, says: I live on high, in holiness, and also with the crushed and the lowly, reviving the spirit of the lowly, reviving the heart of those who have been crushed. (Isa 57:15)

Human one, say to the prince of Tyre, the Lord GOD proclaims: In your arrogance, you say, "I am God, and as God I rule the seas!" Though you claim to have the mind of a god, you are mortal, not divine. So now the Lord GOD proclaims: Because you claim to have the mind of a god, I'll bring foreigners, the most ruthless nations, against you. They will let loose their swords against your fine wisdom, and they will degrade your splendor. (Ezek 28:2, 6-7)	The LORD says: Heaven is my throne, and earth is my footstool. So where could you build a house for me, and where could my resting place be? My hand made all these things and brought them into being, says the LORD. But here is where I will look: to the humble and contrite in spirit, who tremble at my word. (Isa 66:1-2)

2. Desert versus garden. The prophets work skillfully with images of desert/wilderness and garden/oasis, these sometimes carrying literal meanings and other times functioning as signifiers for the spiritual and communal life of their people. Stark contrasts abound in these prophetic oracles; the prophets reflected deeply on the kinds of ecosystems that they saw around them in the ancient Near East. The threats posed by desiccated fields, barren ground, rocky cliffs, and dry streambeds are contrasted in prophetic oracles with the life-giving abundance of vineyards and orchards heavy with fruit, fields bursting with grain, and gardens lush with flowers and produce. Ancient oracles built around images of the desert have relevance as literal signifiers when we consider actual deserts and rough terrain, climatological threats, ecological damage, and constraints on access to fresh water, with the severe challenges that those conditions present to living creatures and to communities. The prophets may also guide our reflections on metaphorical "deserts" of the cultural or theological sort: political and cultural systems in which new life is not allowed to grow, access to replenishing resources is limited or blocked, and living feels more like subsistence or bare survival. We can draw on the Latter Prophets to develop our own prophetic commitments to economic justice, peace-making, and other life-giving postures that will help persons, families, communities, and larger social structures to blossom and flourish.

221

Desert	Garden
The earth dries up and wilts; the world withers and wilts; the heavens wither away with the earth. The earth lies polluted under its inhabitants, for they have disobeyed instruction, swept aside law, and broken the ancient covenant. Therefore, a curse devours the earth; its inhabitants suffer for their guilt. (Isa 24:4-6)	If you remove the yoke from among you, the finger-pointing, the wicked speech; if you open your heart to the hungry, and provide abundantly for those who are afflicted, your light will shine in the darkness, and your gloom will be like the noon. The LORD will guide you continually and provide for you, even in parched places. He will rescue your bones. You will be like a watered garden, like a spring of water that won't run dry. (Isa 58:9-11)
The fields are devastated, the ground mourns; for the grain is destroyed, the new wine dries up, the olive oil fails. The grapevine is dried up; the fig tree withers. Pomegranate, palm, and apple— all the trees of the field are dried up. Joy fades away from the people. What a terrible day! The day of the LORD is near; it comes like chaos from the Almighty. (Joel 1:10, 12, 15)	I will be like the dew to Israel; he will blossom like the lily; he will cast out his roots like the forests of Lebanon. His branches will spread out; his beauty will be like the olive tree, and his fragrance like that of Lebanon. They will again live beneath my shadow, they will flourish like a garden; they will blossom like the vine, their fragrance will be like the wine of Lebanon. (Hos 14:5-7)

He will stretch out his hand against the north and will cause Assyria to perish. Let him make Nineveh a desolation, a desolate place like the wilderness. Flocks will lie down in its midst, every living thing of the nation. Moreover, the owl and the porcupine will spend the night on its columns. A bird's call will resound from the window. Desolation will be on the sill, for the cedar will be stripped bare. (Zeph 2:13-14)	They will come shouting for joy on the hills of Zion, jubilant over the LORD's gifts: grain, wine, oil, flocks, and herds. Their lives will be like a lush garden; they will grieve no more. (Jer 31:12)

3. Ruination versus rebuilding. Over the centuries in Israel and Judah, the prophets witnessed everything from social instability and cultural anxiety to terrible trauma as waves of imperial aggression swept across the ancient Near East. They saw unwalled villages, larger towns, and walled cities reduced to rubble; they saw the ruination of religious and social structures that had grounded and nourished their people for generations. The books of the Latter Prophets speak truth about these times of desolation and destruction. They also use images of rubble and brokenness to articulate how the LORD will bring down the fortified strongholds of enemies and all who wish harm to the covenant people. Prophetic language of ruination can help us stay present to what has been lost when urban or rural structures are decimated, when change has been forced upon persons or communities in violent ways, and when something cherished has become a heap of rubble, literally or figuratively, such that it cannot be repaired. But communities can muster the material resources and the resolve to rebuild, as the prophets saw in Judah after the fall of Jerusalem in 587. Here, prophetic vision is essential. The prophetic imagination can be a catalytic and sustaining force for communities seeking to reconstruct the foundations of who they had been in the past or rebuild in beautiful new ways for the future.

Ruination	Rebuilding
An oracle about Damascus. Look! Damascus is finished as a city; it will become a fallen ruin. The villages of Aroer are abandoned forever. They will be pastures for flocks, which will lie down undisturbed. Ephraim's security will cease, as will Damascus' rule. What's left of Aram will resemble the glory of the Israelites, says the LORD of heavenly forces. (Isa 17:1-3)	I will improve the circumstances of my people Israel; they will rebuild the ruined cities and inhabit them. They will plant vineyards and drink their wine; and they will make gardens and eat their fruit. (Amos 9:14)
On the day I punish the crimes of Israel, I will also visit the altars of Bethel; the horns of the altar will be cut off and will fall to the ground. I will tear down the winter house as well as the summer house; the houses of ivory will perish; the great houses will be swept away, says the LORD. (Amos 3:14-15)	Look, I'm here for you, and I will turn toward you, and you will be farmed and sown. I will populate you with human beings, the whole house of Israel, all of them. The cities will be inhabited, the ruins rebuilt. When I make people and animals increase on you, they will multiply and be fruitful. I will cause you to be inhabited as you were before. I will do more good for you than in the beginning, and you will know that I am the LORD. I will let people walk through you, my people Israel! They will lay claim to you, you will be their inheritance, and you will no longer deprive them of anything. (Ezek 36:9-12)

How terrible for me, due to my injury; my wound is terrible. Yet I said to myself: This is my sickness, and I must bear it. But now my tent is destroyed; all its ropes are cut, and my children are gone for good. There's no one left to set up my tent frame and to attach the fabric. ... Listen! The sound is getting louder, a mighty uproar from the land of the north; it will reduce the towns of Judah to ruins, a den for wild dogs. (Jer 10:19-20, 22)	Your ancient ruins shall be rebuilt; you shall raise up the foundations of many generations; you shall be called the repairer of the breach, the restorer of streets to live in. (Isa 58:12)

To apply wisdom from the ancient prophets as you pursue avenues of transformation in your own community, it may help to visualize a spectrum along which you can connect what the prophets did with your own work of advocacy and creative visioning. How you draw on these sites of connection will depend on the issue you wish to address in a particular contextual moment. Imagine this spectrum:

resilience → resistance → reformation → rejoicing

All of these—resilience, resistance, reformation, and rejoicing—present opportunities for reflection and action aimed at radical change. Each may constitute a site of sustained engagement over weeks or months or years, or a mode you select tactically as circumstances require. Every situation that calls for vision and transformative action is complex. You may find yourself engaged in more than one of these prophetic modes sequentially or even simultaneously.

Resilience: In times when you or your community may be experiencing deprivation, exploitation, or brutality, you have to survive in order to be able to work for transformation. Building communal resilience is vital. You and your community must learn how to find resources that will help you survive and build your strength in adverse circumstances. This is an essential first step for all work for change. Given the ongoing and cyclical nature of oppression in ever-new contexts, learning and practicing resilience will always be important. To fund resilience in yourself and your community, read the Latter Prophets with an eye to ways in which resilience is cultivated.

Resistance: In circumstances in which violence, exploitation, or some other harm is being perpetrated, it is vital to resist as effectively as we can. Many modes of engagement are possible in grassroots organizing, public service, writing, the visual and performance arts, spiritual leadership, and more. We need to use all the creative means at our disposal to contest ideological distortions, to put a stop to policies and actions that reinforce or exacerbate inequity, and to reframe perspectives that keep people mired in pathological or oppressive dynamics. To build the capacity for resistance in yourself and your community, read the Latter Prophets with an eye to ways in which resistance is offered.

Reformation: In times that call for radical change of institutions and social structures, we must transform the ways of thinking, in ourselves and in our communities, that have been maladaptive, unproductive, or harmful to others. This involves attentiveness not only to obvious harms but also to more subtle kinds of repression, silencing, or erasure of the needs and dignity of others. Having begun our own work, we'll also need to facilitate the willing embrace of change within and beyond our communities. To catalyze energy for reformation in yourself and your community, read the Latter Prophets with an eye to ways in which calls to reform are voiced.

Rejoicing: In times that are challenging and in times of peace, folks are sustained by joy. The practice of rejoicing builds our capacity to stay in relationships of trust with one another, to express gratitude for the gifts and hopes that animate our lives, and to look together toward a renewed future. Joy may also be understood as political. When those in positions of less power "dare" to rejoice, they are expressing a strong and jubilant hope for the present and the future. That can galvanize change like nothing else. To empower yourself and your community to rejoice, read the Latter Prophets with an eye to ways in which joy is claimed and celebrated.

Whatever your theological commitments may be, whatever your political stance toward the various systems and policies that govern our communal life, the biblical prophets can help clarify your vision. They can build your strength and skill in resilience, resistance, reformation, and rejoicing. Their ancient witness is rich with possibility. The prophets can serve as cherished companions and indispensable interlocutors as we work for radical change. There is a vast and suffering world waiting for words of truth, postures of solidarity, exhortations to ethical action, and invitations to a renewed sense of the sacred.

Notes

1. Introduction: History, Memory, and Prophetic Texts

1. Stephen Kepnes, *The Future of Jewish Theology* (Oxford: Wiley-Blackwell, 2013), 127.

2. Walter Brueggemann, *Theology of the Old Testament: Testimony, Dispute, Advocacy* (Minneapolis: Fortress, 2012), 625.

3. Detailing thought about the prophets in centuries of rabbinic interpretation and in contemporary Judaism is beyond the scope of this volume. The interested reader may wish to consult the following works and their bibliographies: Martin Buber, *The Prophetic Faith* (based on the 1949 translation by Carlyle Witton-Davies, with a new introduction by Jon D. Levenson [Princeton: Princeton University Press, 2016]); Abraham J. Heschel, *The Prophets* (orig. pub. New York: Harper & Row, 1962, now in a Perennial Classics edition with introduction by Susannah Heschel, 2001); Howard Kreisel, *Prophecy: The History of an Idea in Medieval Jewish Philosophy*, Amsterdam Studies in Jewish Philosophy 8 (Dordrecht: Kluwer, 2001); Kepnes, *Future of Jewish Theology*, esp. chap. 6, "Prophetic Holiness"; Marvin A. Sweeney, "Contemporary Jewish Readings of the Prophets," in *The Oxford Handbook of the Prophets*, ed. Carolyn J. Sharp (Oxford: Oxford University Press, 2016), 447–66.

4. Heschel, *Prophets*, 3–4.

5. Heschel, *Prophets*, 5–6.

6. Heschel, *Prophets*, 19.

7. Robert R. Wilson, *Prophecy and Society in Ancient Israel* (Philadelphia: Fortress, 1980), 58.

8. James Longenbach, *The Virtue of Poetry* (Minneapolis: Graywolf, 2013), 11.

9. Diana Edelman, "From Prophets to Prophetic Books: The Fixing of the Divine Word," in *The Production of Prophecy: Constructing Prophecy and Prophets in Yehud*, ed. Diana V. Edelman and Ehud Ben Zvi (Oakville, CT: Equinox, 2009), 29–54 (41).

10. On political, social, and cultural biases of institutions of higher learning, still illuminating after twenty-five years is the important work by bell hooks, *Teaching to Transgress: Education as the Practice of Freedom* (New York: Routledge, 1994).

11. Iain W. Provan, "Knowing and Believing: Faith in the Past," in *"Behind" the Text: History and Biblical Interpretation*, ed. Craig Bartholomew, C. Stephen Evans, Mary Healey, and Murray Rae, Scripture and Hermeneutics 4 (Grand Rapids: Zondervan, 2003), 229–66 (237). On the pronoun in brackets: genderqueer and other nonbinary persons would be excluded by the quotation's original phrase, laudably inclusive in its time: *him or her.* Throughout this volume, I will be using the epicene singular pronoun *they* in order to avoid gender discrimination and make a space within which genderqueer persons can know themselves to be addressed here. Singular *they* has a venerable historical pedigree, being found in English literature at least since the fourteenth century, and it is linguistically important for gender justice.

12. Louis Stulman and Hyun Chul Paul Kim, *You Are My People: An Introduction to Prophetic Literature* (Nashville: Abingdon, 2010), 11.

13. Dianne Bilyak, a seasoned poet and playwright, has published poems in *The Massachusetts Review, Freshwater*, and elsewhere. See her volume of poems, *Against the Turning* (Amherst, MA: Amherst Writers & Artists Press, 2011).

2. Isaiah: Prophet of Restoration

1. John N. Oswalt, "Righteousness in Isaiah: A Study of the Function of Chapter 56–66 in the Present Structure of the Book," pp. 177–91 in *Writing and Reading the Scroll of Isaiah: Studies of an Interpretive Tradition*, vol. 1, ed. Craig C. Broyles and Craig A. Evans (Leiden: Brill, 1997), 178, 190–91.

2. David L. Petersen, *The Prophetic Literature: An Introduction* (Louisville: Westminster John Knox, 2002), 61–63.

3. Ulrich Berges, "Isaiah: Structures, Themes, and Contested Issues," pp. 153–70 in *The Oxford Handbook of the Prophets*, ed. Carolyn J. Sharp (Oxford: Oxford University Press, 2016), 157.

4. Benjamin D. Sommer, *A Prophet Reads Scripture: Allusion in Isaiah 40–66* (Stanford: Stanford University Press, 1998), 5.

5. Brevard S. Childs, *Isaiah*, OTL (Louisville: Westminster John Knox, 2001), 443.

6. Berges, "Isaiah," 155.

7. Christl M. Maier, *Daughter Zion, Mother Zion: Gender, Space, and the Sacred in Ancient Israel* (Minneapolis: Fortress, 2008), 190.

8. Childs, *Isaiah*, 76.

9. Childs, *Isaiah*, 218.

10. Louis Stulman and Hyun Chul Paul Kim, *You Are My People: An Introduction to Prophetic Literature* (Nashville: Abingdon, 2010), 57, 59–61.

11. See Childs on the Servant Songs in *Isaiah*, 323–27, 381–96, 410–23.

12. See Joseph Blenkinsopp on the Servant Songs in *Isaiah 40–55*, AB 19 (New York: Doubleday, 2002), 84–87, 118–20, 209–12, 298–307, 319–23, 349–57.

13. See Klaus Baltzer on the Servant Songs in *Deutero-Isaiah: A Commentary on Isaiah 40–55*, trans. Margaret Kohl, Hermeneia (Minneapolis: Fortress, 2001), 18–22, 124–37, 305–11, 335–43, 392–429.

14. George Herbert, "The Agony," in *The Complete English Works*, ed. Ann Pasternak Slater (New York: Alfred A. Knopf, 1995), 34.

3. Jeremiah: Prophet of Struggle

1. Abraham J. Heschel, *The Prophets* (New York: HarperCollins Perennial Classics, 2001), 141.

2. Else K. Holt, "The Prophet as Persona," pp. 299–318 in *The Oxford Handbook of the Prophets*, ed. Carolyn J. Sharp (Oxford: Oxford University Press, 2016), 312–13.

3. Christl M. Maier, "Jeremiah as Teacher of Torah," *Int* 62 (2008): 22–32, at 22, 26, and 29.

4. See Louis Stulman, *Order amid Chaos: Jeremiah as Symbolic Tapestry*, BibSem 57 (Sheffield: Sheffield Academic Press, 1998).

5. Robert P. Carroll, *Jeremiah*, OTL (Philadelphia: Westminster, 1986), 297.

6. Kathleen M. O'Connor, *Jeremiah: Pain and Promise* (Minneapolis: Fortress, 2011), 3.

7. Louis Stulman, *Jeremiah*, AOTC (Nashville: Abingdon, 2005), 270.

8. Leslie Allen, *Jeremiah*, OTL (Louisville: Westminster John Knox, 2008), 343.

9. Carroll, *Jeremiah*, 602. Carroll offers, "Sexual connotations may well be present in view of v. 20, and the proverbial nature of the saying . . . may allude to this aspect of community life by means of an oblique reference to future fertility. . . . This reference to vigorous sexual intercourse is shorthand for the renewal of the community. . . . As a bawdy proverb . . . it provides a fine closure of the cycle with 30.6, where the mimicry of pregnancy by men in a time of trouble will be replaced by the real thing when Yahweh creates something new in the land."

10. William L. Holladay, *Jeremiah 2*, Hermeneia (Minneapolis: Fortress, 1989), 154.

11. William McKane, *Jeremiah Vol. II: XXVI–LII*, ICC (Edinburgh: T & T Clark, 1996), 803.

12. Jack R. Lundbom, *Jeremiah 21–36*, AB 21B (New York: Doubleday, 2004), 451. Lundbom explains further, "Jeremiah is expressing shock and surprise at the weakness of Judah's soldiers in defeat. He is saying, 'My, a new thing on earth! the woman must protect the (fighting) man.' Needless to say, it should be the other way around."

13. See O'Connor, *Jeremiah: Pain and Promise*, 109–10.

14. Louis Stulman, "Prophetic Words and Acts as Survival Literature," pp. 319–33 in *The Oxford Handbook of the Prophets*, ed. Carolyn J. Sharp (Oxford: Oxford University Press, 2016), 326.

15. Louis Stulman and Hyun Chul Paul Kim, *You Are My People: An Introduction to Prophetic Literature* (Nashville: Abingdon, 2010), 102.

16. Carroll, *Jeremiah*, 64.

17. John M. Bracke, *Jeremiah 1–29*, WBC (Louisville: Westminster John Knox, 2000), 8–9.

18. Kathleen M. O'Connor, "Jeremiah as Ideal Survivor," *Journal for Preachers* (Lent 2005): 19–24, at 19.

19. O'Connor, *Jeremiah: Pain and Promise*, 113.

20. Stulman and Kim, *You Are My People*, 133.

21. Stulman and Kim, *You Are My People*, 134, 136, 137.

22. See Carolyn J. Sharp, "Embodying Moab: The Figuring of Moab in Jeremiah 48 as Reinscription of the Judean Body," pp. 95–108 in *Concerning the Nations: Essays on the Oracles against the Nations in Isaiah, Jeremiah and Ezekiel*, ed. Else K. Holt, Hyun Chul Paul Kim, and Andrew Mein, LHBOTS 612 (New York: Bloomsbury T & T Clark, 2015).

23. Stulman and Kim, *You Are My People*, 110.

4. Ezekiel: Prophet of Holiness

1. Joseph Blenkinsopp, *A History of Prophecy in Israel* (Louisville: Westminster John Knox, 1996), 180.

2. Blenkinsopp, *History of Prophecy in Israel*, 168.

3. Louis Stulman and Hyun Chul Paul Kim, *You Are My People: An Introduction to Prophetic Literature* (Nashville: Abingdon, 2010), 157.

4. Amy Kalmanofsky, "The Dangerous Sisters of Jeremiah and Ezekiel," *JBL* 130 (2011): 299–312, at 312.

5. Stulman and Kim, *You Are My People*, 155.

6. Rhiannon Graybill, "Voluptuous, Tortured, and Unmanned: Ezekiel with Daniel Paul Schreber," pp. 137–55 in *The Bible and Posthumanism*, ed. Jennifer L. Koosed, SemeiaSt 74 (Atlanta: Society of Biblical Literature, 2014), 144–45. A fuller treatment may be found in chapter 4, "The Unmanning of Ezekiel: The Prophet's Body Voluptuous and Shattered in Ezekiel 1–5," of Graybill's *Are We Not Men: Unstable Masculinity in the Hebrew Prophets* (Oxford: Oxford University Press, 2016).

7. Andrew Mein, "Ezekiel: Structures, Themes, and Contested Issues," pp. 190–206 in *The Oxford Handbook of the Prophets*, ed. Carolyn J. Sharp (Oxford: Oxford University Press, 2016), 203.

8. John J. Collins, "What Is Apocalyptic Literature?" pp. 1–16 in *The Oxford Handbook of Apocalyptic Literature*, ed. John J. Collins (Oxford: Oxford University Press, 2014), 5, 7, 11.

9. Moshe Greenberg, "The Design and Themes of Ezekiel's Program of Restoration," *Interpretation* 38 (1984): 181–208, at 199.

10. Stulman and Kim, *You Are My People*, 161.

11. Stulman and Kim, *You Are My People*, 171.

5. The Book of the Twelve: Prophetic Polyphony

1. See the helpful survey of scholarship in Marvin A. Sweeney, *The Twelve Prophets, Vol. 1: Hosea, Joel, Amos, Obadiah, Jonah*, Berit Olam (Collegeville, MN: Liturgical Press, 2000), xv–xxxix.

2. Sweeney, *Twelve Prophets*, vol. 1, xxxiii.

3. Sweeney, *Twelve Prophets*, vol. 1, xxxii.

4. See Rainer Kessler, "The Twelve: Structure, Themes, and Contested Issues," pp. 207–23 in *The Oxford Handbook of the Prophets*, ed. Carolyn J. Sharp (Oxford: Oxford University Press, 2016), 207–23.

5. Sweeney, *Twelve Prophets*, vol. 1, xxv.

6. Louis Stulman and Hyun Chul Paul Kim, *You Are My People: An Introduction to Prophetic Literature* (Nashville: Abingdon, 2010), 246–47.

7. Joseph Blenkinsopp, *A History of Prophecy in Israel* (Louisville: Westminster John Knox, 1996), 15.

8. Francis I. Andersen and David Noel Freedman, *Hosea: A New Translation with Introduction and Commentary*, AB 24 (New York: Doubleday, 1983), 51–52.

9. For a fuller treatment of this cartographic rhetorical move in Hosea, see my essay, "Hewn by the Prophet: An Analysis of Violence and Sexual Transgression in Hosea with Reference to the Homiletical Aesthetic of Jeremiah Wright," pp. 50–71 in *Aesthetics of Violence in the Prophets*, ed. Chris Franke and Julia M. O'Brien, LHBOTS 517 (New York: T & T Clark, 2010), 50–71.

10. James L. Crenshaw, *Joel*, AB 24C (New York: Doubleday, 1995), 26. For a list of phrases in Joel that Crenshaw says are drawn from other biblical sources, see pp. 27–28.

11. James R. Linville, "What Does 'It' Mean? Interpretation at the Point of No Return in Amos 1–2," *BibInt* 8 (2000): 400–24, at 406, 423.

12. For a fuller discussion of ironies in Amos, with an earlier formulation of points found here, see a subsection, "Hermeneutics of De(con)struction: Amos as Samson *Redivivus*," pp. 151–68 in my *Irony and Meaning in the Hebrew Bible*, ISBL (Bloomington: Indiana University Press, 2009).

13. See the extended treatment in Jörg Jeremias, *Amos*, OTL (Louisville: Westminster John Knox, 1998), 70–73.

14. Francis I. Andersen and David Noel Freedman, *Amos: A New Translation with Introduction and Commentary*, AB 24A (New York: Doubleday, 1989), 490.

15. Robert Alter, *The Art of Biblical Narrative* (New York: Basic Books, 2011), 12.

16. Alter, *Art of Biblical Narrative*, 38.

17. Meir Sternberg, *The Poetics of Biblical Narrative: Ideological Literature and the Drama of Reading*, ISBL (Bloomington: Indiana University Press, 1985), 53.

18. Sternberg, *Poetics of Biblical Narrative*, 323–24.

19. Francis I. Andersen and David Noel Freedman, *Micah: A New Translation with Introduction and Commentary*, AB 24E (New York: Doubleday, 2000), 216.

20. Timothy K. Beal, "The System and the Speaking Subject in the Hebrew Bible: Reading for Divine Abjection," *BibInt* 2 (1994): 171–89, at 182–83.

21. Beal, "System and the Speaking Subject," 186.

22. So, for example, William P. Brown, *Obadiah through Malachi*, WBC (Louisville: Westminster John Knox, 1996), 114.

23. Marvin A. Sweeney, *The Twelve Prophets, Vol. 2: Micah, Nahum, Habakkuk, Zephaniah, Haggai, Zechariah, Malachi*, Berit Olam (Collegeville, MN: Liturgical Press, 2000), 748.

Scripture Index

Index of Modern Authors

CPSIA information can be obtained
at www.ICGtesting.com
Printed in the USA
LVHW042041040419
613046LV00001B/67